Creative Controversy: Intellectual Challenge In The Classroom

Third Edition

David W. Johnson and Roger T. Johnson

Interaction Book Company
7208 Cornelia Drive
Edina, Minnesota 55435
(612) 831-9500

This book is dedicated to David W. Johnson Jr., Catherine E. Johnson, Margaret M. Johnson, Jeremiah W. Johnson, R. Todd Johnson, Kristin E. Johnson, and Timothy S. Johnson who are argued, disagreed, and intellectually challenged us all their lives.

ISBN: 0-0939603-23-3

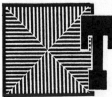

TABLE of CONTENTS

REFACE

How students may be taught the procedures and skills they need to resolve intellectual conflicts constructively has been a relatively ignored issue in teaching. Despite the amount of time teachers and students waste in dealing with destructively managed conflicts, and despite the considerable research evidence indicating that the constructive management of conflict will increase the productivity of the classroom, teachers receive very little training in how to use conflict for instructional purposes and how to teach students the procedures and skills involved in intellectually challenging each other. In essence, teachers have been implicitly taught to avoid and suppress conflicts and to fear them when they burst forth and cannot be denied. Conflicts cannot be suppressed or denied. Trying to do so makes them worse.

This book is about using conflict to create student involvement in learning, intellectual curiosity, intrinsic motivation to learn, higher achievement, and higher-level reasoning. Conflict is the heart of all drama, a major tool for capturing interest and attention. If students are to learn and master the procedures and skills required for managing intellectual conflicts constructively, they must do so in the classroom. The results for your students are well worth your efforts.

It has taken us nearly 30 years to build the theory, research, and practical experience required to write this book. In the 1960's we began by reviewing the research, conducting our initial research studies, and training teachers in the classroom use of constructive conflict (Johnson, 1970; Johnson & F. Johnson, 1975; Johnson & Johnson, 1979). Since then our work has proliferated. Our more recent writings on constructive conflict include **Reaching Out** (Johnson, 1972/1993), **Joining Together** (Johnson & F. Johnson, 1975/1994). and **Productive Organizational Conflict** (Tjosvold & Johnson, 1983). Related work in cooperative learning includes **Cooperation in the Classroom** (Johnson, Johnson, & Holubec, 1984/1993), **Learning Together and Alone** (Johnson & Johnson, 1975/1994) and **Circles of Learning** (Johnson, Johnson, & Holubec, 1984/1993). Yet the concept of constructively managed conflict is much, much older than our work. Our roots reach back to Morton Deutsch and then to Kurt Lewin. We wish to acknowledge our indebtedness to the work of both of these social psychologists.

Many teachers have contributed to our understanding of how to structure academic controversies and have field tested our ideas in their classrooms with considerable success. We have been in their classrooms and we have taught beside them. We appreciate their ideas and celebrate their successes. In addition, our thinking about and understanding of controversy have been enriched by the research of Dean Tjosvold and Karl Smith. We have also had many talented and productive graduate students who have conducted research studies that have made significant contributions to our understanding of controversy. We feel privileged to have worked with them.

Chapter One: What Are Constructive Conflicts?

The Importance Of Intellectual Conflict

Thomas Jefferson noted, *"Difference of opinion leads to inquiry, and inquiry to truth."* Jefferson had a deep faith in the value and productiveness of conflict. He is not alone. A number of 20th-Century theorists have pointed out the value of conflict. Piaget (1950) proposed that it is disequilibrium within a student's cognitive structure that motivates transitions from one stage of cognitive reasoning to another. He believed that conflict among peers is an essential cause of a shift from egocentrism to accommodation of other's perspectives. Piaget proposed that a person, with an existing way of organizing his or her cognitive structures, enters into cooperative interaction with peers. Conflicts inevitably result that create internal disequilibrium and the inability to assimilate current experiences into existing cognitive structures. The person then searches for a new equilibrium by decentering and accommodating the perspectives of others. This creates the need to organize the person's cognitive structures in a new way. Kohlberg (1969) adopted Piaget's formulation as an explanation for the development of moral reasoning.

Conflict theorists noted that conflict had many positive benefits (Coser, 1956; Simmel, 1955). Berlyne (1957, 1966) emphasized that conceptual conflict creates epistemic curiosity which motivates the search for new information and the reconceptualization of the knowledge one already has. Hoffman and Maier (1972) insisted that higher-quality problem solving depended on conflict among group members. Bruner (1961) proposed that conceptual conflict was necessary for discovery learning and could be created by (a) presenting events that are discrepant with what the student already knows and understands, (b) presenting "mysterious" events that seem inexplicable on the basis of students' present knowledge, and (c) having students argue and disagree with the teacher or with each other. Johnson (1970) posited that since knowledge results from social processes (i.e., "truth" is derived by scholars seeking consensus through discussion), then conflict among ideas, theories, and conclusions becomes an essential part of building a conceptual structure that everyone agrees is valid.

The power of conflict may be clearly seen in the arts. Creating a conflict is an accepted writer's tool for capturing an audience. All drama hinges on conflict. Playwrights and scriptwriters create a conflict whenever they want to gain and hold viewer's attention, create viewer interest and emotional involvement, and excite and surprise viewers. A general rule of modern novels is that if a conflict is not created within the first three pages of the book, the book will not be successful. Educators, on the other hand, often avoid and suppress any sort of intellectual conflict in the classroom.

Figure 1.1 Engaging In An Academic Controversy

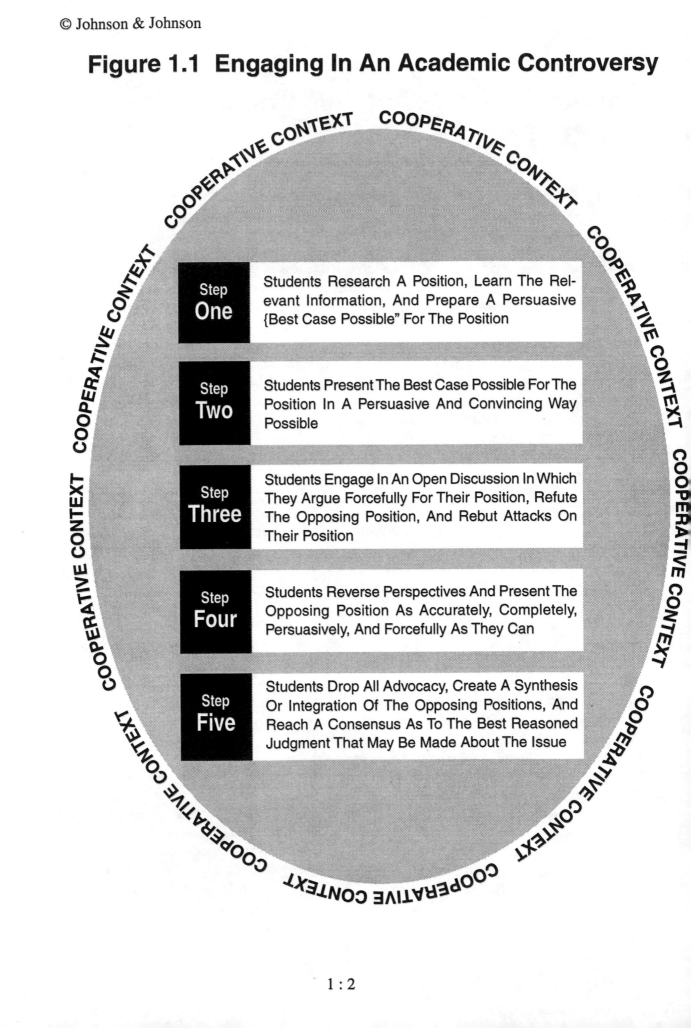

Step One — Students Research A Position, Learn The Relevant Information, And Prepare A Persuasive {Best Case Possible" For The Position

Step Two — Students Present The Best Case Possible For The Position In A Persuasive And Convincing Way Possible

Step Three — Students Engage In An Open Discussion In Which They Argue Forcefully For Their Position, Refute The Opposing Position, And Rebut Attacks On Their Position

Step Four — Students Reverse Perspectives And Present The Opposing Position As Accurately, Completely, Persuasively, And Forcefully As They Can

Step Five — Students Drop All Advocacy, Create A Synthesis Or Integration Of The Opposing Positions, And Reach A Consensus As To The Best Reasoned Judgment That May Be Made About The Issue

COOPERATIVE CONTEXT

Despite the (a) daily demonstration of the power of conflict in dramatic productions and (b) the recommendation by theorists that conflict be an essential aspect of learning and teaching, educators have by and large avoided and suppressed intellectual conflict. Far from being a standard instructional procedure, in most schools creating intellectual conflict is the exception, not the rule. Why do school faculty avoid creating intellectual conflict among and within students? The answer to that question is a somewhat of a mystery.

The Avoidance Of Intellectual Conflicts

There are a number of hypotheses as to why conflict is so avoided and suppressed in academic situations (Johnson, 1970; Johnson & F. Johnson, 1975; Johnson, F. Johnson, & Johnson, 1976; Johnson & R. Johnson, 1979, 1989, 1992). **The first hypothesis is fear blocks faculty and students from engaging in intellectual conflicts**. Since destructively managed conflicts create divisiveness and hostility, when conflicts among students occur, faculty and students may have some anxiety as to whether constructive or destructive outcomes will result. Palmer (1990, 1991), for example, believes that fear of conflict blocks good teaching and learning and recommends that faculty have the courage to promote intellectual conflict among students and between students and faculty despite their apprehensions about doing so.

Hypothesis two is that ignorance of how to engage in intellectual conflict blocks faculty and students from engaging in intellectual conflicts. Until recently there has not been a clear set of instructional procedures that faculty can use in a wide variety of subject areas and with any age student. The development of structured academic controversy gives faculty a clear instructional procedure they can use to structure intellectual conflicts among students in ways that result in increased learning.

The third hypothesis is that lack of training programs to teach faculty how to use intellectual conflict effectively blocks faculty and students from engaging in intellectual conflicts. Most faculty members have not been trained in how to create intellectual conflicts among students and how to use the conflicts to increase students' learning. Such training programs exist only at a few institutions, such as the University of Minnesota. As a consequence, most faculty do not know how to take advantage of the few instructional procedures that are available.

Hypothesis four is that our culture is so anti-conflict that faculty do not see the promotion of intellectual conflicts as a possibility. The view that conflict is a potential positive and powerful force on learning may be culturally unacceptable. The possibility of conflict being constructive is not viewed within the realm of possibility. A general feeling in our society is that conflicts are bad and should be avoided. Many people, consequently, believe that a well-run classroom is one in which there are no conflicts among students.

The fifth hypothesis is that pedagogical norms may block faculty and students from engaging in intellectual conflicts. Current pedagogy promotes the use of a performer-spectator approach to teaching. Faculty lecture, often in an interesting and entertaining way, and students sit and watch and take notes. In an attempt to cover a whole field in a semester or year, students are often exposed to a blizzard of information within a lecture. Departmental chairs and colleagues may equate telling with teaching. In such a learning climate, the norms of what is acceptable teaching practice may not include creating intellectual conflict among students.

Hypothesis six is that inertia, the power of the status quo, may be so great that faculty just do not try anything new. Faculty may choose to play it safe by only lecturing because it is their personal tradition and the tradition of their school and colleagues.

These six barriers are formidable obstacles to overcome if faculty are to utilize the power of intellectual conflict in their teaching. In order to give faculty the courage to change their teaching practices and to include conflict as a center-piece of instruction, faculty members must know what academic controversy is, the outcomes it promotes, and the procedures that operationalize its use in learning situations.

What Is Academic Controversy?

*Have you learned lessons only of
those who admired you, and were tender
with you, and stood aside for you?*

*Have you not learned great lessons
from those who braced themselves
against you, and disputed the passage
with you?*

Walt Whitman, 1860

In an English class students are considering the issue of civil disobedience. They learn that in the civil rights movement, individuals broke the law to gain equal rights for minorities. In numerous literary works, such as Huckleberry Finn, individuals wrestle with the issue of breaking the law to redress a social injustice. Huck wrestles with the issue of breaking the law in order to help Jim, the run-away slave. In the 1970s and 1980s prominent public figures from Wall Street to the White House have felt justified in breaking laws for personal or political gain. In order to study the role of civil disobedience in a democracy, students are placed in a cooperative learning group of four members. The group is then divided into two pairs. One pair is given the assignment of making the best case possible for the constructiveness of civil disobedience in a democracy. The other pair is given the assignment of making the best case possible for the destructiveness of civil disobedience in a democracy. In the resulting conflict, students draw from such sources as the Declaration of Independence by Thomas Jefferson, Civil Disobedience by Henry David Thoreau, Speech at Cooper Union, New York by Abraham Lincoln, and Letter from Birmingham Jail by Martin Luther King, Jr. to challenge each other's reasoning and analyses concerning when civil disobedience is, or is not, constructive.

Subject areas may be taught by giving answers or by asking questions. Students can consider the great questions that have dominated our past and determine our present and future, or they can listen to seemingly isolated facts about people and events. If students are to consider the great questions, the questions must be presented in a way that clarifies alternative answers and opposing points of view. Academic controversy allows faculty to do so. **Academic controversy** exists when one student's ideas, information, conclusions, theories, and opinions are incompatible with those of another, and the two seek to reach an agreement. Controversies are resolved by engaging in what Aristotle called **deliberate discourse** (i.e., the discussion of the advantages and disadvantages of proposed actions) aimed at synthesizing novel solutions (i.e., **creative problem solving**). The teacher guides students through the following steps (Johnson, 1970; Johnson & F. Johnson, 1975; Johnson, F. Johnson, & Johnson, 1976; Johnson & R. Johnson, 1979, 1989):

1. **Research And Prepare A Position**: Each pair develops the position assigned, learns the relevant information, and plans how to present the best case possible to the other pair. Near the end of the period pairs are encouraged to compare notes with pairs from other groups who represent the same position.

2. **Present And Advocate Their Position**: Each pair makes their presentation to the opposing pair. Each member of the pair has to participate in the presentation. Students are to be as persuasive and convincing as possible. Members of the opposing pair are encouraged to take notes, listen carefully to learn the information being presented, and clarify anything they do not understand.

3. **Engage In An Open Discussion In Which They Refute the Opposing Position And Rebut Attacks On Their Own Position**: Students argue forcefully and persuasively for their position, presenting as many facts as they can to support their point of view. The group members analyze and critically evaluate the information, rationale, and inductive and deductive reasoning of the opposing pair, asking them for the facts that support their point of view. They refute the arguments of the opposing pair and rebut attacks on their position. They discuss the issue following a set of rules to help them criticize ideas without criticizing people, differentiate the two positions, and assess the degree of evidence and logic supporting each position. They keep in mind that the issue is complex and they need to know both sides to write a good report.

4. **Reverse Perspectives**: The pairs reverse perspectives and present each other's positions. In arguing for the opposing position, students are forceful and persuasive.

They add any new information that the opposing pair did not think to present. They strive to see the issue from both perspectives simultaneously.

5. **Synthesize And Integrate The Best Evidence And Reasoning Into A Joint Position**: The four members of the group drop all advocacy and synthesize and integrate what they know into factual and judgmental conclusions that are summarized into a joint position to which all sides can agree. They (a) finalize the report (the teacher evaluates reports on the quality of the writing, the logical presentation of evidence, and the oral presentation of the report to the class), (b) present their conclusions to the class (all four members of the group are required to participate orally in the presentation), (c) individually take the test covering both sides of the issue (if every member of the group achieves up to criterion, they all receive bonus points), and (d) process how well they worked together and how they could be even more effective next time.

Structured controversies are most commonly contrasted with concurrence seeking, debate, and individualistic learning. **Debate** exists when two or more individuals argue positions that are incompatible with one another and a judge declares a winner on the basis of who presented their position the best. An example of debate is when each member of a group is assigned a position as to whether more or less regulations are needed to control hazardous wastes and an authority declares as the winner the person who makes the best presentation of his or her position to the group.

Concurrence seeking occurs when members of a group inhibit discussion to avoid any disagreement or arguments, emphasize agreement, and avoid realistic appraisal of alternative ideas and courses of action. An example of concurrence seeking is when a group is to decide whether more or less regulations are needed to manage hazardous waste, with the stipulation that group members are not to argue but rather to compromise quickly whenever opposing opinions are expressed. Concurrence seeking is close to the **groupthink** concept of Janis (1982) in which members of a decision-making group set aside their doubts and misgivings about whatever policy is favored by the emerging consensus so as to be able to concur with the other members. The underlying motivation of groupthink is the strong desire to preserve the harmonious atmosphere of the group on which each member has become dependent for coping with the stresses of external crises and for maintaining self-esteem.

Individualistic efforts exist when individuals work alone at their own pace and with their set of materials without interacting with each other, in a situation in which their goals are unrelated and independent from each other. An example of individualistic efforts is when each individual has to formulate recommendations concerning hazardous waste regulation and is asked to study the pros and cons on his or her own, without discussing it with others, and prepare an individual report that reflects only his or her own reasoning and conclusions.

A key to the effectiveness of conflict procedures for promoting learning is the mixture of cooperative and competitive elements within the procedure (see Table 3.2). The greater the cooperative elements and the less the competitive elements, the more constructive the conflict (Deutsch, 1973). Cooperative elements alone, however, do not ensure maximal productivity. There has to be both cooperation and conflict. Thus, controversy is characterized by both positive goal and resource interdependence as well as by conflict. Debate has positive resource interdependence, negative goal interdependence, and conflict. Within concurrence seeking there is only positive goal interdependence, and within individualistic learning situations there is neither interdependence nor intellectual conflict.

Table 3.1 Controversy, Debate, Concurrence-Seeking, And Individualistic Processes

Controversy	Debate	Concurrence-Seeking	Individualistic
Categorizing And Organizing Information To Derive Conclusions	Categorizing And Organizing Information To Derive Conclusions	Categorizing And Organizing Information To Derive Conclusions	Categorizing And Organizing Information To Derive Conclusions
Presenting, Advocating, Elaborating Position And Rationale	Presenting, Advocating, Elaborating Position And Rationale	Active Presentation Of Position	No Oral Statement Of Positions
Being Challenged By Opposing Views	Being Challenged By Opposing Views	Quick Compromise To One View	Presence Of Only One View
Conceptual Conflict And Uncertainty About Correctness Of Own Views	Conceptual Conflict And Uncertainty About Correctness Of Own Views	High Certainty About The Correctness Of Own Views	High Certainty About The Correctness Of Own Views
Epistemic Curiosity And Perspective Taking	Epistemic Curiosity	No Epistemic Curiosity	No Epistemic Curiosity
Reconceptualization, Synthesis, Integration	Closed-Minded Adherence To Own Point Of View	Closed-Minded Adherence To Own Point Of View	Closed-Minded Adherence To Own Point Of View
High Achievement, Positive Relationships, Psychological Health/Social Competences	Moderate Achievement, Relationships, Psychological Health	Low Achievement, Relationships, Psychological Health	Low Achievement, Relationships, Psychological Health

Inevitability Of Controversy

Intellectual challenge and conflict over ideas, theories, information, and conclusions will occur no matter how hard a teacher tries to suppress them. Anytime students work cooperatively, controversy occurs. Anytime students are asked to make a decision about an academic issue, controversy occurs.

One of the most important sources of controversy is the heterogeneity of students. America has always been a nation of many cultures, races, languages, and religions. In the last eight years alone, over 7.8 million people journeying from over 150 different countries and speaking dozens of different languages came to make the United States their new home. The school increasingly is the meeting ground for students from different cultural, ethnic, social class, and language backgrounds. They come to know each other, appreciate the vitality of diversity, and to internalize a common heritage of being an American that will bind them together. While this diversity represents a source of creativity and energy that few other countries have, it also provides a series of problems concerning how conflicts are managed in the classroom. A wide variety of assumptions about conflict and methods of managing conflict can be found in almost any classroom. Students, therefore, need to be co-oriented as to how the controversy process works.

Table 2: Social Interdependence And Conflict

Individualistic	Controversy	Debate	Concurrence Seeking	
Positive Goal Interdependence	Yes	No	Yes	No
Resource Interdependence	Yes	Yes	No	No
Negative Goal Interdependence	No	Yes	No	No
Conflict	Yes	Yes	No	No

Need For Co-Orientation On How To Manage Controversy

Different students have quite different ideas about how controversies should be resolved. Many students avoid challenging their classmates intellectually. Other students believe that thinking the same as others is the best policy. Some students may confuse physical dominance and intellectual dominance. Other students use verbal attack to ensure that no one disagrees with them. Students who intellectually challenge their classmates may be ostracized. The multiple procedures for managing controversies create some chaos. This is especially true when students are from different cultural, ethnic, social class, and language backgrounds.

In order for education to proceed and learning to occur, students need to be **co-oriented** so that everyone understands and uses the same procedures for managing controversies. All students need to operate under the same norms and adhere to the same conflict resolution procedures. **Norms** are shared expectations about the behavior that is appropriate within the situation. Conflict resolution begins with a common set of norms concerning what behaviors are appropriate and what procedures are to be used to resolve the conflict. These norms must be clearly and publicly established. Intellectual challenge, divergent thinking, and synthesis should be desirable and sought after. Physical violence against oneself or another person, public humiliation and shaming, and lying and deceit should be outlawed.

Types Of Conflicts

Controversy is only one type of conflict. According to the World Book Dictionary, a **conflict** is a fight, struggle, battle, disagreement, dispute, or quarrel. A conflict can be as small as a disagreement or as large as a war. Probably the most influential definition is that of Deutsch (1969), who states that a **conflict** exists whenever incompatible activities occur. An activity that is incompatible with another activity is one that prevents, blocks, or interferes with the occurrence or effectiveness of the second activity. Incompatible activities may originate in one person, between two or more people, or between two or more groups. There are at least four important types of conflicts: controversies, conceptual conflicts, conflict of interests, and developmental conflicts. Closely related to controversies are **conceptual conflicts** which occur when incompatible ideas exist simultaneously in a person's mind or when information being received does not seem to fit with what one already knows (Berlyne, 1957, 1966). An example is when the same amount of water is poured into two glasses—one is tall and skinny and the other is short and fat. The student knows that each glass holds the same amount of water but at the same time believes that the tall glass has more water in it. A **conflict of interests** exists when the actions of one person attempting to maximize his or her wants and benefits prevents, blocks, or interferes with another person maximizing his or her wants and benefits. When two students both want the same library book at the same time, a conflict of interests exists. A **developmental conflict** exists when recurrent incompatible activities between adult and child based on the opposing forces of stability and change within the child cycles in and out of peak intensity as the child develops cognitively and socially. An example is when one year a child is dependent on the teacher and wants to be noticed and approved of by the teacher all the time and the next year the child is independent and does not want the teacher to express approval or liking. The student does not choose to be dependent or independent, there are social developmental imperatives that demand that he or she be so. These imperatives are pushed to the extreme until a teacher (or parent) sets limits and communicates social reality. Conflicts of interest and developmental conflicts are discussed in **Teaching Students to be Peacemakers** (Johnson & Johnson, 1995).

Learning Conflict Skills

Reading a book on physical conditioning exercises will not make you physically fit. Studying books on golf, horse-back riding, or swimming will not make you an expert. Learning the procedures and skills required to manage conflicts constructively is no different. Successful conflict managers are not born, they are trained. You first must **see the need** for becoming a skilled conflict manager, then **understand how to manage** conflicts skillfully, and finally **practice, practice, practice** until skillful management of conflict is an automatic reflex that does not require conscious thought or practice.

With most skills there is a period of slow learning, then a period of rapid improvement, then a period where performance remains the same, and then another period of rapid improvement, then another plateau, and so forth. Individuals have to practice the conflict skills long enough to make it through the first few plateaus and integrate the skills into their behavioral repertoires. There are a set of **stages** that most skill development goes through:

- **Awareness** that the skill is needed.

- **Understanding** of what the skill is.

- Self-conscious, **awkward engagement** in the skill. Practicing any new skill feels awkward. The first few times someone throws a football, plays a piano, or paraphrases, it feels strange.

- Feelings of **phoniness** while engaging in the skill. After a while the awkwardness passes and enacting the skill becomes more smooth. Many individuals, however, feel inauthentic or phony when performing the skill. Encouragement is often needed to move individuals through this stage.

- **Mechanical use** of the skill.

- Automatic, **routine use** where the skill is fully integrated into the person's behavioral repertoire and seems like a natural action to engage in.

You learn any skill (tennis or managing conflict) by:

- Taking a risk by engaging in a challenging action, that is, experimenting to increase one's competence.

- Obtaining feedback on the success or failure of one's efforts.

- Engaging in self-reflection and analysis of the effectiveness of the actions taken.

- Modifying one's actions, and trying again.

- Recycling to Step 2 over and over again.

In learning any skill it is helpful to remember the following advice. "You have to sweat on the practice field before you perform on the playing field!" "You gotta study the lessons before you get the grades!" "You gotta make the call before you get the sale!"

While reading this book you will be expected to learn the procedures and skills you need to manage conflict constructively. You will be asked to try out procedures, assess the effectiveness of your actions, reflect on how you could behave more competently in conflict situations, then try again in a modified way. You will be asked to support and encourage the efforts of your classmates to do likewise. Improving your competence is an exciting and exhilarating experience, but in doing so it is often helpful to remember the stages of skill learning involved. Do not worry about feeling awkward the first time you negotiate or mediate. Persevere and practice and soon the awkwardness will pass.

What Faculty Need To Know

In order to use academic controversies to create intellectual conflicts, faculty must know a number of things:

- What are the benefits to students to participating in an academic controversy?

- How does academic controversy work?

- What is the faculty member's role in using academic controversies?

- How may students be trained to research and prepare intellectual positions?

- How may students be trained to advocate intellectual positions through presentations and open discussion in which they attempt to refute the opposing position and rebut attacks on their position?

- How may students be trained to reverse perspectives and see intellectual issues from both points of view?

- How may students synthesize or integrate the opposing positions and reach consensus on intellectual issues?

- How may controversy be used in faculty decision making?

Each of these questions will be addressed in the following chapters.

Your Challenge

If civilization is to survive, we must cultivate the science of human relationships—the ability of all peoples, of all kinds, to live together, in the same world at peace.

Franklin Delano Roosevelt

History is filled with many exciting examples of constructive conflicts. The major issues of our times have been shaped by past conflicts and will be resolved through future conflicts. A democracy is conflict in continuous action. Just as it is not possible to eliminate conflict from our history, it is not possible to eliminate conflict from school life. It is in the classroom that students will learn how to participate in open and free discussions in ways that enrich their learning and their lives. Your challenge is to teach your students how to manage intellectual conflicts constructively and thereby give them the procedures and competencies that will allow them to live a productive and successful life.

Summary

What people know about managing conflicts is usually learned at a very early age within the family. Students manage conflicts the same way their parents and older siblings do. The authors initially learned how to manage conflicts from our older sister, Helen. Helen was an early maturing female in a family of late maturing males (she was 5'4" when we were 2'6"). Her basic rule was, "Save time, see it my way now!" In conflicts she tended to strike out emotionally, accusing and blaming us in ways to induce guilt and shame. "You did it, it's all your fault, if you were not such a rotten person, then I would not have obliterated you," were some of her favorite statements. Most characteristic of all, she gleefully believed that all our hostile actions were caused by our nasty and vicious personalities while any hostile behavior she (a remarkably sweet, gentle, and kind person) engaged in was the result of circumstances and situational factors (this is called the **fundamental attribution error**). She loved to "demonize" us. "Let's discuss your degree of rottenness," was one of her favorite topics of conversation. Helen, of course, now works for a professional football team, ruling the players with an iron fist. While she taught us how to bully and blame others, make the fundamental attribution error, and demonize our enemies, none of that has helped us live happy and fulfilling lives. We, like so many other people, have had to relearn how to manage conflict constructively.

It is a mistake to avoid conflicts. Conflicts are pervasive. They cannot be avoided or suppressed. Even if conflicts could be suppressed, no one would want to. Without conflict there would be no creativity, high-level reasoning, and cognitive development. Conflicts lead to growth, development, and change. This is true of individuals, groups, organizations, and even societies. Because of the highly constructive potential of conflicts, all students need to learn the procedures and skills required to resolve conflicts constructively. Especially when the conflicts involve academic subject matter.

There are both theoretical and practical reasons to believe that aroursing intellectual conflict one of the most important and powerful instructional procedures available to faculty. Yet most faculty avoid and suppress intellectual conflict, perhaps (a) out of fear it will be divisive, (b) because they have never been trained in how to use instructional procedures that maximize the likelihood that intellectual conflict will be constructive, not destructive, or (c) because the current societal and pedagogical norms discourage them from doing so. This situation needs to change, and intellectual conflict needs to become part of day-to-day student life.

The pathway to using intellectual conflict for instructional purposes primarily lies through academic controversy. **Controversy** exists when one individual's ideas, information, conclusions, theories, and opinions are incompatible with those of another, and the two seek to reach an agreement. To engage in a controversy students must research and prepare a position, present and advocate their position, refute opposing positions and rebut attacks on their own position, reverse perspectives, and create a synthesis that all group members can agree to. Structured academic controversies are most often contrasted with concurrence seeking, debate, and individualistic learning. For instance, students can inhibit discussion to avoid any disagreement and compromise quickly to reach a consensus while they discuss the issue (**concurrence-seeking**). Or students can appoint a judge and then debate the different positions with the expectation that the judge will determine who presented the better position (**debate**). Finally, students can work independently with their own set of materials at their own pace (**individualistic learning**).

Controversies are (a) an inherent aspect of sciencing, decision making, problem solving, reasoned judgment, and critical thinking, and (b) inevitable. If students get intellectually and emotionally involved in academic learning, controversies will occur no matter what teachers do. Since controversies are inevitable and cannot be avoided, educators are well-advised to co-orient all students by teaching them the procedures and skills they need to intellectually challenge each other constructively.

⟫⟪ CONTROVERSY CONTRACT ⟫⟪

Major Learnings	Implementation Plans

Date _____   Date of Progress Report Meeting _____

Participant's Signature   _____

Signatures of Other Group Members   _____ _____

_____   _____   _____

❧ CONTROVERSY PROGRESS REPORT ❧

NAME _____ SCHOOL _____

AGE LEVEL _____ SUBJECT _____

Day and Date	Description of Tasks and Activities Performed	Successes Experienced	Problems Encountered

Description of critical or interesting incidents:

1 : 15

❧ CONTROVERSY LOG SHEET ❧

WK.	LESSONS PLANNED AND/OR TAUGHT	COLLAB. SKILL STRESSED	PLANNED WITH	OBSERVED BY	GIVEN AWAY TO
1					
2					
3					
4					
5					
6					
7					
8					
9					
10					
11					
12					
13					
14					
15					
GRP					
TOTAL					

1 : 16

EXERCISE MATERIALS

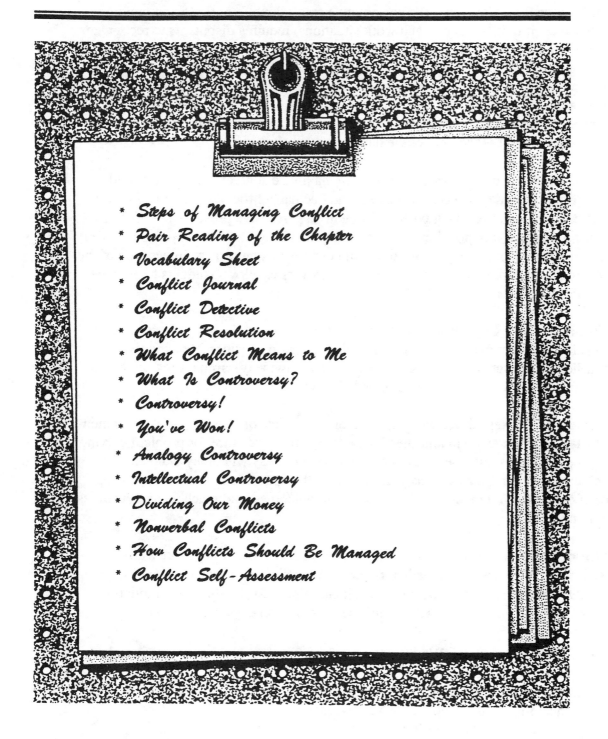

* Steps of Managing Conflict
* Pair Reading of the Chapter
* Vocabulary Sheet
* Conflict Journal
* Conflict Detective
* Conflict Resolution
* What Conflict Means to Me
* What Is Controversy?
* Controversy!
* You've Won!
* Analogy Controversy
* Intellectual Controversy
* Dividing Our Money
* Nonverbal Conflicts
* How Conflicts Should Be Managed
* Conflict Self-Assessment

STEPS of MANAGING CONFLICT

1. **Create A Cooperative Context**: The constructive resolution of conflict in an ongoing relationship (such as in family, school, and work situations) requires disputants to recognize that their long-term relationship is more important than the result of any short-term conflict. In order for long-term mutual interests to be recognized and valued, individuals have to perceive their interdependence and be invested in each other's well-being. To teach students the procedures and skills they need to manage conflicts constructively, furthermore, a cooperative experiences must be provided. The easiest way to do so is to use cooperative learning procedures at least 60 percent of the day.

2. **Structure Academic Controversies**: In order to maximize student achievement and higher-level reasoning, students need to engage in intellectual conflicts. The procedure for doing so is researching and preparing positions, making a persuasive presentation of their position, refuting the opposing position while rebutting attacks on their own position, viewing the issue from a variety of perspectives, and creating a synthesis or integration of the opposing positions. The frequent use of academic controversies allows students to practice their conflict skills daily.

3. **Teach Students To Be Peacemakers**: All students must be taught how to negotiate and mediate and gain enough experience doing so that they develop considerable expertise in resolving conflicts constructively. Doing so creates a schoolwide discipline program based on giving students the tools to regulate their own behavior.

- **Teach Students To Negotiate**: In order to resolve conflicts of interest and developmental conflicts constructively, students need to be taught the procedure for problem-solving negotiations. Students must be able to communicate honestly what they want and how they feel, explain interests as well as positions, take the opposing perspective, create a number of optional agreements that maximize joint outcomes, and reach an agreement as to which option to adopt.

- **Teach Students To Mediate**: When students cannot successfully negotiate a constructive resolution to their conflicts, mediators should be available. Mediating involves ending hostilities, ensuring commitment to the mediation process, facilitating negotiations, and formalizing the agreement. All students need mediation experience.

- **Arbitrate Student Conflicts**: When mediation fails, the teacher or administrator arbitrates the conflict. Arbitration involves listening carefully to both sides in a conflict and deciding who is right and who is wrong. Arbitration is a last resort because it can leave at least one student resentful and angry toward the arbitrator.

VOCABULARY SHEET

Working with a partner, learn the definitions of the words below.

1. Define each word in two ways.

    First, write down what you think the word means.

    Second, look it up in the book and write down its definition.

    Note the page on which the definition appears.

2. For each word write a sentence in which the word is used.

3. Make up a story in which all of the words are used.

4. Learn how to spell each word. They will be on your spelling test.

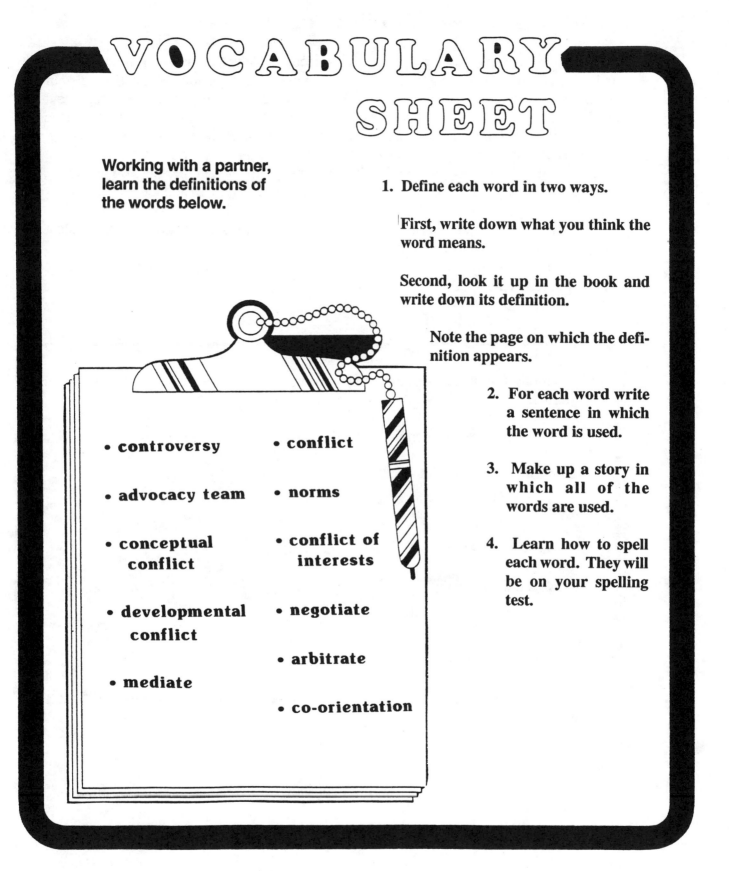

- controversy
- advocacy team
- conceptual conflict
- developmental conflict
- mediate
- conflict
- norms
- conflict of interests
- negotiate
- arbitrate
- co-orientation

∞ **Conflict Journal** ∽

You are to make a conflict journal in which you record what you are learning about yourself and how you behave in conflict situations. A **journal** is a personal collection of your significant thoughts about conflict. Include specific information you have learned about conflict resolution, effective behavior in conflict situations, and the extent to which you have mastered the conflict skills. Personalize it with art, poetry, cartoons, and creative writing. The most important thing about journal writing is to express your ideas freely without judging them. Whatever you write is OK. Spelling, grammar, and neatness do not count. The only thing that matters is writing freely about your experiences and ideas.

The purposes of the journal are to collect (a) thoughts that are related to the book's content (the best thinking often occurs when you are driving to or from school, about to go to sleep at night, and so forth) and (b) newspaper and magazine articles and references that are relevant to resolving conflicts constructively.

Entries

1. Each day find a conflict in the newspaper or on television and describe it in your journal.

   Each day describe one conflict you were involved in during the day:

   a. What was the conflict about?

   b. Who was involved?

   c. The strategies you used to manage the conflict.

   d. How did you feel?

   e. How was it resolved?

   f. What did you learn about managing conflicts constructively?

(Note: If you publish your journal as did John Holt, Hugh Prather, and others, all we ask is a modest 10 percent of the royalties.)

Journal Entry One

Conflicts always occur, and you can profit from them if you have the necessary skills. It is important, therefore, to master the skills necessary for resolving conflicts constructively. The first step for doing so is to become more aware of your most frequently used strategies for managing conflicts.

Think back over the interpersonal conflicts you have been involved in during the past few years. These conflicts may be with students, administrators, parents, or colleagues.

1. Describe a recent conflict with a schoolmate, teacher, administrator, or parent.

2. What kind of emotional reaction do you have to these or other classroom or school-related conflicts? Check the ones that are appropriate.

   _____Anger   _____Resignation   _____Depression

   _____Frustration   _____Fear   _____Excitement

   _____Annoyance   _____Sadness

3. What were the strategies you used to resolve the conflicts?

4. Compare your answers with those of the person next to you.

INK

 Conflict detective

Conflicts go on continually everywhere. As a conflict detective you need to investigate conflicts daily. The two major sources of conflicts are the newspaper, TV entertainment programs, and TV news programs.

1. **Investigate the newspaper each day.** Find an example of a conflict in an article. It can be a small conflict (neighbors quarreling about a barking dog) or a large conflict (nations disagreeing). Bring in the article for the Conflict Bulletin Board. Or you can put the article in your Conflict Journal.

2. **Investigate TV entertainment programs.** Watch one and write down each conflict that occurs. Write down the name of the program, the date, the conflicts that occur, and the strategies used to manage the conflicts.

3. **Investigate TV news programs.** Watch one and write down each conflict that is discussed. Write down who is involved in the conflict and what strategies they are using to resolve it.

Name _____   **Date** _____

CONFLICT RESOLUTION

WORD HUNT

WORDS FOUND   **BONUS WORDS**

_____ _____   _____

_____ _____   _____

_____ _____   _____

_____ _____   _____

_____ _____   _____

_____ _____   _____

_____ _____   _____

_____ _____   _____

_____ _____   _____

_____ _____   _____

_____ _____   _____

_____ _____   _____

For this activity, you and your partner have to put your heads together to find as many words as you can from the phrase CONFLICT RESOLUTION. You may use as few or as many letters in each word as you like, arranged in any order, as long as the letter appears in CONFLICT RESOLUTION. Write each of the words you find in the columns on the left. You may also write each word in the Bonus Column if you can write a sentence on the back of this sheet using the word. THE SENTENCE MUST HAVE SOMETHING TO DO WITH CONFLICT. Good luck in your conflict word hunt!

EXAMPLE: You and your partner find the word it. Write it in a Words Found space. On the back of your paper you write the sentence: When Sue called me "fatty," I told her I would like to talk about it. (Any sentence you write will count as long as it deals with conflict in some way.)

1 : 23

Name _____ Date _____

What CONFLICT Means to Me

Think of what CONFLICT means to you. Is it scary or exciting? Is it interesting or yukky? Write in the circles words that come into your mind when you think of conflict. [Make additional circles if you need to.]

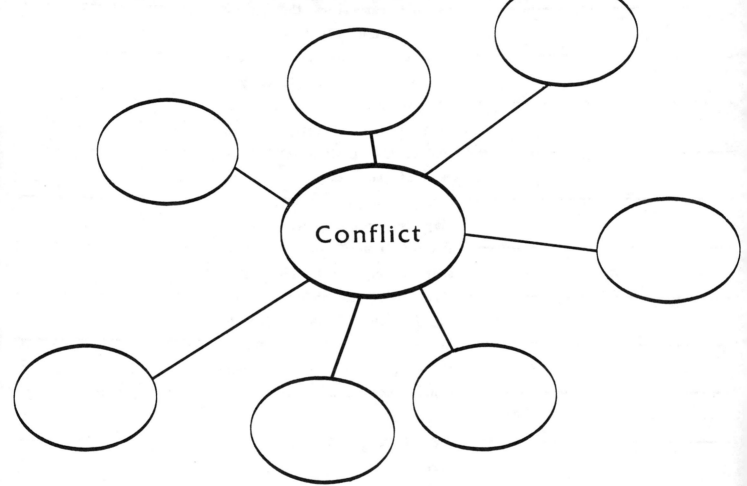

Now compare your words with those of the other members of your group. Decide as a group what conflict means and write the meaning below.

_____

_____

Instructions For Associations Mapping

Individualistic Task:

Think of what the word "**conflict**" means and what associations and memories it evokes. When you think of conflict, do negative or positive, scary or delightful, hostile or caring images come to mind? Each time you think of something write it down in one of the inner circles. Then write down all the words you associate with each of the new words. Add additional circles if you need to.

Cooperative Task:

Compare with associations with those of the other three members of your group:

1. How would you define the concept "**conflict**."

2. What elements do all conflicts have in common?

3. What causes conflict?

4. What makes conflicts destructive?

5. What makes conflicts constructive?

Individualistic Task:

Write down answers to the following:

1. What did you learn about your associations with conflict?

2. What did you learn about the nature of conflict and how most people perceive it?

WHAT IS CONTROVERSY?

Working as a pair, write out your answers to the following questions. There should be one set of answers for the two of you, both of you have to agree on the answers, and both of you have to be able to explain your answers to the teacher or the entire class. When you have finished, find another pair and compare answers. Take some of their ideas and make your answers better.

1. Controversy begins when two people must reach an agreement and their ideas, information, conclusions, theories, and opinions are incompatible. When one person says, "Germany builds the best cars" and another person says, "Japan builds the best cars," a controversy exists. What do you think a controversy is? Define the word **controversy** in your own words, using your own ideas.

2. Are controversies good _____ or bad _____?

Give three examples of good controversies. Give three examples of bad controversies. Then list three small and three large controversies you know about. Finally, list three controversies at home and three controversies at school.

	Good	Bad
1		
2		
3		

	Small	Large
1		
2		
3		

	Home	School
1		
2		
3		

3. What is more important:

_____ Having everyone agree with your ideas

or

_____ Making the best decision possible.

Working as a pair, write out your answers to the following questions. There should be one set of answers for the two of you, both of you have to agree on the answers, and both of you have to be able to explain your answers. When you have finished, find another pair and compare answers. Take some of their ideas and make your answers better.

Controversy begins when two people disagree. When one person says, "Hunting and gathering societies were generally happy and carefree" and another person says, "Hunting and gathering societies were generally harsh and oppressive, " a controversy exists. Define the word **controversy** in your own words, using your own ideas.

Controversy Quiz

1. An argument a day makes student involvement stay.

   _____ True   _____ False

2. Controversy (after cooperative learning) is the teacher's best friend.

   _____ True   _____ False

3. A lesson without controversy is like a day without sunshine--things are gloomy, depressing, and drag along slowly.

   _____ True   _____ False

4. All intellectual growth depends on the collision of adverse opinions.

   _____ True   _____ False

1:28

5. It is controversy that adds to instruction the spark of curiosity, the flame of interest, the heat of involvement, and the power of creativity.

_____ True   _____ False

Define These Terms

Listen to the Monty Python episode, **Argument**, carefully. Write down the definition of the following words.

 Argument

 Contradiction

1:29

YOU'VE WON!!

Congratulations!

Your group has just won an all-expense-paid field trip for one week to the spot of your choosing. It can be anywhere in the world. Since it is a field trip, you will have no school for that week. Now comes the hard part -- where will your group choose to go?

1. Think of three places you would like to go. Write down your reasons for wanting to go there.

	Place	Reason
Place 1 .		
Place 2 .		
Place 3 .		

2. In order to make that choice, form pairs. Each pair will think up a list of three places that would be special to them to visit. The pairs will write down their choices and talk over reasons why they think their choices are wise ones. (A trip to someone's grandparent's house may be a fine choice, if that person can suggest things that all the group members would enjoy there.)

   a. Person A states where he or she wants to go. Person B states where he or she wants to go.

   b. Person A states his or her reasons. Person B states his or her reasons.

   c. The two reach an agreement as to where they would like to go as a pair and why.

3. After each pair has made its selection of places, two pairs combine to make a group of four. The group meets to choose a field-trip spot. The group must reach consensus in order to claim their prize.

4. Divide into two pairs. Working as a pair, define the words negotiate, negotiating, and negotiations.

❧ Analogy Controversy ❧

1. You and your partner have been assigned one of the answers to the following question. Prepare the best case possible for your answer being correct. Each of you needs to be able to present your case.

2. You have been assigned to a group of four. Your group is to make a decision as to what the answer is to the following question.

   a. Each member represents one of the answers for the question given below. Present the "best case" for your alternative.

   b. After all alternatives have been advocated, each member points out why the answer represented by the person on his or her right is incorrect. Defend your alternative from attacks by other group members.

3. Reverse perspectives by presenting the best case for the answer represented by the person on your right.

4. Drop all advocacy and decide by consensus on the correct answer.

ASSERTION is to DISPROVED as ACTION is to:

Intellectual Controversy

Task: In the book, **Peter Pan,** a case is made for staying young forever in Never-Never Land. Is this a good idea? Would you like to live in Never-Never Land and never grow up? Write a report on the issue, **Was Peter Pan right or wrong? Should you grow up or stay a child?"** The report should present a position and the reasons why the position is valid.

Cooperative: Write one report for the group, everyone has to agree, and everyone has to be able to explain the choice made and the reasons why the choice is a good one.

Procedure:

1. **Research And Prepare Your Position:** Your group of four has been divided into two pairs. One pair has been assigned the pro position and the other pair has been assigned to the con position. With your partner, plan how to present to the other pair the best case possible for your assigned position in order to make sure it receives a fair and complete hearing. Research your position and get as much information to support it as possible. Make sure both you and your partner are ready to present.

2. **Present And Advocate Your Position:** Forcefully and persuasively present the best case for your position to the opposing pair. Be as convincing as possible. Take notes and clarify anything you do not understand when the opposing pair presents.

3. **Open Discussion:** Argue forcefully and persuasively for your position, presenting as many supporting facts as you can. Critically evaluate the opposing pair's arguments, challenge their information and reasoning, and defend your position from their attacks. Keep in mind that you need to know both sides to write a good report.

4. **Reverse Perspectives:** Reverse perspectives and present the best case for the opposing position. The opposing pair will do the same. Strive to see the issue from both perspectives simultaneously.

5. **Synthesis:** Drop all advocacy. Synthesize and integrate the best evidence and reasoning from both sides into a joint position that all members can agree to. Then (a) finalize the group report, (b) present your conclusions to the class, (c) individually take the test covering both sides of the issue, and (d) process how well you worked together as a group and how you could be even more effective next time.

Controversy Rules ○ ○ ○

1. I am critical of ideas, not people. I challenge and refute the ideas of the opposing pair, but I do not indicate that I personally reject them.

2. I remember that we are all in this together, sink or swim. I focus on coming to the best decision possible, not on **winning**.

3. I encourage everyone to participate and to master all the relevant information.

4. I listen to everyone's ideas, even if I don't agree.

5. I restate what someone has said if it is not clear.

6. I first bring out **all** ideas and facts supporting both sides, and then I try to put them together in a way that makes sense.

7. I try to understand both sides of the issue.

8. I change my mind when the evidence clearly indicates that I should do so.

Thumb Wrestling: Lock fingers with another person with your thumbs straight up. Tap your thumbs together three times and then try to pin the other's thumb so that the other cannot move it.

Slapping hands: Person A puts her hands out, palms down. Person B extends his hands, palms up, under Person A's hands. The object of the exercise is for Person B to try to slap the hands of Person A by quickly moving his hands from the bottom to the top. As soon as Person B makes a move, Person A tries to pull her hands out of the way before Person B can slap them.

NONVERBAL
CONFLICTS

Exercise

How Conflicts Should Be Managed

1. Working with a partner, write out five rules for resolving your controversies. There should be one set of answers for the two of you, both of you have to agree on the answers, and both of you have to be able to explain your answers to the teacher or the entire class.

    1.

    2.

    3.

    4.

    5.

2. Combine with another pair. Share your rules. Listen carefully to theirs. Use their ideas to improve your list.

    1.

    2.

    3.

    4.

    5.

Here is a list from another class:

1. Deal with the issue, not the person (ancient history does not count).
2. No name calling (it only makes things worse).
3. No pushing, shoving, or hitting (physical violence makes things worse).
4. Stand up for your ideas and opinions (You have a perfect right).
5. Explore the differences between what you and the other person think before you try to agree.
6. Try to see the issue from both perspectives at the same time.
7. Synthesize, don't win.

Conflict Self-Assessment

1. Rate your ability to resolve conflicts constructively on the criteria given in the table below.

Low 1--2--3--4--5--6--7--8--9--10 High

2. Then rate the ability of your classmates (students) to resolve conflicts constructively.

Low 1--2--3--4--5--6--7--8--9--10 High

3. Share ratings with partner. Compare your ratings of yourself and others.

Rating of Me	Criteria	Rating of Others
	Engage In Controversies (Academic Conflict) Frequently	
	Knowledge Of Controversy Procedures	
	Challenge Other's Information And Logic To Spark Inquiry	
	Argue With Others To Increase Own And Others' Learning	
	Able To Argue In Ways That Increase Trust, Liking, Respect	
	Improve Conflict Skills Each Time Academic Conflict Is Resolved	

I am _____
   am not _____   satisfied with the way I now solve conflicts.

I would _____
   would not _____   like to learn ways to solve conflicts.

Chapter Two: Using Academic Controversy: The Research Promise

Introduction

In a course on ethical decision making in a nursing school, the instructor explains that (a) with the expanded use of technological advances in health care accompanied by the need for moral decisions, there is a growing pressure on nurses to be proficient in ethical decision making, and (b) the development of their ethical decision making skills will be promoted through use of structured controversy as a learning strategy (Pederson, Ducket, Maruyama, & Ryden, 1990). *"Should nutrition and/or hydration be given to a patient by artificial means for whom there is no hope of recovery and who is no longer conscious?"* the instructor asks. *"Your task is to write a report giving your best reasoned judgment as to when, ideally, the responsibility of medical personnel to treat a patient ends. I want one report from your group of four. Everyone must agree on the contents of the report and everyone must be able to explain the group's final judgment to the rest of the class."* The instructor then divides the groups into two-person advocacy teams with one team being given the *"Medical personnel must prolong as long as possible"* position and the other team being given the *"Family members should determine whether medical care should be extended beyond hope of recovery"* position. In addition to their textbooks, the advocacy teams are given materials supporting their assigned position. Students then engage in the controversy procedure involving preparing positions, presenting them, refuting the positions of others while rebutting criticisms of one's own positions, taking the perspectives of opposition, and deriving a synthesis or integration of the positions.

There is considerable research evidence validating the use of academic controversies. Over the past 20 years, we (with such colleagues as Dean Tjosvold and Karl Smith) have developed and tested a theory of controversy (Johnson, 1970, 1978, 1980; Johnson & F. Johnson, 1975; Johnson, F. Johnson, & R. Johnson, 1976; Johnson & R. Johnson, 1979, 1989, 1992; Tjosvold & Johnson, 1983; Watson & Johnson, 1972). We have conducted over 20 experimental and field-experimental studies on controversy. In all our studies subjects were randomly assigned to conditions, the studies lasted from one to thirty hours of instructional time, all were conducted on intermediate elementary and school individuals, and all have all been published in journals. In connection with our research, we have developed a series of curriculum units on energy and environmental issues structured for academic controversies. The use of academic controversy has been field-tested in schools and schools throughout the United States, Canada, and a number of other countries. We are not, however, the only researchers interested in this field of inquiry.

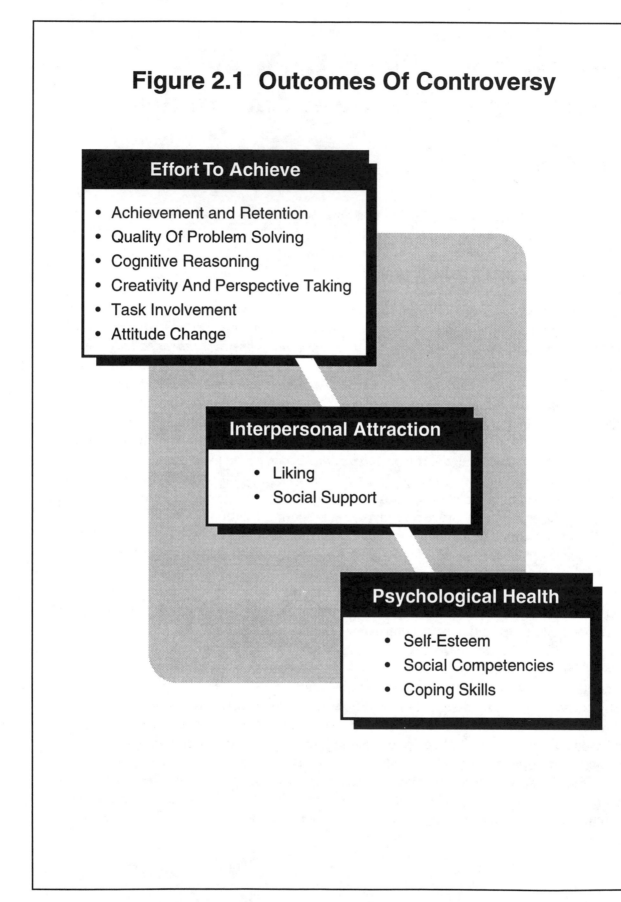

Figure 2.1 Outcomes Of Controversy

Effort To Achieve

- Achievement and Retention
- Quality Of Problem Solving
- Cognitive Reasoning
- Creativity And Perspective Taking
- Task Involvement
- Attitude Change

Interpersonal Attraction

- Liking
- Social Support

Psychological Health

- Self-Esteem
- Social Competencies
- Coping Skills

General Characteristics Of Controversy Research

Table 2.1 General Characteristics Of Studies

	No.	%
1970-1979	11	42
1980-1989	15	58
Random Assign Subjects	20	77
No Random Assignment	6	23
Grade 1-3	6	23
Grade 4-6	7	27
Grades 10-12	1	4
College	11	42
Adult	1	4
Journals	26	100
1 Session	11	42
2-9 Sessions	6	23
10-20 Sessions	7	27
20+ Sessions	2	8

The research on controversy has all been conducted in the last 25 years within an experimental and field-experimental format (see Table 2.1). Over 75 percent of the studies randomly assigned subjects to conditions. About 50 percent of the studies were conducted on elementary and secondary school students and the other half were conducted on college students and adults. They have all been published in journals. The studies have lasted from one to over 60 hours.

To analyze the results of the research a meta-analysis was conducted. To ensure that all studies were weighted equally, an average effect size for each dependent variable for each study was conducted. To compensate for number of students included in each study, a weighted effect size was conducted.

Outcomes Of Controversy

Numerous outcomes of controversy have been documented by the research. They may be classified into three broad categories: achievement, positive interpersonal relationships, and psychological health.

Achievement, Problem Solving, Creativity, Task Involvement

From Table 2.2 it may be seen that in the research conducted to date controversy produced higher productivity, achievement, and quality of decision making than did concurrence-seeking, debate, or individualistic efforts. When controversy was compared with concurrence-seeking, controversy produced significantly higher achievement in over 56 percent of the cases while concurrence-seeking produced significantly higher achievement about 11 percent of the time. The average controversy participant performed at over 1/3 a standard deviation above the average person working within concurrence-seeking cooperative groups. The z-scores for these two comparisons indicate that the likelihood that these findings were found by chance is less than one in a

Table 2.2 Meta-Analysis Of Controversy Studies: Achievement

	Average Effect Size			Weighted Effect-Size				Z-Score		
	Mean	sd	n	d+	sd	k	Cld95%	Z	n	fsn
Achievement										
Contro/Concurrence	0.68	0.41	15	0.70	0.01	15	0.16	14.22	55	4,028
Contro/Debate	0.40	0.43	6	0.44	0.02	6	0.25	4.07	21	107
Contro/Individual	0.87	0.47	19	0.81	0.01	19	0.16	16.85	56	5,787
Cog Reasoning										
Contro/Concurrence	0.62	0.44	2	0.60	0.03	2	0.58	2.68	5	8
Contro/Debate	1.35	0.00	1	1.35	0.04	1	0.79	1.39	6	2
Contro/Individual	0.90	0.48	15	0.84	0.01	15	0.18	14.28	43	3,177
Perspective Taking										
Contro/Concurrence	0.91	0.28	9	0.86	0.01	9	0.20	9.03	17	493
Contro/Debate	0.22	0.42	2	0.26	0.04	2	0.39	0.17	6	6
Contro/Individual	0.86	0	1	0.86	0	1	0.55	5.48	4	40
Motivation										
Contro/Concurrence	0.75	0.46	12	0.69	0.01	12	0.17	11.12	33	1466
Contro/Debate	0.45	0.44	5	0.53	0.02	5	0.27	4.95	9	72
Contro/Individual	0.71	0.21	4	0.72	0.02	4	0.29	7.31	9	168
Interpersonal Attr										
Contro/Concurrence	0.24	0.44	8	0.27	0.01	8	0.20	1.26	19	8
Contro/Debate	0.72	0.25	6	0.68	0.02	6	0.25	5.76	14	158
Contro/Individual	0.81	0.11	3	0.80	0.03	3	0.33	6.44	10	142
Debate/Individual	0.46	0.13	2	0.46	0.04	2	0.41	3.39	8	26
Social Support										
Contro/Concurrence	0.32	0.44	8	0.31	0.01	8	0.18	3.15	30	79
Contro/Debate	0.92	0.42	6	0.89	0.02	6	0.26	13.82	30	2,075
Contro/Individual	1.52	0.29	3	1.48	0.03	3	0.36	11.20	10	451
Debate/Individual	0.85	0.01	2	0.85	0.05	2	0.42	6.85	6	98
Attitudes										
Contro/Concurrence	0.58	0.29	5	0.62	0.02	5	0.22	7.49	19	392
Contro/Debate	0.81	0.00	1	0.81	0.14	1	0.74	3.34	8	25
Contro/Individual	0.64	0	1	0.64	0.08	1	0.54	1.92	6	2

Self- Esteem										
Contro/Concurrence	0.39	0.15	4	0.37	0.02	4	0.25	2.75	7	12
Contro/Debate	0.51	0.09	2	0.51	0.02	2	0.41	1.02	4	2
Contro-Individual	0.85	0.04	3	0.65	0.01	3	0.22	5.26	5	46
Debate/Individual	0.45	0.17	2	0.45	0.02	2	0.41	1.41	3	1

Note 1: Neg = Negative, NoD = No Difference, Pos = Positive, sd = standard deviation, n = number, fsn= fail safe n, Contro = Controversy, Attr = Attraction, Cog = Cognitive

Note 2—Homogeneity Statistics: **Achievement**: Qwithin = 26.77, df = 18, p = 0.08, Qbetween = 1.18, df = 2, p = 0.55, Qtotal = 27.95, df = 20, p = 0.11; **Cognitive Reasoning**: Qwithin = 14.44, df = 15, p = 0.49, Qbetween = 2.65, df = 2, p = 27, Qtotal = 17.09, df = 12, p = 0.45; **Perspective- Taking**: Qwithin = 7.05, df = 9, p = 0.63, Qbetween = 7.34, df = 2, p = 0.03, Qtotal = 14.39, df = 11, [= 0.21; **Motivation**: Qwithin = 5.71, df = 11, p = 0.89, Qbetween = 0.61, df = 2, p = 0.74, Qtotal = 6.32, df = 13, p = 0.94; **Interpersonal Attraction**: Qwithin = 13.87, df = 15, p = 0.54, Qbetween = 10.53, df = 3, p = 0.02, Qtotal = 24.40, df = 18, p = 0.14; **Social Support**: Qwithin = 21.88, df = 15, p = 0.11, Qbetween = 30.30, df = 3, p = 0.00, Qtotal = 52.22, df = 18, p = 0.00; **Attitudes**: Qwithin = 3.24, df = 5, p = 0.66, Qbetween = 0.19, df = 2, p = 0.91, Qtotal = 3.43, df = 7, p = 0.84.

hundred. Finally, it would take over one thousand new studies that found exactly no difference between controversy and concurrence-seeking to reduce the **z**-score to nonsignificance. The comparisons between controversy and debate and individualistic efforts is even more positive with effect sizes of 0.77 and 0.62 respectively. In the three studies that compared debate and individualistic learning, debate tended to produce somewhat higher achievement (effect size = 0.36).

While the research findings on productivity may be summarized into overall statistical analyses, the specific studies on achievement, problem solving, creativity, and task involvement may be examined separately.

Achievement And Retention

Controversy has been found to result in greater mastery and retention of the material and skills being learned than did concurrence-seeking (effect size = 0.68), debate (effect size = 0.40), or individualistic learning (effect size = 0.87). Nemeth and his associates (1990), for example, found that subjects exposed to a credible alternative view (a) recalled more correct information, (b) were better able to transfer learning to new situations, and (c) used more complex and higher-level reasoning strategies in recalling and transferring information learned. Furthermore, individuals who experienced conceptual conflict resulting from controversy were better able to generalize the principles they learned to a wider variety of situations than were individuals not experiencing conceptual conflict (Inagaki & Hatano, 1968, 1977). Finally, controversy tends to promote greater motivation to learn than do concurrence seeking (effect size = 0.67), debate (effect size = 0.82), and individualistic learning (effect size = 0.65).

Quality of Problem Solving

The purpose of controversy within a group is to arrive at the highest quality problem solution or decision that is possible. There is evidence that the occurrence of a controversy within a group resulted in a higher quality problem solution and decision than did concurrence-seeking, debate, or individualistic learning (Boulding, 1964; Glidewell, 1953; Hall & Williams, 1966, 1970; Hoffman, Harburg, & Maier, 1962; Hoffman & Maier, 1961; Maier & Hoffman, 1964; Maier & Solem, 1952).

Tjosvold (1990) interviewed 27 pilots, first officers, and second officers, and 8 flight attendants on how specific incidents that threatened the safety of the airplane were managed. Respondents were asked to describe in detail a recent, significant incident in which they managed an air safety problem effectively and one they managed ineffectively. Sixty incidents were provided. Hierarchical regression analyses indicated that the open discussion of conflicting views and ideas within a cooperative context were powerful antecedents to using safe procedures expeditiously. Pederson, Ducket, Maruyama, and Ryden (1990) demonstrated that the use of structured academic controversy improves the quality of decisions that involve ethical dilemmas nursing students make about patients.

What happens when erroneous information is presented by participants? Can the advocacy of two conflicting but wrong solutions to a problem create a correct one? In most of the studies conducted, two conflicting but legitimate alternative solutions were advocated by members of problem-solving groups. There are creative contributions, however, that may be made by opposing positions, even when they are wrong. **The value of the controversy process lies not so much in the correctness of an opposing position, but rather in the attention and thought processes it induces.** More cognitive processing may take place when individuals are exposed to more than one point of view, even if the point of view is incorrect. Nemeth and Wachtler (1983) found that subjects exposed to a credible minority view generated more solutions to a problem and more correct solutions than did subjects exposed to a consistent single view, even if the minority view was incorrect.

Cognitive Reasoning

From Table 2 it may be seen that controversy promotes more higher-level reasoning than do concurrence seeking (effect size = 0.62), debate (effect size = 1.35), or individualistic learning (effect size = 0.90). A number of studies on cognitive reasoning have focused on the ways in which nonconserving, cognitively immature children can be influenced to gain the critical insights into conservation. Presenting immature children with erroneous information that conflicts with their initial position has been found to promote some cognitive growth, although not as much growth as when they received correct information (Cook & Murray, 1973; Doise, Mugny, & Perret-Clermont, 1976; Murray, 1972). On subsequent posttests taken individually after the controversy, significant gains in performance were recorded. Ames and Murray (1982) compared the impact of controversy, modeling, and nonsocial presentation of information on the performance of nonconserving, cognitively immature children on conservation tasks. The immature children were presented with erroneous information that conflicted with their initial position. Ames and Murray found modest but significant gains in conservation performance. Three children with scores of 0 out of 18 scored between 16 and 18 out of 18 on the posttest, and 11 children with initial scores of 0 scored between 5 and 15. They conclude that conflict **qua** conflict is not only cognitively motivating, but that the resolution of the conflict is likely to be in the direction of correct performance. In this limited way, two wrongs came to make a right.

Creativity

By blending the breath of the sun and the shade,
true harmony comes into the world.

Tao Te Ching

Controversy tends to promote creative insight by influencing individuals to (a) view problems from different perspectives and (b) reformulate problems in ways that allow the emergence of new orientations to a solution. From Table 2 it may be seen that controversy promotes more accurate and complete understanding of opposing perspectives than do concurrence seeking (effect size = 0.91), debate (effect size = 0.22), and individualistic learning (effect size = 0.86). Controversy also increases the number of ideas, quality of ideas, feelings of stimulation and enjoyment, and originality of expression in creative problem- solving (Bahn, 1964; Bolen & Torrence, 1976; Dunnette, Campbell & Jaastad, 1963; Falk & Johnson, 1977; Peters & Torrance, 1972; Torrance, 1970, 1971, 1973; Triandis, Bass, Ewen, & Mikesell, 1963). Being confronted with credible alternative views has resulted in the generation of more novel solutions (Nemeth & Wachtler, 1983), varied strategies (Nemeth & Kwan, 1985b), and original ideas (Nemeth & Kwan, 1985a). And there is also evidence that controversy resulted in more creative problem solutions, with more member satisfaction, compared to group efforts that did not include controversy (Glidewell, 1953; Hall & Williams, 1966, 1970; Hoffman, Harburg, & Maier, 1962; Maier & Hoffman, 1964; Rogers, 1970). These studies further demonstrated that controversy encouraged group members to dig into a problem, raise issues, and settle them in ways that showed the benefits of a wide range of ideas being used, as well as resulting in a high degree of emotional involvement in and commitment to solving the problems the group was working on.

Task Involvement

John Milton, in **Doctrine and Discipline**, stated *"Where there is much desire to learn, there of necessity will be much arguing, much writing, many opinions; for opinion in good men is but knowledge in the making."* Intellectual disagreement tends to arouse emotions and increase task involvement. **Task involvement** refers to the quality and quantity of the physical and psychological energy that individuals invest in their efforts to achieve. Task involvement is reflected in the attitudes participants have toward the:

1. **Task:** Individuals who engaged in controversies tended to **like the task** better than did individuals who engaged in concurrence-seeking discussions (effect size = 0.63). Participants and observers reported a high level of student involvement in a controversy (LeCount, Evens, & Maruyama, 1992).

2. **Controversy Experience:** Individuals involved in controversy (and to a lesser extent, debate) **liked the procedure** better than did individuals working individualistically (Johnson & Johnson, 1985) and participating in a controversy consistently promoted positive attitudes toward the experience (Johnson, Johnson, Pierson, & Lyons, 1985; Johnson, Johnson & Tiffany, 1984; R. Johnson, Brooker, Stutzman, Hultman, & Johnson, 1985; Lowry & Johnson, 1981; Smith, Johnson, & Johnson, 1981, 1984).

The effectiveness of any management or instructional strategy is directly related to the capacity of the strategy to increase task involvement. Participants' time and energy are finite resources and success can be evaluated in terms of increasing the time and energy individuals will commit to their success.

Attitude Change

Johnson, Johnson, and Tiffany (1984) found that in a controversy participants reevaluated their attitudes about the issue and incorporated opponent's arguments into their own attitudes. LeCount, Maruyama, Petersen, and Basset (1991) demonstrated that participating in the academic controversy procedure results in attitude change beyond what occurs when individuals read about the issue immediately after the controversy ended. LeCount, Evens, and Maruyama (1992) found that participating in a controversy resulted in a shift of attitudes on gender issues that maintained over a period of one week after the controversy ended. They conclude that the attitude change is relatively stable and not merely a response to the controversy experience itself.

Interpersonal Attraction Among Participants

It is often assumed that the presence of controversy within a group will lead to difficulties in establishing good interpersonal relations and will promote negative attitudes toward fellow group members, and it is also often assumed that arguing leads to rejection, divisiveness, and hostility among peers (Collins, 1970). Within controversy and debate there are elements of disagreement, argumentation, and rebuttal that could result in individuals disliking each other and could create difficulties in establishing good relationships. On the other hand, conflicts have been hypothesized potentially to create positive relationships among participants (Deutsch, 1962; Johnson, 1971; Johnson & F. Johnson, 1994), but in the past there has been little evidence to validate such a hypothesis.

From Table 2 it may be seen that controversy promoted greater liking among participants than did concurrence-seeking (effect size = 0.24), debate (effect size = 0.72), or individualistic efforts (effect size = 0.81). Concurrence seeking and debate tended to promote greater interpersonal attraction among participants than did individualistic efforts. The more cooperative the context, the greater the cooperative elements in the situation, and the greater the confirmation of each other's competence, the greater the resulting interpersonal attraction (Johnson & Johnson, 1989).

From Table 2 it may also be seen that controversy promoted greater perceptions of social support from other students than did concurrence seeking (effect size = 0.32), debate (effect size = 0.92), and individualistic learning (effect size = 1.52). Debate within cooperative groups tended to promoted greater perceptions of social support than did individualistic learning (effect size = 0.85). These findings corroborate previous findings that cooperative experiences promote greater perceptions of peer task support than do competitive or individualistic learning situations (Johnson & Johnson, 1983).

The combination of frank exchange of ideas coupled with a positive climate of friendship and support not only leads to more productive decision making and greater learning, it disconfirms the myth that conflict leads to divisiveness and dislike.

Psychological Health And Social Competence

The aspect of psychological health that has been most frequently examined in the research on controversy is self-esteem. From Table 2 it may be seen that controversy promoted higher self-esteem than did concurrence seeking (effect size = 0.39), debate (effect size = 0.51), and individualistic learning (effect-size = 0.85). Debate promoted higher self-esteem than did individualistic learning (effect size = 0.45).

In a series of studies on resilience in the face of adversity Ann Mastern and Norman Garmezy at the University of Minnesota found problem-solving skills and qualities such as empathy to be directly related to students and students' long-term coping with adversity. Mastern states that both problem-solving skills and empathy can be improved through training in conflict management. There are a number of challenges that students face. One is processes such as (a) changes associated with puberty, (b) poverty, (c)

disabilities or handicaps, or (d) racial prejudice. Another is catastrophes such as the death of a family member or friend. In addition, there are a variety of everyday conflicts. Competent students tend to be more cooperative (as opposed to disruptive) and more proactive and involved (as opposed to withdrawn). **The more students learn how to take a cooperative approach to managing conflicts through joint problem-solving, the healthier psychologically they tend to be and the better able they are to deal with stress and adversity.** Students who cannot cope with the challenges they face tend to not know what to do when faced with conflicts and misfortune. **Controversy skills are carried with the adolescent wherever he or she goes and, once acquired, cannot be taken away.** Having procedures and skills to derive creative syntheses that solve joint problems prepares students and students to handle conflict and cope with life's challenges and unforeseen adversities.

Summary

Academic controversy, which structured appropriately, results in (a) increased achievement and retention, higher quality problem solving and decision making, more frequent creative insight, more thorough exchange of expertise, and greater task involvement, (b) more positive interpersonal relationships among students, and (c) greater social competence, self-esteem, and ability to cope with stress and adversity. The next question is by what process those outcomes are derived.

Creative Conflict Contract

Major Learnings	Implementation Plans

Date _____   Date of Progress Report Meeting _____

Participant's Signature _____

Signatures of Other Group Members _____ _____

_____   _____   _____

Research Rationale Statement

Task: Write an explanation why you are using academic controversies. The written rationale statement should include:

1. An introduction that includes the statement that conflict is the key to arousing and maintaining students' interest in an academic area and motivating students to learn.

2. A definition of academic controversy that includes an example.

3. A summary of the more important outcomes of academic controversy. State that, *"There is a great deal of research validating the use of academic controversy."* Then include information about:

   a. The importance of curiosity and motivation on learning.

   b. The impact of intellectual challenge on learning, retention, and higher-level reasoning.

   c. The importance of conflict resolution skills for successful living.

   d. The research outcomes most important to you and to the eprson asking, "Why?"

4. At least one classroom incident that illustrates the power of academic controversy.

5. A summary or conclusion.

Cooperative: All members must sign each other's rationale statements indicating that they have edited each other's statements, agree with its contents, and verify its quality.

Criteria For Success: A well-written research rationale statement by each participant that they can deliver orally.

Individual Accountability: Each person presents his or her rationale statement persuasively.

Expected Behaviors: Suggesting ideas, summarizing, explaining and listening.

Intergroup Cooperation: Whenever it is helpful to do so, check procedures and information with another group.

⚜ CONTROVERSY Questionnaire ⚜

Each of the following questions describes an action taken during a controversy. For each question put a 5 if you <u>always</u> behave that way, 4 if you <u>frequently</u> behave that way, 3 if you <u>occasionally</u> behave that way, 2 if you <u>seldom</u> behave that way, and 1 if you <u>never</u> behave that way.

5-4-3-2-1   1.   When I disagree with other group members, I insist that they change their opinions to match mine.

5-4-3-2-1   2.   If someone disagrees with my ideas and opinions, I feel hurt and rejected.

5-4-3-2-1   3.   I often infer that persons who disagree with me are incompetent and ignorant.

5-4-3-2-1   4.   When others disagree with me, I try to view the issue from all points of view.

5-4-3-2-1   5.   I try to avoid individuals who argue with me.

5-4-3-2-1   6.   When others disagree with me, I view it as an interesting opportunity to learn and to improve the quality of my ideas and reasoning.

5-4-3-2-1   7.   When I get involved in a argument with others, I become more and more certain that I am correct and argue more and more strongly for my own point of view.

5-4-3-2-1   8.   When others disagree with my ideas, I get hostile and angry at them.

5-4-3-2-1   9.   When I disagree with others, I am careful to communicate respect for them as persons while I criticize their ideas.

5-4-3-2-1 10.   I am careful to always paraphrase thinking and feelings of others when they present ideas and opinions that are different from mine.

5-4-3-2-1 11.   When others disagree with me, I generally keep my ideas and opinions to myself.

5-4-3-2-1 12.   When others disagree with me, I encourage them to express their ideas and opinions fully, and seek to clarify the differences between their position and perspective and mine.

5-4-3-2-1 13.   I view my disagreements with others as opportunities to see who "wins" and who "loses."

5-4-3-2-1 14.   I often insult those who criticize my ideas and opinions.

Taken from: <u>Joining Together: Group Theory and Group Skills</u> (4th ed.) by D. W. Johnson and F. P. Johnson. Englewood Cliffs, NJ: Prentice-Hall, 1991.

CONTROVERSY Questionnaire (cont.)

5-4-3-2-1   15.   When another person and I disagree, I carefully communicate, "I appreciate you, I am interested in your ideas, but I disagree with your current position."

5-4-3-2-1   16.   When others disagree with me, I keep thinking of my ideas and opinions so that I do not forget them or get confused.

5-4-3-2-1   17.   I am careful not to share my ideas and opinions when I think others may disagree with them.

5-4-3-2-1   18.   When I disagree with others, I listen carefully to their ideas and opinions and change my mind when doing so is warrented by their information and reasoning.

5-4-3-2-1   19.   When others and I disagree, I try to overpower them with my facts and reasoning.

5-4-3-2-1   20.   I tend to dislike those who disagree with my ideas and opinions.

5-4-3-2-1   21.   When I am disagreeing with and criticizing others' ideas and opinions, I let them know that I like them as persons.

5-4-3-2-1   22.   I try to view the situation and issue from my opponent's shoes when involved in a disagreement about ideas and opinions.

5-4-3-2-1   23.   I refuse to get into a argument with anyone.

5-4-3-2-1   24.   When others disagree with me, I try to clarify the differences among our ideas and opinions, clarify the points of agreement, and seek a creative integration of all our ideas and information.

5-4-3-2-1   25.   When others and I disagree, I have to convince them that I am right and they are wrong.

5-4-3-2-1   26.   When others disagree with my ideas and opinions, it means that they are angry with me and dislike me.

5-4-3-2-1   27.   While I am disagreeing with others, I let them know that I appreciate their ability to present a challenging and thought-provoking position.

5-4-3-2-1   28.   When I am involved in an argument, I restate and summarize the opposing positions.

5-4-3-2-1   29.   When others disagree with me I stay very quiet and try to avoid them in the future.

5-4-3-2-1   30.   When I am involved in an argument, I never forget that we are trying to make the best decision possible by combining the best of all our facts and reasoning.

CONTROVERSY Questionnaire

Write your scores in the spaces provided below. If your score is above 15, it means that you are likely to engage in this strategy. If your score is less than 15, it means that you are not likely to engage in this strategy.

Add the scores of all group members for each strategy and divide by the number of members in the group. This will give you your group average for each strategy.

Constructive Strategy	Your Score	Group Average	Destructive Strategy	Your Score	Group Average
Problem Solving			Win-Lose		
Confirmation			Rejection		
Perspective Taking			Avoidance		

Procedure

1. Compare your scores for the constructive and destructive strategies.

2. Compare your scores with your actual behavior (as reported by observer) in the controversy exercise.

3. Discuss the strategies that are difficult for you to engage in.

4. On the basis of the group average scores and on the actual behavior of the group members in the controversy exercise, characterize the group's tendencies toward constructive and destructive controversy.

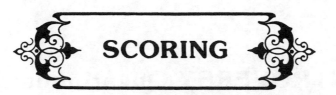

SCORING

Write your answer for each question in the space provided and total your answers for each controversy-managing strategy. The higher the total score for each controversy strategy, the more frequently you tend to use that strategy; the lower the total score for each controversy strategy, the less frequently you tend to use it. Add the scores of all group members for each strategy and divide by the number of members in the group. This will give your group average for each strategy.

WIN-LOSE

_____ 1.
_____ 7.
_____ 13.
_____ 19.
_____ 25.
_____ TOTAL
_____ GRP AVE

REJECTION

_____ 2.
_____ 8.
_____ 14.
_____ 20.
_____ 26.
_____ TOTAL
_____ GRP AVE

CONFIRMATION

_____ 3.*
_____ 9.
_____ 15.
_____ 21.
_____ 27.
_____ TOTAL
_____ GRP AVE

PERSPECTIVE-TAKING

_____ 4.
_____ 10.
_____ 16.*
_____ 22.
_____ 28.
_____ TOTAL
_____ GRP AVE

AVOIDANCE

_____ 5.
_____ 11.
_____ 17.
_____ 23.
_____ 29.
_____ TOTAL
_____ GRP AVE

PROBLEM-SOLVING

_____ 6.
_____ 12.
_____ 18.
_____ 24.
_____ 30.
_____ TOTAL
_____ GRP AVE

Reverse the scoring on this question by substituting 1 for 5, 2 for 4, and so on.

Chapter Three: How Controversy Works

Introduction

Rique Campa, a Professor in the Department of Fisheries and Wildlife at Michigan State University, asked his class, *"Can a marina be developed in an environmentally sensitive area where piping plovers (a shorebird) have a breeding ground?"* He assigns students to groups of four, divides each group into two pairs, and assigns one pair the *"Developer-Position"* and the other pair the *"Department of Natural Resources Position."* He then follows the structured academic controversy procedure over several class periods and requires students to do extensive research on the issue. Students research the issue, prepare a persuasive case for their position, present their position in a compelling and interesting way, refute the opposing position while rebutting criticisms of their position, take the opposing perspectives, and derive a synthesis or integration of the positions. In conducting the controversy, Professor Campa is operationalizing the theoretical process by which controversy works.

Process Of Controversy, Debate, Concurrence Seeking

Since the general or prevailing opinion on any subject is rarely or never the whole truth, it is only by the collision of adverse opinion that the remainder of the truth has any chance of being supplied.

John Stuart Mill

Given that controversy tends to promote higher productivity, more positive relationships, and higher self-esteem than do concurrence-seeking, debate, or individualistic efforts, the question has to be asked, *How does it do so? What are the underlying processes?* A number of developmental (Hunt, 1964; Kohlberg, 1969; Piaget, 1928, 1950), cognitive (Berlyne, 1966; Hammond, 1965, 1973), social (Janis, 1982; Johnson, 1970, 1979, 1980; Johnson & F. Johnson, 1975; Johnson, F. Johnson, & Johnson, 1976; Johnson & R. Johnson, 1979, 1989, 1992; Johnson, Johnson, & Smith, 1988; Maier, 1970), and organizational (Maier, 1970) psychologists have theorized about the processes through which conflict leads to the above outcomes. On the basis of their work, we have proposed the following process:

1. When individuals are presented with a problem or decision, they have an initial conclusion based on categorizing and organizing incomplete information, their limited experiences, and their specific perspective.

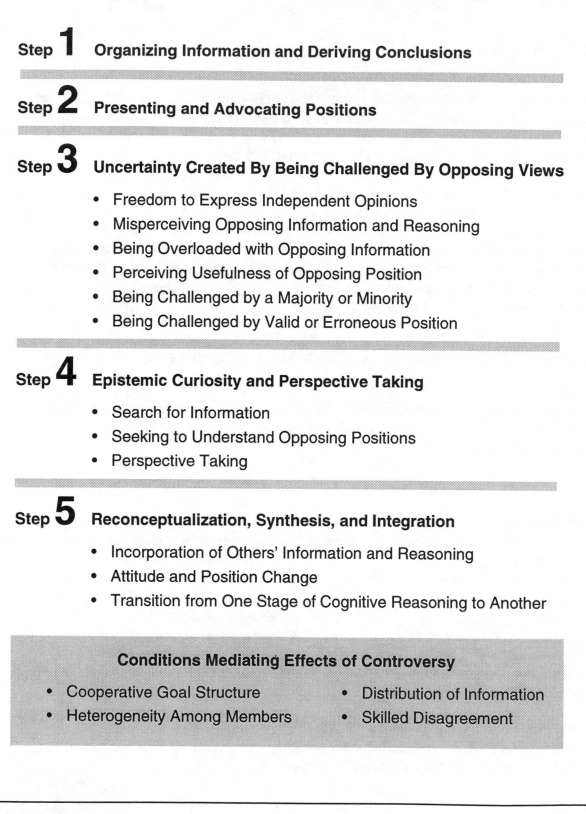

Figure 3.1 Process Of Controversy

Step 1 Organizing Information and Deriving Conclusions

Step 2 Presenting and Advocating Positions

Step 3 Uncertainty Created By Being Challenged By Opposing Views

- Freedom to Express Independent Opinions
- Misperceiving Opposing Information and Reasoning
- Being Overloaded with Opposing Information
- Perceiving Usefulness of Opposing Position
- Being Challenged by a Majority or Minority
- Being Challenged by Valid or Erroneous Position

Step 4 Epistemic Curiosity and Perspective Taking

- Search for Information
- Seeking to Understand Opposing Positions
- Perspective Taking

Step 5 Reconceptualization, Synthesis, and Integration

- Incorporation of Others' Information and Reasoning
- Attitude and Position Change
- Transition from One Stage of Cognitive Reasoning to Another

Conditions Mediating Effects of Controversy

- Cooperative Goal Structure
- Heterogeneity Among Members
- Distribution of Information
- Skilled Disagreement

2. When individuals present their conclusion and its rationale to others, they engage in cognitive rehearsal, deepen their understanding of their position, and discover higher-level reasoning strategies.

3. When individuals are confronted by other people with different conclusions based on other people's information, experiences, and perspectives, they become uncertain as to the correctness of their views. A state of conceptual conflict or disequilibrium is aroused.

4. Uncertainty, conceptual conflict, and disequilibrium motivate an active search for more information, new experiences, and a more adequate cognitive perspective and reasoning process (i.e., **epistemic curiosity**) in hopes of resolving the uncertainty. Divergent attention and thought are stimulated.

5. By adapting their cognitive perspective and reasoning through understanding and accommodating the perspective and reasoning of others, a new, reconceptualized, and reorganized conclusion is derived. Novel solutions and decisions that, on balance, are qualitatively better are detected.

Step 1: Organizing Information And Deriving Conclusions

The controversy process begins with students being asked to consider a problem, issue, or question. To do so, they must conceptualize and avoid barriers to conceptualizing adequately. This involves (a) forming concepts, (b) interrelating them into a conceptual structure, and (c) logically deriving conclusions. Among other things, conceptualizing promotes learning, retention, and transfer and application of learning.

Anything that interferes with the conceptualizing process is a barrier to problem solving, decision making, and learning. Three interrelated barriers are (a) uncritically giving one's dominant response to the situation, (b) mental sets, and (c) fixation on the first satisfactory solution generated. First, responses may be arranged hierarchically (Berlyne, 1965, Maier, 1970) and, when confronted with a problem, individuals may quickly respond with their **dominant response** (without thinking of, evaluating, and choosing among the proper alternatives). Dominant responses based on physical states such as hunger can affect which stimuli a person attends to (Levine, Chein, & Murphy, 1942; McClelland & Atkinson, 1948), psychological states such as attitudes and beliefs (Allport & Postman, 1945; Iverson & Schwab, 1967; Shiplet & Veroff, 1952), and one's general cultural frame of reference (Bartlett, 1932). Second, **mental sets** can cause the same words to have different meanings for different persons (Foley & MacMillan, 1943), the adoption of solutions that have been previously useful (Luchins, 1942), the perception only of what is expected (Neisser, 1954), and the interpretation of ambiguous events in ways that confirm expectations (Bruner & Minturn, 1955). Third, individuals may become **fixated** on the first reasonable solution thought of (Simon, 1976)--this is called **satisficing**.

In many instances people are lazy cognitive processors (they do not actively process the information that is available or do not fully consider the alternative ways of understanding such information [Langer, Blank, & Chanowitz, 1978; Taylor, 1980]) and do not think divergently. **Divergent thinking** results in more ideas (fluency) and more classes of ideas (flexibility) (Guilford, 1956). To ensure that divergent thinking takes place and all major alternatives to the problem being considered are given a fair hearing, each alternative has to be presented in a complete and persuasive way.

Controversy involves assigning the major alternatives to advocacy subgroups and having each subgroup (a) develop its alternative in depth and (b) plan how to present the best case possible for its alternative to the rest of the group. Preparing a position to be advocated within a problem-solving group has clear effects on how well the position is understood and the level of reasoning used in thinking about the position. There is evidence that when individuals know that they will have to present the best case possible for Alternative A to the group as a whole, and try to convince the other group members to decide to adopt Alternative A, they tend to understand Alternative A better than if they had simply considered it for their own use (Allen, 1976; Benware, 1975; Gartner, Kohler, & Reissman, 1971). Higher-level conceptual understanding and reasoning are promoted when individuals teach each other a common way to think about problem situations (Johnson & Johnson, 1979, 1983; Murray, 1983). The way people conceptualize and organize material cognitively has been found to be markedly different when they learned material to teach to others than when they learned material for their own benefit (Annis, 1983; Bargh & Schul, 1980; Murray, 1983). Material learned to be taught was learned at a higher conceptual level than was material learned for one's own use.

The development of a position involves:

1. **Formulating a thesis statement or claim.** A **thesis statement/claim** is a statement that the person wants accepted, but which he or she expects to be challenged. It often includes qualifiers and reservations. **Qualifiers** are those ways of communicating how confident the speaker is in his or her claim and involve words such as "probably," "sometimes," "never," and "always." **Reservations** are the circumstances under which the speaker would decide not to defend a claim and involve words such as "unless" and "until."

2. **Listing and detailing the facts, information, and theories gathered that validate the thesis statement.** Solid evidence and sound reasoning are strived for.

3. **Deriving a conclusion on the basis of principles of scientific inquiry and deductive and inductive logic.** The facts are arranged, composed, and linked together in a logical structure that leads to the conclusion and thereby makes the case for the thesis statement.

There are conditions under which individuals will gather and organize facts, information, and theories into a rationale to support a thesis statement and there are conditions under which they will not. Three of the conditions that may affect the adequacy of a person's preparation are:

1. **The social and cognitive skills involved in formulating a rationale to support the thesis statement.** The person needs the skills of searching out relevant evidence and organizing it into a coherent and logical rationale. Doing so as part of a team requires a wide variety of interpersonal and small group skills (Johnson & F. Johnson, 1991).

2. **The effort expended doing so.** The more effort expended, the more the position is valued. Individuals generally have an enhanced regard for their own productions relative to others' (Greenwald & Albert, 1968) and the effort spent in preparing a position may be a source of enhanced regard for one's position (Zimbardo, 1965).

3. **The ego- or task-orientation underlying the person's efforts. Ego-oriented efforts** tend to focus on proving one is "right" and "better," while **task-oriented efforts** tend to focus on contributing to a process of making the best decision possible (Nicholls, 1983).

Thus, adequate preparation of the position to be advocated is dependent on being skilled in searching out relevant evidence and working with others to organize it into a coherent and logical rationale, on being willing to expend considerable effort in doing so, and on being task-oriented.

Step 2: Presenting and Advocating Positions

Advocacy may be defined as the presenting of a position and providing reasons why others should adopt it. Most students have very little experience with presenting and advocating a position and get few opportunities to do so. Within a controversy participants present and advocate positions to others who, in turn, are advocating opposing positions. Through a process of argument and counter-argument students attempt to persuade others to adopt, modify, or drop positions. This has a number of benefits. Advocating a position and defending it against refutation require engaging in considerable cognitive rehearsal and elaboration. A number of research studies have found that individuals engaged in controversy (compared with those engaged in debate, concurrence-seeking, and individualistic efforts) contributed more information to the discussion, more frequently repeated information, shared new information, elaborated the material being discussed, presented

more ideas, presented more rationale, made more higher-level processing statements, made more comments aimed at managing their efforts to make high quality decisions, made fewer intermediate level cognitive processing statements, and made more statements managing the group's work (Johnson & Johnson, 1985; Johnson, Johnson, Pierson, & Lyons, 1985; Johnson, Johnson, & Tiffany, 1984; Lowry & Johnson, 1981; Nijhof & Kommers, 1982; Smith, Johnson, & Johnson, 1981, 1984). Disagreements within a group have been found to provide a greater amount of information and variety of facts as well as changes in the salience of known information (Anderson & Graesser, 1976; Kaplan, 1977; Kaplan & Miller, 1977; Vinokur & Burnstein, 1974). Peers, furthermore, have frequently been found to be more effective in teaching information to their peers than specially trained experts (Fisher, 1969; Sarbin, 1976). Finally, people were particularly prone to increase their commitment to a cause that they attempted to persuade another to adopt (Nel, Helmreich, & Aronson, 1969).

Edward R. Murrow, the journalist, said, *To be persuasive we must be believable; to be believable we must be credible; to be credible, we must be truthful.* For the presentation to be credible, and to have impact on the other participants in a controversy, a position must be persistently presented with consistency and confidence and, if possible, advocated by more than one person (Nemeth, Swedlund, & Kanki, 1974; Nemeth & Wachter, 1983).

Step 3: Uncertainty Created By Being Challenged By Opposing Views

In controversy, individuals' conclusions are challenged by the advocates of opposing positions. Members critically analyze each other's positions in attempts to discern weaknesses and strengths. They attempt to refute opposing positions while rebutting the attacks on their position. At the same time, they are aware that they need to learn the information being presented and understand the perspective of the other group members. Students tend to experience conceptual conflict and uncertainty when faced with (a) opposing positions and (b) challenges to the validity of their own position. The direct evidence does indicate that the greater the disagreement among group members, the more frequently disagreement occurs, the greater the number of people disagreeing with a person's position, the more competitive the context of the controversy, and the more affronted the person feels, the greater the conceptual conflict and uncertainty the person experiences (Asch, 1952; Burdick & Burnes, 1958; Festinger & Maccoby, 1964; Gerard & Greenbaum, 1962; Inagaki & Hatano, 1968, 1977; Lowry & Johnson, 1981; Tjosvold & Johnson, 1977, 1978; Tjosvold, Johnson, & Fabrey, 1980; Worchel & McCormick, 1963).

In order for cognitive conflict and uncertainty to be maximized, students must (a) be free to express their opinions, (b) accurately perceive opposing information and reasoning, (c) not be overloaded with information, (d) see opposing information as useful, (e) be challenged by a majority of group members, and (f) be challenged by valid information.

Freedom To Express Independent Opinions

Exposure to more than one point of view decreases the tendency to conform to the majority opinion and to uncritically accept the opinions of others (Asch, 1956). Hearing opposing views being advocated gives participants freedom to examine alternative and original solutions to problems without the stress of noncompliance to the majority opinion (Nemeth, 1986).

Misperceiving Opposing Information And Reasoning

Seeking to understand the rationale supporting opposing positions is not a simple enterprise. There are a number of ways in which understanding information contradicting one's position and reasoning is subject to bias and selective perception. **First**, individuals tend to seek out, learn, and recall information that confirms and supports their beliefs (Levine & Murphy, 1943; Nisbett & Ross, 1980; Snyder & Cantor, 1979; Swann & Reid, 1981). Levine and Murphy (1943), for example, found that individuals learned and retained information congruent with their positions better than they did statements that ran counter to their positions. **Second**, individuals with certain expectations will perceive some information and events but not others (Dearborn & Simon, 1958; Foley & MacMillan, 1943; Iverson & Schwab, 1967; Neisser, 1954; Postman & Brown, 1952). **Third**, individuals' preconceptions and perspectives affect the understanding and recall of information (Allport & Postman, 1945; Bartlett, 1932; Pepitone, 1950). **Finally**, individuals who hold strong beliefs about an issue are apt to subject disconfirming evidence to highly critical evaluation while accepting confirming evidence at face value (Lord, Ross, and Lepper, 1979).

Being Overloaded With Opposing Information

Some danger of information overload and becoming confused with the complexity of the issues exists when we are required to learn opposing views and contrary information (Ackoff, 1967). There is a limit to the amount of information that human beings can process at any given time. If they are exposed to more information than they can handle, much of it will be lost. Sometimes, in the interests of accuracy or objectivity, so much information is packed into such a short period of time that nearly everything is lost. This is called **information overload**.

Perceiving Usefulness Of Opposing Position

There is also evidence that if individuals are planning to use contrary information to improve the quality of their learning, problem solving, and decision making, they will learn and utilize the information. Jones and Aneshansel (1956), for example, found that when individuals have to learn information counter to their position because they have to be ready to argue from that viewpoint at a later time, they learn it better than will those who agree with the information and therefore already have such arguments at hand.

Being Challenged By A Majority Or Minority

Whether individuals' views are challenged by a majority or by a minority of group members has important implications on the outcomes of controversy. **Majorities** exert more influence than do minorities (see Tanford & Penrod, 1984 for a review). Majorities may influence through compliance (through a comparison process) or conversion (through a validation process). In most groups, there is movement toward the majority opinion. Kalven and Zeisel (1966), for example, documented in a study of 225 juries that the majority position on the first ballot (i.e., held by 7-11 jury members) was the final verdict in over 85 percent of the cases. Such movement to the majority position is assumed to be based on information influence (majority judgments give information about reality) and normative influence (individuals want to be accepted and avoid disapproval) (Deutsch & Gerard, 1955). Majorities start with positive judgments and expectations (e.g., they are correct and their approval is important). Movement to the majority position usually occurs early within the group discussion (Asch, 1956). Majority viewpoints seem to be seriously considered from the beginning. Majority influence often results in overt compliance without private or latent change to majority views (Allen, 1965; Moscovici & Lage, 1976). Two types of conflict are aroused by the majority: the fear of being deviant and the fear of being wrong.

Majorities induce a concentration on the position they propose (Nemeth, 1976, 1986). Persons exposed to opposing majority views focus on the aspects of the stimuli pertinent to the position of the majority, they think in convergent ways, and they tend toward adoption of the proposed solution to the neglect of novel solutions or decisions. The quality of the solution or decision depends on the validity of the initial majority position.

Being influenced by a **minority** is different. Minorities have to convert through validating their position. The conflict aroused is based on the fear of being wrong (resistance to agreeing with a minority position, however, may be aroused by not wanting to lose membership in the majority). Minorities are often viewed negatively, sometimes with downright derision (Nemeth & Wachtler, 1983). Movement to the minority position often occurs late in the group discussion (Nemeth, Swedlund, & Kanki, 1974; Nemeth & Wachtler, 1974, 1983). Minority viewpoints need time because it is the consistency and confidence with which the minority positions are argued that leads them to receive serious consideration (Moscovici & Faucheaux, 1972; Moscovici & Nemeth,

1974). Minority influences may be latent, being detected in subsequent situations where individuals make solitary judgments (Moscovici & Lage, 1976; Moscovici, Lage, & Naffrechoux, 1969; Mugny, 1980; Nemeth & Wachtler, 1974).

Minorities, compared with majorities, stimulate a greater consideration of other alternatives and, therefore, persons exposed to opposing minority views exert more cognitive effort (Nemeth, 1976, 1986). Those exposed to minority views are stimulated to attend to more aspects of the situation, they think in more divergent ways, and they are more likely to detect novel solutions or come to new decisions. On the balance, these solutions and decisions are "better" or "more correct." Initially, opposing minority views are considered to be incorrect and are dismissed. With consistency and confidence on the minority's part over time, individuals may ask, "How can they be so wrong and yet so sure of themselves?" As a result, they are stimulated to reappraise the entire situation, which may include alternatives other than that being proposed by the minority. In other words, the thought processes are marked by divergence and, hence, the potential for detecting novel solutions or decisions.

Much more stress is reported in majority influence situations than in minority influence ones, presumably because in the former individuals feared that they were wrong and that the majority would reject them while in the latter individuals could deride the minority and their opposing views (Asch, 1956; Maass & Clark, 1984; Nemeth, 1976; Nemeth & Wachtler, 1983). The stress induced by the majority would be expected to narrow the focus of attention and increase the likelihood that the strongest and most dominant response would be engaged in (Zajonc, 1965). The more moderate stress experienced when facing minority opposition may stimulate individuals to consider more aspects of the situation and more possible conclusions.

Being Challenged By Valid Or Erroneous Position

There is some question as to whether a minority challenge based on erroneous information and reasoning will have the same impact as will a challenge based on valid information and reasoning. As was discussed earlier, there are creative contributions made by being confronted with opposing positions, even when they are wrong. The value of the controversy lies not so much in the correctness of an opposing position, but rather in the attention and thought processes it induces. More cognitive processing may take place when individuals are exposed to more than one point of view, even if the point of view is incorrect (Nemeth & Wachtler, 1983). Subjects exposed to a credible but erroneous minority view generated more solutions to a problem and more correct solutions than did subjects exposed to a consistent single view. The advance to a higher-level reasoning process has been

demonstrated to be sparked by being confronted with an opposing erroneous point of view (Cook & Murray, 1973; Doise, Mugny, & Perret-Clermont, 1976; Murray, 1974).

Summary

The direct evidence indicates that opposing information is learned more accurately within controversies than within debate, concurrence-seeking, or individualistic situations. Hearing opposing views being advocated, furthermore, stimulates new cognitive analysis and frees individuals to create alternative and original conclusions. When contrary information is not clearly relevant to completing the task at hand it may be ignored, discounted, or perceived in biased ways in favor of supporting evidence. When individuals realize, however, that they are accountable for knowing the contrary information some time in the near future, they will tend to learn it. Too much information can result in information overload. Opposing views are more effective in promoting divergent thinking and effective problem solving when they are presented by a nonmajority. Even being confronted with an erroneous point of view can result in more divergent thinking and the generation of novel and more cognitively advanced solutions.

Step 4: Epistemic Curiosity And Perspective Taking

Macbeth said, *Stay, you imperfect speakers, tell me more.* When faced with intellectual opposition within a cooperative context, individuals tend to ask each other for more information. Conceptual conflict is hypothesized to motivate an active search for more information (often called **epistemic curiosity**) in hopes of resolving the uncertainty. The direct evidence indicates that individuals engaged in controversy (compared to persons involved in noncontroversial discussions, concurrence-seeking discussions, and individualistic efforts) are motivated to know others' positions and to develop understanding and appreciation of them (Tjosvold & Johnson, 1977, 1978; Tjosvold, Johnson, & Fabrey, 1980; Tjosvold, Johnson, & Lerner, 1981) and develop a more accurate understanding of the other positions (Smith, Johnson, & Johnson, 1981; Tjosvold & Johnson, 1977, 1978; Tjosvold, Johnson, & Fabrey, 1980). Indices of epistemic curiosity include individuals' actively (a) searching for more information, (b) seeking to understand opposing positions and rationales, and (c) attempting to view the situation from opposing perspectives.

Search For Information

There is evidence that controversy results in an active search for more information. Lowry and Johnson (1981) found that individuals involved in controversy, compared with persons involved in concurrence seeking, read more relevant material, reviewed more relevant materials, more frequently gathered further information during their free time, and more frequently requested information from others. Smith, Johnson, and Johnson (1981) found that controversy, compared with both concurrence- seeking and individualistic efforts, promoted greater use of relevant materials and more frequently giving up free time to gather further information. Johnson and Johnson (1985) and Johnson, Johnson, and Tiffany (1984) found that controversy, compared with debate and individualistic efforts, promoted greater search for more information outside of class. R. Johnson, Brooker, Stutzman, Hultman, and Johnson (1985) found that individuals engaged in controversy had greater interest in learning more about the subject being discussed than did persons engaged in concurrence seeking or individualistic efforts. Beach (1974) found that small discussion groups working cooperatively consulted more books in writing papers for a school psychology course than did individuals in a traditional lecture-competition format. Hovey, Gruber, and Terrell (1963) found that individuals who participated in cooperative discussion groups during a school psychology course engaged in more serious reading to increase their knowledge and demonstrated more curiosity about the subject matter following a course experience than did individuals in a traditional lecture-competition course format.

Seeking To Understand Opposing Positions

Individuals engaged in controversy have been found to be motivated to know others' positions and to develop understanding and appreciation of them (Tjosvold & Johnson, 1977, 1978; Tjosvold, Johnson, & Fabrey, 1980; Tjosvold, Johnson, & Lerner, 1981). Attempting to understand opposing positions pays off. Individuals involved in a controversy developed a more accurate understanding of other positions than did persons involved in noncontroversial discussions, concurrence-seeking discussions, and individualistic efforts (Smith, Johnson, & Johnson, 1981; Tjosvold & Johnson, 1977, 1978; Tjosvold, Johnson, & Fabrey, 1980).

Perspective Taking

In order to arrive at a synthesis that is acceptable to all group members, the issue must be viewed from all perspectives. Understanding the facts being presented by other advocacy teams is not enough. The perspective from which opposing members are speaking must also be clearly understood. Group members need to be able to both comprehend the information being presented by their opposition and to understand the cognitive perspective their opposition is using to organize and interpret the information. A **cognitive perspective** consists of the cognitive organization being used to give meaning to a person's knowledge, and the structure of a person's reasoning. Tjosvold and Johnson (1977, 1980) and Tjosvold, Johnson, and Fabrey (1978) conducted three experiments in which they found that the presence of controversy promoted greater understanding of another person's cognitive perspective than did the absence of controversy. Individuals engaging in a controversy were better able subsequently to predict what line of reasoning

their opponent would use in solving a future problem than were persons who interacted without any controversy.

In his dissertation, Karl Smith (1980; Smith, Johnson, and Johnson, 1981) compared the relative impact of controversy, concurrence seeking, and individualistic efforts. Eighty-four sixth-grade individuals were randomly assigned to conditions (and to groups of four within the two group conditions) stratifying for ability and sex. The study lasted for ten ninety-minute periods. Two issues were studied—the advisability of allowing logging, mining, and the use of snowmobiles and motor boats in the Boundary Waters National Park and the advisability of strip mining of coal. He found that individuals engaged in a controversy were more accurate in understanding their opponents' perspective than were persons involved in concurrence-seeking discussions or individualistic efforts. Johnson, Johnson, Pierson, and Lyons (1985) also found that individuals in the controversy condition were better able to take the opposing perspective than were individuals participating in concurrence-seeking discussions.

Perspective-taking skills are important for exchanging information and opinions within a controversy, affecting the amount of information disclosed, communication skills, accuracy of understanding and retention of opposing positions, and friendliness of the information exchange process (Johnson, 1971).

Step 5: Reconceptualization, Synthesis, And Integration

Andre Gide said, *One completely overcomes only what one assimilates.* Nothing could be more true of controversy. When overt controversy is structured within a problem-solving, decision-making, or learning group by identifying alternatives and assigning members to advocate the best case for each alternative, the purpose is not to choose the best alternative. The purpose is to create a synthesis of the best reasoning and conclusions from all the various alternatives. **Synthesizing** occurs when individuals integrate a number of different ideas and facts into a single position. It is the intellectual bringing together of ideas and facts and engaging in inductive reasoning by restating a large amount of information into a conclusion or summary. Synthesizing is a creative process involving seeing new patterns within a body of evidence, viewing the issue from a variety of perspectives, and generating a number of optional ways of integrating the evidence. The dual purposes of synthesis are to arrive at the best possible decision or solution and to find a position that all group members can agree on and commit themselves to. It may be hypothesized that the quality of individuals' reconceptualization, synthesis, and integration depends on the accuracy of their perspective-taking, their incorporation of others' information and reasoning into their own position, their attitude and position change, and their transition to higher stages of cognitive reasoning.

Incorporation of Others' Information and Reasoning

A more accurate understanding of the opponents' position, reasoning, and perspective has been hypothesized to result in greater incorporation of the opponents' reasoning into one's own position. There is evidence that participation in a controversy, compared with participating in noncontroversial discussions, concurrence-seeking discussions, and individualistic efforts, resulted in greater incorporation of opponents' arguments and information (Johnson & Johnson, 1985; Johnson, Johnson, & Tiffany, 1984; Tjosvold, Johnson, & Lerner, 1981).

The critical question is under what conditions will opposing information be incorporated into one's reasoning and under what conditions will it not be. Two conditions hypothesized to affect the incorporation of opposing information are (a) whether cooperative or competitive elements dominate the situation and (b) whether the participants disagree skillfully or unskillfully. Tjosvold and Johnson (1978) conducted a study utilizing 45 under-graduate individuals at Pennsylvania State University. Three conditions were included: controversy within a cooperative context, controversy within a competitive context, and no controversy. Subjects worked on resolving a moral dilemma by individually deciding what course of action should be taken, prepared for a discussion about the moral dilemma with a partner, discussed the moral dilemma with a person from another group, and were debriefed. The experimental session lasted ninety minutes. They found that when the context was cooperative there was more open-minded listening to the opposing position. When controversy occurred within a competitive context, a closed-minded orientation was created in which individuals comparatively felt unwilling to make concessions to the opponent's viewpoint, and closed-mindedly refused to incorporate any of it into their own position. Within a competitive context the increased understanding resulting from controversy tended to be ignored for a defensive adherence to one's own position.

Lowin (1969) and Kleinhesselink and Edwards (1975) found that when individuals were unsure of the correctness of their position, they selected to be exposed to disconfirming information when it could easily be refuted, presumably because such refutation could affirm their own beliefs. Van Blerkom and Tjosvold (1981) found that individuals selected to discuss an issue with a peer with an opposing position more frequently when the context was cooperative rather than competitive, and that individuals in a competitive situation more often selected a less competent peer to discuss an issue with. Tjosvold (1982) and Tjosvold and Deemer (1980) found that when the context was competitive, participants in a controversy understood but did not use others' information and ideas, but when the context was cooperative the information and ideas provided by opponents was used.

In addition to whether a cooperative or competitive climate dominates the situation, the skill with which individuals disagree with each other also affects the degree to which opponents' reasoning is incorporated into one's own position. Tjosvold, Johnson, and Fabrey (1980) and Tjosvold, Johnson, and Lerner (1981) found that when individuals involved in a controversy have their personal competence disconfirmed by their opponent, a closed-minded rejection of the opponent's position, information, and reasoning results. The amount of defensiveness generated influenced the degree to which individuals incorporated the opponent's information and reasoning into decision-makers' position, even when they understood accurately their opponent's position.

Attitude And Position Change

Involvement in a controversy tends to result in attitude and position change. Disagreements within a group have been found to provide a greater amount of information and variety of facts, and a change in the salience of known information which, in turn, resulted in shifts of judgment (Anderson & Graesser, 1976; Kaplan, 1977; Kaplan & Miller, 1977; Nijhof & Kommers, 1982; Vinokur & Burnstein, 1974). Controversy has promoted greater attitude change than did concurrence-seeking, no-controversy, and individualistic efforts (Johnson & Johnson, 1985; R. Johnson, Brooker, Stutzman, Hultman, & Johnson, 1985). Putnam and Geist (1985) found that the likelihood of an agreement requiring position change was highest when there were strong pro and con arguments followed by the development of qualifiers and reservations as ways of finding an acceptable consensus.

Transition from One Stage of Cognitive Reasoning to Another

Cognitive development theorists (Flavell 1963; Kohlberg, 1969; Piaget, 1948, 1950) have posited that it is repeated interpersonal controversies (in which individuals are forced again and again to take cognizance of the perspective of others) that promote (a) cognitive and moral development, (b) the ability to think logically, and (c) the reduction of egocentric reasoning. Such interpersonal conflicts are assumed to create disequilibrium within individuals' cognitive structures, which motivate a search for a more adequate and mature process of reasoning. J. Murray (1972) and Silverman and Stone (1972) paired preoperational children with operational peers and had them argue until they came to an agreement or stalemate about the solutions to various problems. When tested alone after the interaction, 80 percent to 94 percent of the lower level pupils made significant gains in performance compared to the very much lower rates of success reported in studies of more traditional training attempts (Beilin, 1977; F. Murray, 1978). In Murray (1972) 8 out of 15 children who scored 0 out of 12 on the pretest had scores of 11 or 12 out of 12 on the various posttests.

There are several studies that demonstrated that pairing a conserver with a nonconserver, and giving the pair conservation problems to solve and instructing them to argue until there is agreement or stalemate, resulted in the conserver's answer prevailing on the great majority of conservation trials and in the nonconserver learning how to conserve (Ames & Murray, 1982; Botvin & Murray, 1975; Doise & Mugny, 1979; Doise, Mugny, & Perret-Clermont, 1976; Knight-Arest & Reid, 1978; Perret- Clermont, 1980; Miller &

Brownell, 1975; Mugny & Doise, 1978; Murray, 1972; Murray, Ames, & Botvin, 1977; Silverman & Geiringer, 1973; Silverman & Stone, 1972; Smedslund, 1961a, 1961b). Inagaki (1981) and Inagaki and Hatano (1968, 1977) found that individuals (2/3 of whom were nonconservers) who were placed in small groups and given a conservation task and who argued among themselves, gave more adequate and higher level explanations than did the control subjects who did not argue with one another. Experimental subjects showed greater progress in generalizing the principle of conservation to a variety of situations and tended to resist extinction more often when they were shown an apparently nonconserving event. The discussion of the task per se did not produce the effects. There had to be conflict among individuals' explanations for the effects to appear.

The impact of controversy on cognitive and moral reasoning has been found in pairs (Silverman & Geiringer, 1973; Silverman & Stone, 1972), two on one (F. Murray, 1972), and three on two (Botvin & Murray, 1975), in kindergarten, first, second, third, and fifth grades with normal and learning disabled, although not with those disabled by communication disorders (Knight-Arest & Reid, 1978), with blacks and whites, and with middle and low socioeconomic status groups. Borys and Spitz (1979), however, did not find social interaction to be especially effective with mentally retarded institutionalized adolescents (IQ = 66, mental age = 10 years, chronological age = 20 years). Agreement is often reached quickly. Miller and Brownell (1975) found that nearly half the agreements were reached in less than 50 seconds and rarely took longer than 4 or 5 minutes. The advanced children did not prevail because of any greater social influence or higher IQ or because they were more skillful arguers. In arguments about best TV shows and other concepts that have no developmental or necessity attributes, the advanced children won only 41 of 90 arguments, lost 38, and stalemated 11 (Miller & Brownell, 1975). The advanced children seem to initiate discussion slightly more often, state their answer slightly more often, give good reasons, counter the others slightly more often, move stimuli more often, and appear slightly more flexible in their arguments than do the immature children, who tend to repetitiously focus on their original opinion and its justifications (Miller & Brownell, 1975; Silverman & Stone, 1972). Growth tended to occur only for the children who yield, which they do 60 to 80 percent of the time (Silverman & Geiringer, 1973). Growth tended to occur through actual insight, not through parroting the answers of the advanced peers (Botvin & Murray, 1975; Doise, Mugny, & Perret-Clermont, 1976; Gelman, 1978; Murray, 1981). Change tended to be unidirectional and nonreversible. Children who understood conservation did not adopt erroneous strategies while nonconservers tended to advance toward a greater understanding of conservation (Miller & Brownell, 1975; Silverman & Geiringer, 1973). Even two immature children who argued erroneous positions about the answer tended to make modest but significant gains toward an understanding of conservation (Ames & Murray, 1982).

Similar studies have been conducted on moral reasoning. Typically, an individual who used lower-level moral reasoning to resolve a moral dilemma was placed in a cooperative pair with a peer who used a higher-level strategy, and the two were given the assignment of making a joint decision as to how a moral dilemma should be resolved. A controversy inevitably resulted. The studies utilizing this procedure found that it tended to result in initially immature individuals increasing their level of moral reasoning (Blatt, 1969; Blatt & Kohlberg, 1973; Crockenberg & Nicolayev, 1977; Keasey, 1973; Kuhn, Langer, Kohlberg, & Haan, 1977; LeFurgy & Woloshin, 1969; Maitland & Goldman, 1974; Rest, Turiel, & Kohlberg, 1969; Turiel, 1966).

Taken together, these studies provide evidence that controversies among individuals promoted transitions to higher stages of cognitive and moral reasoning. Such findings are important as there is little doubt that higher levels of cognitive and moral reasoning cannot be directly taught (Inhelder & Sinclair, 1969; Sigel & Hooper, 1968; Sinclair, 1969; Smedslund, 1961a, 1961b; Turiel, 1973; Wallach & Sprott, 1964; Wallach, Wall, & Anderson, 1967; Wohowill & Lowe, 1962).

Summary

Students arrive at a synthesis by using higher level thinking and reasoning processes, critically analyzing information, and using both deductive and inductive reasoning. Synthesis requires that students keep conclusions tentative, accurately understand opposing perspectives, incorporate new information into their conceptual frameworks, and change their attitudes and positions.

Conditions Mediating Effects Of Controversy

Although controversies can operate in a beneficial way, they will not do so under all conditions. As with all types of conflicts, the potential for either constructive or destructive outcomes is present in a controversy. Whether there are positive or negative consequences depends on the conditions under which controversy occurs and the way in which it is managed. These conditions and procedures include:

1. The goal structure within which the controversy occurs.

2. The heterogeneity of participants.

3. The amount of relevant information distributed among participants.

4. The social skills of participants.

Cooperative Goal Structure

Deutsch (1973) emphasizes that the context in which conflicts occur has important effects on whether the conflict turns out to be constructive or destructive. There are two possible contexts for controversy: cooperative and competitive. A cooperative context

3 : 16

facilitates constructive controversy and a competitive context promotes destructive controversy in several ways (Johnson & Johnson, 1983):

1. In order for controversy to be constructive, information must be accurately communicated. Communication of information is far more complete, accurate, encouraged, and utilized in a cooperative context than in a competitive context (Johnson, 1974).

2. Constructive controversy requires a supportive climate in which group members feel safe enough to challenge each other's ideas. Cooperation provides a far more supportive climate than competition (Johnson & Johnson, 1991).

3. In order for controversy to be constructive, it must be valued. Cooperative experiences promote stronger beliefs that controversy is valid and valuable (Johnson, Johnson, & Scott, 1978; Lowry & Johnson, 1981; Smith, Johnson, & Johnson, 1981).

4. Constructive controversy requires dealing with feelings as well as with ideas and information. There is evidence that cooperativeness is positively related and competitiveness is negatively related to the ability to understand what others are feeling and why they are feeling that way (Johnson, 1971; 1975a, 1975b).

5. How controversies are defined has a great impact on how constructively they are managed. Within a competitive context controversies tend to be defined as "win-lose" situations (Deutsch, 1973).

6. Constructive controversy requires a recognition of similarities between positions as well as differences. Group members participating in a controversy within a cooperative context identify more of the similarities between their positions than do members participating in a controversy within a competitive context (Judd, 1978).

Evidence supports the argument that a cooperative context aids constructive controversy. Tjosvold and Johnson (1978) found that when the context was cooperative there was more open-minded listening to the opposing position. When controversy occurred within a competitive context, a closed-minded orientation was created in which individuals comparatively felt unwilling to make concessions to the opponent's viewpoint, and closed-mindedly refused to incorporate any of it into their own position. Within a competitive context the increased understanding that resulted from controversy tended to be ignored for a defensive adherence to one's own position. Van Blerkom and Tjosvold (1981) found that participants in a controversy within a cooperative context sought out individuals with opposing opinions to test the validity of their ideas and reap the benefits of controversy, while participants in a controversy within a competitive context attempted to strengthen their opinions either by choosing a more competent partner with the same opinion or a less competent discussant with an opposing view. Tjosvold and Deemer (1980) and Tjosvold (1982) found that **controversy within a cooperative context** induced (a) feelings of comfort, pleasure, and helpfulness in discussing opposing opinions; (b) expectations of the other being helpful; (c) feelings of trust and generosity towards the opponent; (d) uncertainty about the correctness of the opponent's position; (e) motivation to hear more about the opponent's arguments; (f) more accurate understanding of the opponent's position; and (g) the reaching of more integrated positions where both one's own and one's opponent's conclusions and reasoning are synthesized into a final position. **Controversy within a competitive context** promoted closed-minded disinterest and rejection of the opponent's ideas and information. **Avoidance of controversy** resulted in little interest in or actual knowledge of opposing ideas and information and the making of a decision that reflected one's own views only. Within a competitive context, however, Lowin (1969) and Kleinhesselink and Edwards (1975) found that when individuals were unsure of the correctness of their position, they selected to be exposed to disconfirming information when it could easily be refuted, presumably because such refutation could affirm their own beliefs.

Heterogeneity Among Members

Differences among individuals in personality, sex, attitudes, background, social class, reasoning strategies, cognitive perspectives, information, ability levels, and skills lead to diverse organization and processing of information and experiences, which, in turn, begin the cycle of controversy. Such differences have been found to promote achievement and productivity (Fiedler, Meuwese, & Conk, 1961; Frick, 1973; Johnson, 1977; Torrance, 1961; Webb, 1977). The greater the heterogeneity among individuals, the greater the amount of time spent in argumentation (Nijhof & Kommers, 1982). Heterogeneity among individuals leads to potential controversy, and to more diverse interaction patterns and resources for achievement and problem-solving.

Distribution of Information

If controversy is to lead to achievement, individuals must possess information that is relevant to the completion of the tasks on which they are working. The more information individuals have about an issue, the greater their achievement and successful problem solving tends to be (Goldman, 1965; Laughlin, Branch, & Johnson, 1969). Having relevant information available, however, does not mean that it will be utilized. Individuals need the interpersonal and group skills necessary to ensure that all individuals involved contribute their relevant information and that the information is synthesized effectively (Hall & Williams, 1966; Johnson, 1977).

Skilled Disagreement

Controversy requires a complex set of procedures and skills that takes some time to master. When unskilled individuals who have no previous experience with the controversy process are required to engage in it, no advantage is expected. Susan Lund (1980), for example, in her PhD dissertation compared the effectiveness of the presence and absence of controversy and systematic evaluation on quality of decision making.

Subjects were 154 graduate and undergraduate individuals at the University of Minnesota. They were randomly assigned to the four conditions and to groups from four to seven members within conditions. None of the subjects had previously participated in a structured controversy. The subjects participated in a one-hour experimental session in which they were instructed to follow the procedure of controversy or concurrence seeking or vigilant or nonvigilant decision-making behaviors. No significant differences in quality of decision making were found. She concludes that the one-hour time limit was too short for subjects to learn the procedures of controversy and skillfully engage in them.

In order for controversies to be managed constructively, individuals need a number of collaborative and conflict management skills (Johnson, 1990; Johnson & F. Johnson, 1991; Johnson, Johnson, & Holubec, 1991). One of the most important is to be able to **disagree with each other's ideas while confirming each other's personal competence**. Disagreeing with others, and at the same time imputing that they are incompetent, tends to increase their commitment to their own ideas and their rejection of one's information and reasoning (Tjosvold, 1974). Tjosvold, Johnson, and Fabrey (1980) and Tjosvold, Johnson, and Lerner (1981) found that when individuals involved in a controversy had their personal competence disconfirmed by their opponent, a closed-minded rejection of the opponent's position, information, and reasoning resulted. The amount of defensiveness generated influenced the degree to which individuals incorporated the opponent's information and reasoning into their position, even when they understood accurately their opponent's position. Disagreeing with others while simultaneously confirming their personal competence, however, results in being better liked and in the opponents being less critical of one's ideas, more interested in learning more about one's ideas, and more willing to incorporate one's information and reasoning into their own analysis of the problem (Tjosvold, Johnson, & Fabrey, 1980; Tjosvold, Johnson, & Lerner, 1981).

Another important set of skills for exchanging information and opinions within a controversy is **perspective taking**. More information, both personal and impersonal, is disclosed when one is interacting with a person engaging in perspective-taking behaviors such as paraphrasing to demonstrate understanding and communicating the desire to understand accurately. Perspective-taking ability increases one's capacity to phrase messages so that they are easily understood by others and to comprehend accurately the messages of others. Engaging in perspective taking in conflict situations tends to increase understanding and retention of the opponent's information and perspective; facilitate the achievement of creative, high quality problem solving; and promote more positive perceptions of the information-exchange process, fellow group members, and the group's work (Falk & Johnson, 1977; Johnson, 1971, 1977). The greater the clarity of group members' understanding of all sides of the issues and the more accurate the assessment of their validity and relative merits, the more creative the synthesis of all positions in a controversy tends to be.

Summary

It is not enough to know that academic controversies result in (a) increased achievement and retention, higher quality problem solving and decision making, more frequent creative insight, more thorough exchange of expertise, and greater task involvement, (b) closer and more positive relationships, and (c) greater social competence and self-esteem. The process by which they do so must also be understood. The process consists of:

1. Individuals are given a problem to solve, a decision to make, or a question to answer. They have an initial conclusion based on categorizing and organizing incomplete information, their limited experiences, and their specific perspective.

2. Individuals present their conclusion and its rationale to others, thereby engaging in cognitive rehearsal, deepening their understanding of their position, and discovering higher-level reasoning strategies.

3. Individuals are confronted by other people with different conclusions based on other people's information, experiences, and perspectives. The result is that individuals become uncertain as to the correctness of their views. A state of conceptual conflict or disequilibrium is maximized when students (a) are free to express their opinions, (b) accurately perceive opposing information and reasoning, (c) are not overloaded with information, (d) see opposing information as useful, (e) are challenged by a majority of group members, and (f) are challenged by valid information.

4. A state of uncertainty, conceptual conflict, and disequilibrium motivates an active search for more information, new experiences and a more adequate cognitive perspective and reasoning process (i.e., **epistemic curiosity**) in hopes of resolving the uncertainty. Divergent attention and thought are stimulated.

5. A new, reconceptualized, and reorganized conclusion is derived by adapting their cognitive perspective and understanding and accommodating the perspective and reasoning of others. Individuals incorporate others' information and reasoning into their thinking, change their attitudes and position, and use higher-level reasoning strategies. Novel solutions and decisions that, on balance, are qualitatively better are detected.

Controversies tend to be constructive when the situational context is cooperative, there is some heterogeneity among group members, information and expertise is distributed within the group, and members have the necessary conflict skills. While the controversy process sometimes occurs naturally within cooperative learning groups, it may be considerably enhanced when teachers structure academic controversies. The faculty's role in structuring academic controversies.

⟶✦⟦ CONTROVERSY CONTRACT ⟧✦⟵

Major Learnings	Implementation Plans

Date _____   Date of Progress Report Meeting _____

Participant's Signature _____

Signatures of Other Group Members _____   _____

_____   _____   _____

EXERCISE MATERIALS

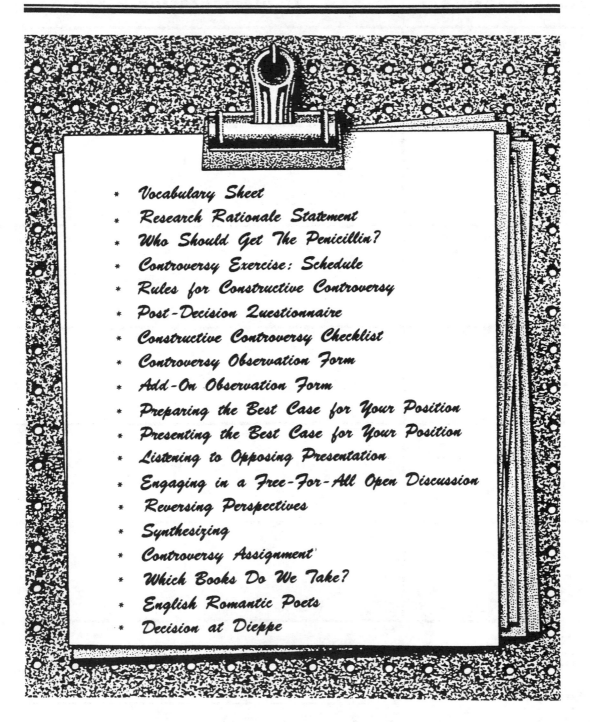

* *Vocabulary Sheet*
* *Research Rationale Statement*
* *Who Should Get The Penicillin?*
* *Controversy Exercise: Schedule*
* *Rules for Constructive Controversy*
* *Post-Decision Questionnaire*
* *Constructive Controversy Checklist*
* *Controversy Observation Form*
* *Add-On Observation Form*
* *Preparing the Best Case for Your Position*
* *Presenting the Best Case for Your Position*
* *Listening to Opposing Presentation*
* *Engaging in a Free-For-All Open Discussion*
* *Reversing Perspectives*
* *Synthesizing*
* *Controversy Assignment*
* *Which Books Do We Take?*
* *English Romantic Poets*
* *Decision at Dieppe*

VOCABULARY SHEET

Working with a partner, learn the definitions of the words below.

1. Define each word in two ways.

   First, write down what you think the word means.

   Second, look it up in the book and write down its definition.

   Note the page on which the definition appears.

2. For each word write a sentence in which the word is used.

3. Make up a story in which all of the words are used.

4. Learn how to spell each word. They will be on your spelling test.

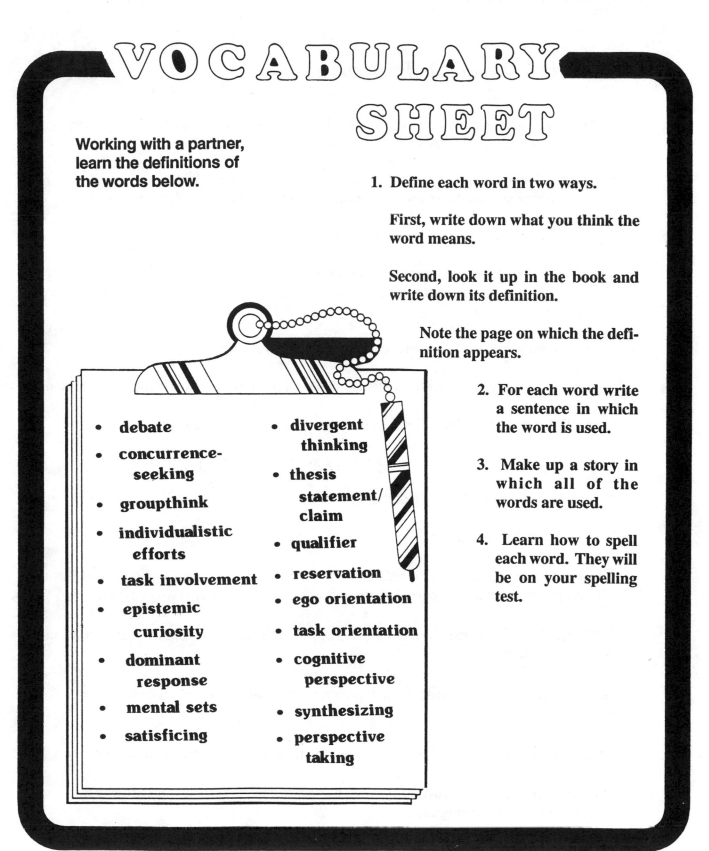

- debate
- concurrence-seeking
- groupthink
- individualistic efforts
- task involvement
- epistemic curiosity
- dominant response
- mental sets
- satisficing
- divergent thinking
- thesis statement/claim
- qualifier
- reservation
- ego orientation
- task orientation
- cognitive perspective
- synthesizing
- perspective taking

Research Rationale Statement

Task: Write an explanation why you are using academic controversies. The written rationale statement should include:

1. An introduction that includes the statement that conflict is the key to arousing and maintaining students' interest in an academic area and motivating students to learn.

2. A definition of academic controversy that includes an example.

3. A summary of the more important outcomes of academic controversy. State that, "*There is a great deal of research validating the use of academic controversy.*" Then include information about:

   a. The importance of curiosity and motivation on learning.

   b. The impact of intellectual challenge on learning, retention, and higher-level reasoning.

   c. The importance of conflict resolution skills for successful living.

   d. The research outcomes most important to you and to the eprson asking, "Why?"

4. At least one classroom incident that illustrates the power of academic controversy.

5. A summary or conclusion.

Cooperative: All members must sign each other's rationale statements indicating that they have edited each other's statements, agree with its contents, and verify its quality.

Criteria For Success: A well-written research rationale statement by each participant that they can deliver orally.

Individual Accountability: Each person presents his or her rationale statement persuasively.

Expected Behaviors: Suggesting ideas, summarizing, explaining and listening.

Intergroup Cooperation: Whenever it is helpful to do so, check procedures and information with another group.

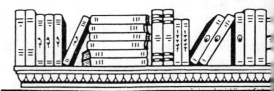

WHO SHOULD GET THE PENICILLIN?

DAVID and ROGER JOHNSON

Minneapolis,
MN

Subject Area: Social Studies

Grade Level: Intermediate to Adult

Lesson Summary: Pairs of students prepare positions on the distribution of penicillin during the North African campaign in World War II. In groups of four the pairs argue their positions, discuss and question each other, then change sides and argue for the opposition. The group of four reaches a consensus, then organizes the rationale into a written report.

Instructional Objectives: The purpose of this lesson is to promote learning about World War II through the use of a structured academic controversy.

Materials:

ITEM	NUMBER NEEDED
Situation Sheet	One per group
Controversy Schedule	One per group
Rules Sheet	One per group
Military Viewpoint Sheet	One per group
Medical Viewpoint Sheet	One per group
Post-Decision Questionnaire	One per group
Constructive Controversy Checklist	One per group

Time Required: Three one-hour class periods

≈ Decisions ≈

Group Size: Four

**Assignment
to Groups:** Form random, heterogeneous groups

Roles: None

≈ The Lesson ≈

Instructional Task:

Review (a) the overall cooperative goal of the lesson and (b) the sequence of controversy and the basic rules to be followed.

Divide into two pairs. One pair takes a copy of Position 1 and the other pair takes a copy of Position 2. Prepare your position in the following manner:

1. Learn the information supporting your assigned position and make sure your partner also learns the supporting information.

2. Add any information you and your partner know about World War II that will support your assigned position.

3. Plan how to teach your position and its supporting rationale to the other pair and summarize the major points.

Each member of your pair must present half of the time. Your position should be presented using more than one media (i.e., visual aids, music). Plan how to present your assigned position strongly and sincerely, whether you believe it or not. Save a few points for the discussion.

Then meet with another pair from another group representing the same position as you. Your task is to ensure that both pairs are ready to advocate their assigned position sincerely and forcefully. Share your plans for advocating your assigned position and any new information or visual aids you have developed to help you do so. Combine the best of your ideas with the best of theirs.

The next step is to meet with the other members of your group so that each pair may advocate its position. The overall goal of the lesson is for the group to come to a decision about the issue that all four members can agree to. The decision should represent the best reasoning of the entire group.

1. *Each pair presents its assigned position as forcefully and persuasively as it can (each member of the pair must do half of the presenting). Help your partner to "get in role."*

2. *The opposing pair takes notes and clarifies anything the two members do not fully understand.*

Discuss the issue:

1. *Argue forcefully and persuasively for your assigned position, presenting as many facts as you can to support it.*

2. *Listen critically to the opposing position, asking the other pair for supporting facts and rationale, presenting rebuttals and counter-arguments, while ensuring that you learn and understand the opposing position. Be ready to use the phrases:* **"I disagree." "Do you have facts to back up that statement?"** *and* **"Your reasoning is flawed in this way . . ."**

This is a complex issue and members need to know both sides in order to come to a thoughtful decision.

At this point reverse perspectives. Present the opposing position as if you were they. Be as forceful and persuasive as you can. Add as many new facts and arguments to support their position as you can think of. Help your partner to "get in role." Correct errors in the other pair's presentation of your position.

It is now time to arrive at a group decision:

1. *Drop advocacy of assigned position.*

2. *Summarize and synthesize the best arguments for both positions.*

3. *Add as much information about the situation as you can.*

4. *Develop a number of optional positions and syntheses.*

5. *Reach a consensus about the option that is most supported by facts and logic.*

6. *Organize the rationale supporting your group's position into a written report that will be orally presented to the rest of the class. Be ready to defend the validity of your decision to groups who may have come to a different decision.*

Positive Interdependence

In addition to the written report, which will be a cooperative group effort, you will complete the post-decision questionnaire. Determine the group mean for each question. I will ask each group to summarize its decision and rationale and the results of the post-decision questionnaire.

Individual Accountability

Each member of the group will be responsible for helping your pair develop its position and present its case and for helping the entire group reach consensus and write the position paper. One member of each group will be selected at random to summarize orally.

⪽ Monitoring and Processing ⪼

Processing: Process how well the group worked together, using the checklist as a tool for this evaluation.

3 : 28

WHO SHOULD GET THE PENICILLIN? Exercise

Situation

In 1943 penicillin, which is used for the prevention and cure of infection, was in short supply among the U.S. armed forces in North Africa. Decisions had to be made whether to use this meager supply for the thousands of hospitalized victims of venereal disease or for the thousands of victims of battle wounds at the front. If you were a member of a team of medical and military personnel, whom would you use the penicillin for and why?

_____ Victims of venereal disease

_____ Victims of battle wounds

Share your position and rationale with your group. Stick to your guns unless you are logically persuaded otherwise. At the same time, help your group achieve consensus on this issue.

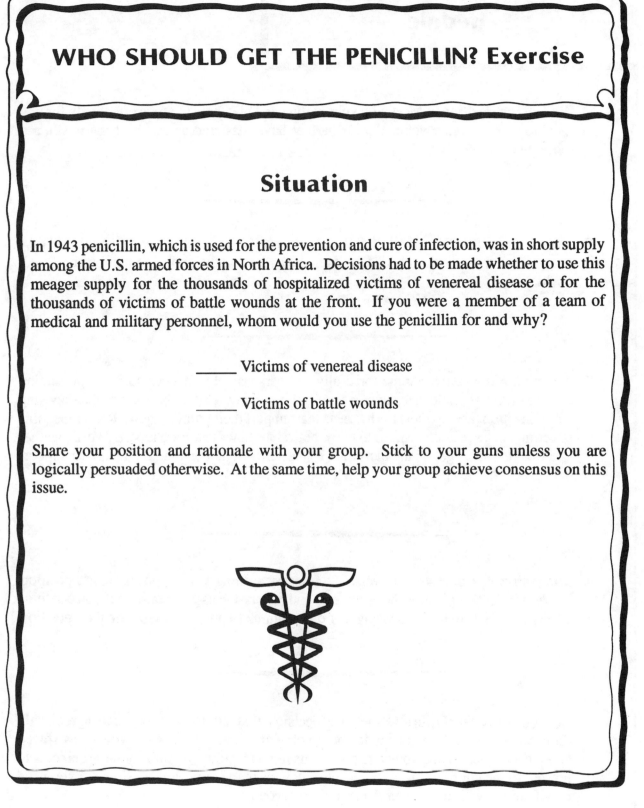

Controversy Exercise:
Schedule

1. **Preparing Positions:** Meet with your partner and plan how to argue effectively for your position. Make sure you and your partner have mastered as much of the position as possible.

---

2. **Presenting Positions:** Be forceful and persuasive in presenting your position. Take notes and clarify anything you do not understand when the opposing pair presents their position.

---

3. **Discussing the Issue:** Argue forcefully and persuasively for your position, presenting as many facts as you can to support your point of view. Critically listen to the opposing pair's position, asking them for the facts that support their point of view. Remember, this is a complex issue and you need to know both sides to write a good report. Work together as a total group to get all the facts out. Make sure you understand the facts that support both points of view.

---

4. **Reversing Perspectives:** Reverse the roles by arguing your opposing pair's position. In arguing for this position, be as forceful and persuasive as you can. See if you can think of any new facts that the opposing pair did not think to present. Elaborate their position.

---

5. **Reaching A Decision:** Come to a decision that all four of you can agree with. Summarize the best arguments for both points of view. Detail what you know (facts) about each side. When you have consensus in your group, organize your arguments to present to the entire room. Other groups may make the opposite decision and you need to defend the validity of your decision to everyone.

Rules for Constructive Controversy

1. I am critical of ideas, not people. I challenge and refute the ideas of the opposing pair, but I do not indicate that I personally reject them.

2. Remember, we are all in this together, sink or swim. I focus on coming to the best decision possible, not on **winning.**

3. I encourage everyone to participate and to master all the relevant information.

4. I listen to everyone's ideas, even if I don't agree.

5. I restate what someone has said if it is not clear.

6. I first bring out **all** ideas and facts supporting both sides, and then I try to put them together in a way that makes sense.

7. I try to understand both sides of the issue.

8. I change my mind when the evidence clearly indicates that I should do so.

Post-Decision Questionnaire

1. To what extent did other members of the group listen to, and understand your ideas?

   (Not at all) 1 : 2 : 3 : 4 : 5 : 6 : 7 : 8 : 9 (Completely)

2. How much influence do you feel you had on the group's decision?

   (None at all) 1 : 2 : 3 : 4 : 5 : 6 : 7 : 8 : 9 (Complete)

3. To what extent do you feel committed to, and responsible for, the group's decision?

   (Not at all) 1 : 2 : 3 : 4 : 5 : 6 : 7 : 8 : 9 (Completely)

4. To what extent are you satisfied with your group's performance?

   (Very dissatisfied) 1 : 2 : 3 : 4 : 5 : 6 : 7 : 8 : 9 (Very satisfied)

5. How much did you learn about the issue under discussion?

   (Nothing at all) 1 : 2 : 3 : 4 : 5 : 6 : 7 : 8 : 9 (A great deal)

6. Write two adjectives describing the way you now feel.

   _____   _____

⇒ **Constructive Controversy Checklist** ⇐

☐ 1. There was no winner or loser, only a successful, creative, and productive solution. The cooperativeness of group members should outweigh by far their competitiveness.

☐ 2. Disagreements among members' positions were initiated.

☐ 3. All members actively participated in the group discussions, sharing their information, conclusions, and perspectives.

☐ 4. Every member's contributions were listened to, respected, and taken seriously.

☐ 5. Effective communication skills were used, including paraphrasing and other listening skills and "I" messages and other sending skills.

☐ 6. Issues and problems were viewed from all available perspectives.

☐ 7. Group members criticized ideas and positions, not individuals. Members disagreed with each other while confirming each other's competence.

☐ 8. Group members viewed disagreement as an interesting situation from which something could be learned, not as personal rejection or a sign that they were being perceived as incompetent or ignorant.

☐ 9. There was appropriate pacing of differentiation and integration of member's positions. Differentiation took place first, followed by integration.

☐ 10. Emotions were allowed and members were encouraged to express them.

☐ 11. The rules of rational argument were followed. Members presented organized information to support their positions, reasoned logically, and changed their minds when others presented persuasive and convincing arguments and proof.

☐ 12. The arguments of all members were given equal consideration, regardless of how much formal power a member had.

World War II: Military Viewpoint

Your position is to give the penicillin to the V.D. patients. *Whether or not you agree with this position, argue for it as strongly as you can. Take the military viewpoint honestly, using arguments that make sense and are rational. Be creative and invent new supporting arguments. Seek out information that supports your position. If you do not know needed information, ask members of other groups who may know.*

1. Our responsibility is to win the war for our country at all costs. If we lose Africa, we will lose Europe to Hitler, and eventually we will be fighting in the United States.

2. Our strategies to win must be based on the premise of **"the greatest good for the greatest number."** We may have to sacrifice soldiers in order to win the war and save our democracy and "free" Europe.

3. Troop morale is vital. Our soldiers must be able to fight harder than the German soldiers. Nothing raises troop morale like seeing fresh troops arrive at the front.

4. Morale at home is vital. People must make sacrifices to produce the goods and materials we need to fight the war. Nothing raises morale at home like hearing of battles won and progress being made in winning the war. Victories give our people hope and dedication.

5. At this point, the war is going badly in North Africa. Rommel and the German Army are cutting through our lines like butter. We are on the verge of being pushed out of Africa, which means we will lose the war. Rommel must be stopped at all costs!

6. Penicillin is a wonder drug that will send the V.D. into remission and within 24 hours the V.D. patients will be free from pain and able to function effectively on the battlefield.

World War II: Medical Viewpoint

Your position is to give the penicillin to the battle-wounded. *Whether or not you agree with this position, argue for it as strongly as you can. Take the medical viewpoint honestly, using arguments that make sense and are rational. Be creative and invent new supporting arguments. Seek out information, ask members of other groups who may know.*

1. Our responsibility is to treat the wounded and save as many lives as possible. Without the penicillin many of the wounded will needlessly die. Minor wounds will get infected and become major, life-threatening wounds.

2. Our strategies must be based on the premise that human life is sacred. If one person dies needlessly, we have failed in our responsibility. The soldiers who have sacrificed so much to help us win the war must be treated with all the care, concern, and resources we can muster. Our soldiers must be able to fight harder than the German soldiers.

3. Troop morale is vital. Nothing raises troop morale as knowing that if they are wounded, they will receive top-notch medical treatment.

4. Morale at home is vital. People must make sacrifices to produce the goods and materials we need to win the war. Nothing raises morale at home more than knowing that their sons and brothers are receiving as effective medical care as is humanly possible. It would be devastating for word to reach the United States that we were needlessly letting soldiers die for lack of medical care.

5. Even though we are at war, we must not lose our humanity. It will do no good to defeat Germany if we become Nazis in the process.

6. At this point, the war is going badly in North Africa. Rommel and the German Army are cutting through our lines like butter. We are on the verge of being pushed out of Africa, which means we will lose the war. Rommel must be stopped.

7. Fresh troops and supplies are unavailable. The German submarines control the Atlantic and we cannot get troop ships or supply ships into African ports. We have to make due with what we have.

8. Penicillin is a wonder drug that will save countless lives if it is used to treat the wounded.

CONTROVERSY OBSERVATION FORM

Behaviors	Participants			Total
Contributes ideas and opinions				
Asks others for their ideas and opinions				
Emphasizes mutual goals				
Emphasizes win-lose competition				
Asks others for proof, facts, and rationale				
Paraphrases, summarizes				
Criticizes and disagrees with others' ideas				
Criticizes other members as persons				
Differentiates positions				
Integrates positions				
Total				

Insert the name of each group member above the columns. Then record the frequency with which each member engages in each behavior.

Taken from: Joining Together: Group Theory and Group Skills by D. W. Johnson and F. P. Johnson (4th Ed.). Englewood Cliffs, NJ: Prentice Hall, 1991.

ADD-ON OBSERVATION SHEET

Start by teaching one skill and observing for it. Show students how well they do in practicing that skill; praise and otherwise reward their efforts. When they have mastered one skill, add and teach a second skill, etc.

DATE _____ PERIOD _____ OBSERVER _____

Controversy Skills	Group Members			

Other Observation Notes:

PREPARING the BEST CASE

for YOUR POSITION

1. **Research (Look):** Gather evidence to support your assigned position. **Research** your position by gathering and collecting of all relevant facts, information, and experiences.

2. **Conceptualize (Think):** Organize what you know into a reasoned position and persuasive argument by (a) arranging the information into a **thesis statement or claim** that asserts something is "true," (b) arranging the supporting facts, information, experiences, and other evidence into a coherent, reasoned, valid, and logical **rationale**, and (c) making the conclusion that the claim is "true" (the conclusion is the same as the original thesis statement). Your aim is to lead listeners **step-by-step** from lack of knowledge to an informed conclusion that agrees with your thesis statement.

3. **Leap To Conclusion:** Reach a tentative conclusion based on your current understanding of the issue. Your **conclusion** has to be the same as your original thesis statement.

4. **Present (Tell):** Plan how to advocate your position forcefully and persuasively.

Thesis Statement / Claim:

Rationale (Given That):

    1.

    2.

    3.

    4.

    5.

Conclusion (Then):

PRESENTING the BEST CASE

for

YOUR POSITION

There are a number of ways you can increase your persuasiveness in presenting and advocating the best case possible for your position. You want to persuade the other group members to agree with your thesis statement and accept its validity. The following guidelines will help you do so.

1. I will begin and end with a strong, sincere, and enthusiastic appeal for the listeners to agree with my position.

2. I will present several points of evidence organized in a logical way.

3. During my initial presentation, I will select a few major points, four or five at the most, and expand on them by using examples, stories, and anecdotes. In order to ensure that the important facts supporting my position are not missed by the audience, I will a point, say it again in different words, illustrate the point with an example or anecdote, and then state it once more.

4. I will make eye contact with all members of the audience.

5. I will keep my presentation within the time limits.

6. I will use more than one media in my presentation. I have developed visual aides to help make my case.

7. I have practiced my presentation. I am comfortable delivering it.

LISTENING
to
OPPOSING PRESENTATION

You need to learn the opposing position as well as your own for at least two reasons:

1. To write a dynamic group report that synthesizes both positions and pass an individual test covering all sides of the issue.

2. To be able to better and more incisively refute it. If you do not know the other position, you cannot challenge it effectively.

Listen carefully to the opposing position. Write down (a) the points strongly supporting it and (b) its weaknesses. Then rate each point on a one-to-ten scale from very important (10) to very unimportant (1).

Strong Points	Rating	Weaknesses	Rating

～ ENGAGING IN A FREE-FOR-ALL OPEN DISCUSSION ～

1. **Continue To Advocate Your Position.** Present your arguments forcefully and persuasively. Emphasize facts, evidence, and rationale. Try out the "tricks of the trade" to see if you can (a) win with fallacious arguments and (b) add humor and interest to the discussion. Occasionally try **ignoratio elenchi** (missing the point), arguing from analogy, sneaky ways of using questions, **reduction ad absurdum**, and **argumetum ad hominem**.

2. **Learn The Evidence And Information Contained In The Opposing Position.** Keep in mind that the overall goal is to make a reasoned judgment about the issue. You need to know both sides thoroughly.

3. **Refute The Evidence Presented By The Opposition:**

   a. Differentiate between facts and opinions.

   b. Determine if the evidence supports the claim. If the claims are vague, ambiguous, or meaningless, or if euphemisms are used, then the claim is not supportable.

   c. Determine if the evidence is of sufficient quantity and quality to validate the claim.

   d. Determine if the evidence is reliable enough to support the claim. If the opponent overgeneralizes, oversimplifies, does not cite credible sources, slants information, or appeals to emotion, then the evidence is not reliable.

4. **Refute The Reasoning Used By The Opposition.** Look for erroneous reasoning based on:

   a. Errors of perception (faulty ways of seeing reality).

   b. Errors of judgment (flaws in reasoning such as overgeneralizing, hasty conclusions, unwarranted assumptions, and failure to make distinctions).

   c. Errors of reaction (defensively explaining away, shifting the burden of proof, or attacking the other person).

   d. Errors of interrelating evidence (check the **and**, **but**, and **therefore** relationships).

e. Errors in the use of inductive and deductive reasoning. Especially look for denying the antecedent and affirming the consequence.

5. **Defend Your Evidence And Reasoning By Rebutting The Attacks Of The Opposition.** Present counter-arguments, clarifications, and extensions. Rebuild your case. Clarify your evidence and reasoning and present further evidence.

6. **Reduce Your Uncertainty By Seeking Further Evidence And Reconceptualizing The Issue.** The fire of the refutation not only tempers and strengthens the evidence being considered, it creates uncertainty, conceptual conflict, and disequilibrium. Uncertainty tends to motivate an active search for more information (often called **epistemic curiosity**) in hopes of resolving the conceptual conflict.

7. **Use The Appropriate Social And Cognitive Skills.** Refutation and rebuttal require the use of a number of social and cognitive skills, including criticizing ideas (not people) and clarifying differences between the two positions.

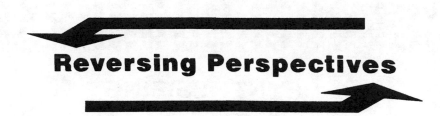

Reversing Perspectives

Reverse perspectives and present the best case for the opposing position. The opposing pair will do the same. Strive to see the issue from both perspectives simultaneously. **Perspective reversal** is taking the opposing pair's position and sincerely and completely presenting their position as if it were one's own.

Overall

1. Change chairs, buttons, hats, and so forth.

2. Caucus briefly with your partner and plan your presentation.

Presenting Opposing Position (Reversing Perspectives)

1. Take the opposing perspective and present opposing arguments as if they were yours. Present the best case for the opposing position.

2. Be forceful and persuasive.

3. Add new facts and evidence if you can.

Listening To Opposition Present Your Position

1. Correct errors in the other pair's presentation of your position.

2. Note omissions in the other pair's presentation of your position.

❖ SYNTHESIZING ❖

1. **Drop all advocacy.** Step back, be objective, and see the issue from a variety of perspectives. See new patterns within a body of evidence.

2. **Summarize and synthesize the best evidence and reasoning from all sides of the issue into a joint position that all group members can agree to.** The alternative syntheses are considered on their merits. Synthesizing involves at least three processes:

   a. **Generate optional ways of integrating the evidence** (the more alternatives suggested, the less group members will be "frozen" to their original positions):

      1.

      2.

      3.

      4.

   b. **Summarize the evidence in fewer words** (gather all the facts, information, and experiences and integrate them into one or a set of conclusions).

   c. **Create a new position that subsumes the previous ones:** Create a new position that unifies the previous ones, brings them into harmony, and unites their best features at a higher level. The previous positions are seen as parts to be combined into a whole.

3. **Write a joint report** that (a) explains the group's synthesis and (b) is based on a group consensus supported by evidence. The report should include a new thesis statement, a rationale, and a conclusion.

4. **Present your conclusions to the class.** Your presentation should be both informative and interesting.

5. **Individually take the test** covering both sides of the issue.

6. **Process how well you worked together as a group** and how you could be even more effective next time. Celebrate the group's success.

CONTROVERSY ASSIGNMENT

Tasks:

1. Prepare, present, and defend two opposing positions.

2. Write a report synthesizing the best ideas from both positions.

Cooperative: One report from the group, everyone has to agree, everyone has to be able to explain the rationale and facts supporting the group's position.

Evaluation:

1. All group members receive the grade for their report.

2. All group members individually take a test covering both positions. If all members score 80 percent correct or above, each receives 10 bonus points.

Individual Accountability:

1. One group member will be selected randomly to present group's position to the class.

2. Test covering both positions.

Expectations:

1. Everyone participates.

2. Rules of constructive controversy will be followed.

English Romantic Poets

Tasks: Analyze what makes a poet great, using the English romantic poets as examples. Build a set of criteria as to what makes a poet great. Read several poems by Wadsworth, Shelley, Byron, Browning, and other assigned poets. Apply the criteria to choose the greatest romantic poet.

Cooperation: Work in a triad. All members must agree, be able to explain the criteria, and be able to explain why the poet picked best fits the criteria.

Procedure:

1. You are assigned to triads. Each triad works cooperatively to develop their criteria and makes a decision as who is the greatest romantic poet.

2. You are now assigned to a group of four. Each member represents a different poet. Your group is to follow this procedure:

   a. Each members presents his or her position.

   b. An open discussion is held in which each member presents a refutation of the opposing positions and defends his or her choice as the most correct one. The strong and weak points of each poet should be identified.

   c. Each member reverses perspectives by presenting the best case for the poet advocated by the person on the member's right.

   d. The group comes to a decision as to who is the greatest romantic poet and why. It does not matter which poet is chosen. What matters is the quality of analysis and understanding of what makes a poet great. Tell each member, "Good job."

   e. Members return to their original triads and report on what happened in their groups of four. Then they write a group report on the strengths and weaknesses of each poet studied.

3. Identify at least one thing each member of your triad did to contribute to the quality of the group's work. Identify one thing members could do to improve group effectiveness. Then celebrate the group's success.

OZYMANDIAS

by Percy Bysshe Shelley (1818)

I met a traveler from an antique land
Who said: Two vast and trunkless legs of stone
Stand in the desert.... Near them, on the sand
Half sunk, a shattered visage lies, whose frown
And wrinkled lip, and sneer of cold command,
Tell that its sculptor well those passions read
Which yet survive, stamped on these lifeless things,
The hand that mocked them, and the heart that fed:
And on the pedestal these words appear:
"My name is Ozymandias, King of Kings:
Look on my works, ye Mighty, and despair!"
Nothing beside remains. Round the decay
Of that colossal wreck, boundless and bare
The lone and level sands stretch far away.

> Ozymandias is the Greek name for Rameses II, 13th-century B.C. pharaoh of Egypt. According to a first-century B.C. Greek historian, Diodorus Siculus, the largest statue in Egypt was inscribed: "I am Ozymandias, king of kings. If anyone wishes to know what I am and where I lie, let him surpass me in some of my exploits."

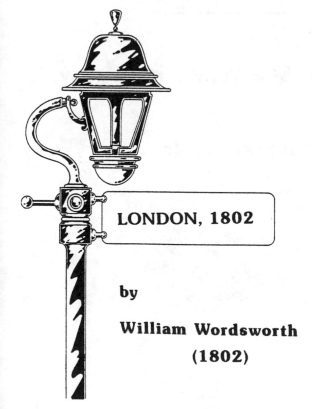

LONDON, 1802

by

**William Wordsworth
(1802)**

Milton! thou should'st be living at this hour:
England hath need of thee: she is a fen
Of stagnant waters: altar, sword, and pen,
Fireside, the heroic wealth of hall and bower,
Have forfeited their ancient English dower
Of inward happiness. We are selfish men
Oh! raise us up, return to us again;
And give us manners, virtue, freedom, power.
Thy soul was like a star, and dwelt apart...
Thou hadst a voice whose sound was like the sea:
Pure as the naked heavens, majestic, free,
So didst thou travel on life's common way
In cheerful godliness; and yet thy heart
The lowliest duties on herself did lay.

fen means marsh and **dower** means inheritance

3:47

How Do I Love Thee?

How do I love thee? Let me count the ways.
I love thee to the depth and breadth and height
My soul can reach, when feeling out of sight
For the ends of Being and ideal Grace.
I love thee to the level of every day's
Most quiet need, by sun and candlelight.
I love thee freely, as men strive for Right;
I love thee purely, as they turn from Praise;
I love thee with the passion put to use
In my old griefs, and with my childhood's faith.
I love thee with a love I seemed to lose
With my lost saints--I love thee with the breath,
Smiles, tears of all my life!--and, if God choose,
I shall but love thee better after death.

Elizabeth Barrett Browning (1850)

She walks in beauty, like the night
Of cloudless climes and starry skies;
And all that's best of dark and bright
Meet in her aspect and her eyes:
Thus mellowed to that tender light
Which heaven to gaudy day denies.

One shade the more, one ray the less,
Had half impaired the nameless grace
Which waves in every raven tress,
Or softly lightens o'er her face;
Where thoughts serenely sweet express
How pure, how dear their dwelling place.

And on that cheek, and o'er that brow,
So soft, so calm, yet eloquent,
The smiles that win, the tints that glow
But tell of days in goodness spent
A mind at peace will all below
A heart whose love is innocent!

She Walks in Beauty

by George Gordon, Lord Byron

(June 12, 1814)

3:48

Chapter Four: The Teacher's Role In Structuring Academic Controversies

Teacher's Role In Academic Controversies

Conflict is the gadfly of thought. It stirs us to observation and memory. It instigates invention. It shocks us out of sheeplike passivity, and sets us at noting and contriving...Conflict is a "sine qua non" of reflection and ingenuity.

John Dewey, Human Nature and Conduct: Morals Are Human

"Are wolves a national treasure that should be allowed to roam freely while being protected from hunting and trapping? Or are wolves a renewable resource that should be managed for sport and revenue? Ecologist say that wolves should be a protected species. But many farmers, ranchers, and sportsmen believe that wolves should be managed. What do you think? Can you prove you are right? A science teacher asks her class to take a stand on the wolf. *"You,"* she says to her class, *"must write a a report in which you explain what should happen to the wolf in the continental United States and why! To ensure that the reports represent your best thinking, you will write it cooperatively with several of your classmates!"* She then randomly assigns students to heterogeneous groups of four. She then divides each group into two pairs. One pair is assigned the position that wolves should be a protected species. The other pair is assigned the position that wolves should be a managed species.

The teacher has prepared the way for structuring an academic controversy by:

1. Choosing a topic that has content manageable by the students and on which at least two well-documented positions (pro and con) can be prepared.

2. Structuring cooperative learning by assigning students to learning groups of four.

3. Creating resource interdependence by giving each pair half of the materials.

4. Highlighting the cooperative goals of reaching a consensus on the issue, writing a group report on which all members will be evaluated, and preparing each member to take a test on the information studied.

She is now ready to conduct the controversy, which involves a structured, but complex, process.

Figure 4.1 Teacher's Role In Structuring Controversies

Context For Conflict

- Competitive Context
- Cooperative Context

Cooperative Learning

- Positive Interdependence
- Individual Accountability
- Face-To-Face Promotive Interaction
- Social Skills
- Group Processing

Teacher's Role In Structuring Academic Controversies

Step 1: *Preinstructional Decisions And Preparations*

- Setting Objectives And Selecting Topic
- Deciding On Size Of Group
- Assigning Students To Groups
- Arranging The Room
- Planning Instructional Materials
- Assigning Roles

Step 2: *Orchestrating Academic Task, Cooperative Structure, Controversy Procedure*

- Explaining Academic Task
- Structuring Positive Interdependence
- Structuring The Controversy
- Structuring Individual Acountability
- Explaining Criteria For Success
- Specifying Desired Behaviors

Step 3: *Monitoring And Intervening*

- Observing Interaction Among Group Members
- Ensuring Adherence To Controversy Procedure
- Providing Academic Assistance
- Teaching Controversy Skills

Step 4: *Evaluating And Processing*

- Providing Closure
- Assessing And Evaluating Students' Learning
- Group Processing
- Group Celebration

Creating A Cooperative Context

The first step in managing conflict effectively is to establish a constructive context. The context within which conflicts occur largely determines whether the conflict is managed constructively or destructively (Deutsch, 1973; Johnson & Johnson, 1989; Tjosvold & Johnson, 1983; Watson & Johnson, 1972). There are two possible contexts for conflict: cooperative and competitive (in individualistic situations individuals do not interact and, therefore, no conflict occurs).

Competitive Context

For competition to exist, there must be scarcity. I must defeat you to get what I want. Rewards are restricted to the few who perform the best. In a competitive situation, individuals work against each other to achieve a goal that only one or a few can attain. You can attain your goal if and only if the other people involved cannot attain their goals. Thus, competitors seek outcomes that are personally beneficial but detrimental to all others in the situation.

Conflicts usually do not go well in a competitive context. Within competitive situations, individuals typically have a short-term time orientation where all energies are focused on winning. Little or no attention is paid to maintaining a good relationship. Within competitive situations (Deutsch, 1973; Johnson & Johnson, 1989; Tjosvold & Johnson, 1983; Watson & Johnson, 1972):

1. Communication tends to be avoided and when it does take place it tends to contain misleading information and threats. Threats, lies, and silence do not help students resolve conflicts with each other. Competition gives rise to espionage or other techniques to obtain information about the other that the other is unwilling to communicate, and "diversionary tactics" to delude or mislead the opponent about oneself.

2. There are frequent and common misperceptions and distortions of the other person's position and motivations that are difficult to correct. Students engage in self-fulfilling prophecies by perceiving another person as being immoral and hostile and behaving accordingly, thus evoking hostility and deceit from the other person. Students see small misbehaviors of opponents while ignoring one's own large misbehaviors (mote-beam mechanism). Double standards exist. Because preconceptions and expectations influence what is perceived, and because there is a bias towards seeing events in a way that justifies one's own beliefs and actions, and because conflict and threat impair perceptual and cognitive processes, the misperceptions are difficult to correct.

3. In a competitive situation, individuals have a suspicious, hostile attitude toward each other that increases their readiness to exploit each other's wants and needs and refuse each other's requests.

4. In a competitive situation, individuals tend to deny the legitimacy of others' wants, needs, and feelings and consider only their own interests.

Cooperative Context

For cooperation to exist there must be mutual goals that all parties are committed to achieving. I am not successful unless you are successful. The more successful you are, the more I benefit and the more successful I am. In a cooperative situation students work together to accomplish shared goals. Students seek outcomes that are beneficial to everyone involved. They are committed to each other's, as well as their own, well-being and success.

Conflicts usually go well in a cooperative context. Within cooperative situations, individuals typically have a long-term time orientation where energies are focused both on achieving goals and on building good working relationships with others. Within cooperative situations (Deutsch, 1973; Johnson & Johnson, 1989; Tjosvold & Johnson, 1983; Watson & Johnson, 1972):

1. Effective and continued communication is of vital importance in resolving a conflict. Within a cooperative situation, the communication of relevant information tends to be open and honest, with each person interested in informing the other as well as being informed. Communication tends to be more frequent, complete, and accurate.

2. Perceptions of the other person and the other person's actions are far more accurate and constructive. Misperceptions and distortions such as self-fulfilling prophecies and double standards occur less frequently and are far easier to correct and clarify.

3. Individuals trust and like each other and, therefore, are willing to respond helpfully to each other's wants, needs, and requests.

4. Individuals recognize the legitimacy of each other's interests and search for a solution accommodating the needs of both sides. Conflicts tend to be defined as mutual problems to be solved in ways that benefit everyone involved.

Conclusions

Conflicts cannot be managed constructively within a competitive context. When competitive and individualistic learning dominates a classroom and school, conflicts will inevitably be destructive. Instead of trying to solve interpersonal problems, students will think short-term and go for the "win." In order to use academic controversies effectively, a teacher first has to establish a cooperative context, primarily through the use of cooperative learning. A complete and thorough discussion of cooperative learning may be found in Johnson, Johnson & Holubec (1993).

Cooperative Learning

Together we stand, divided we fall.

Watchword Of The American Revolution

Teachers may structure academic lessons so that students are (a) in a win-lose struggle to see who is best, (b) learning individually on their own without interacting with classmates, or (c) learning in pairs or small groups helping each other master the assigned material. When lessons are structured **competitively**, students work against each other to achieve a goal that only one or a few students can attain. When lessons are structured **individualistically**, students work by themselves to accomplish learning goals unrelated to those of their classmates. When lessons are structured **cooperatively**, students work together to accomplish shared goals. There is far more to cooperative learning, however, than a seating arrangement. Seating students together can result in competition at close quarters or individualistic efforts with talking. Simply placing students in groups and telling them to work together does not in and of itself result in cooperative efforts. It is only when five basic elements are carefully structured in a group that the group is cooperative (Johnson & Johnson, 1989; Johnson, Johnson, & Holubec, 1993):

1. **Positive Interdependence:** Positive interdependence is the perception that you are linked with others in a way so that you cannot succeed unless they do (and vice versa), that is, their work benefits you and your work benefits them. It promotes a situation in which students work together in small groups to maximize the learning of all members, sharing their resources, providing mutual support, and celebrating their joint success. Positive interdependence is the heart of cooperative learning. Students must believe that they sink or swim together. Within every cooperative lesson positive goal interdependence must be established through **mutual learning goals** (learn the assigned material and make sure that all members of your group learn the assigned material). In order to strengthen positive interdependence, **joint rewards** (if all members of your group score 90 percent correct or better on the test, each will receive 5 bonus points), **divided resources** (giving each group member a part of the total information required to complete an assignment), and **complementary roles** (reader, checker, encourager, elaborator) may also be used. For a learning situation to be cooperative, students must perceive that they are positively interdependent with other members of their learning group.

2. **Face-To-Face Promotive Interaction:** Once teachers establish positive interdependence, they need to maximize the opportunity for students to promote each

other's success by helping, assisting, supporting, encouraging, and praising each other's efforts to learn. There are cognitive activities and interpersonal dynamics that only occur when students get involved in promoting each other's learning. This includes orally explaining how to solve problems, discussing the nature of the concepts being learned, teaching one's knowledge to classmates, and connecting present with past learning. Accountability to peers, ability to influence each other's reasoning and conclusions, social modeling, social support, and interpersonal rewards all increase as the face-to-face interaction among group members increase. In addition, the verbal and nonverbal response of other group members provide important information concerning a student's performance. Silent students are uninvolved students who are not contributing to the learning of others as well as themselves. Promoting each other's success results in both higher achievement and in getting to know each other on a personal as well as a professional level. To obtain meaningful face-to-face interaction the size of groups needs to be small (2 to 4 members).

3. **Individual Accountability:** Individual accountability exists when the performance of each individual student is assessed and the results given back to the group and the individual. It is important that the group knows who needs more assistance, support, and encouragement in completing the assignment. It is also important that group members know that they cannot "hitch-hike" on the work of others. The purpose of cooperative learning groups is to make each member a stronger individual in his or her right. Students learn together so that they can subsequently perform higher as individuals. To ensure that each member is strengthened, students are held individually accountable to do their share of the work. Common ways to structure individual accountability include (a) giving an individual test to each student, (b) randomly selecting one student's product to represent the entire group, or (c) having each student explain what they have learned to a classmate.

4. **Social Skills:** Contributing to the success of a cooperative effort requires interpersonal and small group skills. Placing socially unskilled individuals in a group and telling them to cooperate does not guarantee that they will be able to do so effectively. Persons must be taught the social skills for high quality cooperation and be motivated to use them. Leadership, decision-making, trust-building, communication, and conflict-management skills have to be taught just as purposefully and precisely as academic skills. Procedures and strategies for teaching students social skills may be found in Johnson (1991, 1993) and Johnson and F. Johnson (1994).

5. **Group Processing:** Group processing exists when group members discuss how well they are achieving their goals and maintaining effective working relationships. Groups need to describe what member actions are helpful and unhelpful and make decisions about what behaviors to continue or change. Students must also be given the time and procedures for analyzing how well their learning groups are functioning and the extent to which students are employing their social skills to help all group members to achieve and to maintain effective working relationships within the group. Such processing (a) enables learning groups to focus on group maintenance, (b) facilitates the learning of

social skills, (c) ensures that members receive feedback on their participation, and (d) reminds students to practice collaborative skills consistently. Some of the keys to successful processing are allowing sufficient time for it to take place, making it specific rather than vague, maintaining student involvement in processing, reminding students to use their social skills while they process, and ensuring that clear expectations as to the purpose of processing have been communicated.

Since academic controversies take place within cooperative learning groups, each of these basic elements need to be carefully structured when faculty create an academic controversy.

Using Academic Controversies

To conduct an academic controversy, teachers:

1. Specify the objectives for the lesson.

2. Make a number of preinstructional decisions.

3. Clearly explain the task, the positive interdependence, and the controversy procedure to the students.

4. Monitor the effectiveness of cooperative learning groups and intervene to provide assistance in (a) completing the task, (b) following the controversy procedure, or (c) using the required interpersonal and group skills.

5. Evaluate students' achievement and help students process how well they functioned as a group.

Preinstructional Decisions And Preparations

Objectives And Topic

There are two types of objectives that a Teacher needs to specify before the lesson begins. The **academic objective** needs to be specified at the correct level for the students and matched to the right level of instruction according to a conceptual or task analysis. The **social skills objective** details what interpersonal and small group skills are going to be emphasized during the lesson. A common error many teachers make is to specify only academic objectives and ignore the social skills needed to train students to cooperate and disagree constructively with each other.

In specifying the objectives you, the Teacher, must choose a topic for the controversy. Criteria for the selection include that at least two well-documented positions can be prepared and that the content be manageable by the students. Almost any issue being studied can be turned into a controversy. Most environmental, energy, public policy, social studies, literature, and scientific issues are appropriate. It should also be noted that whenever students work together in cooperative learning groups, natural controversies will arise in their decision-making and problem-solving activities. By participating in structured academic controversies, students will learn the procedures and skills to use when unplanned, natural controversies suddenly arise.

Deciding On the Size Of Group

Unless you plan to use an observer, cooperative learning groups of four should be used for structured controversies. Each position usually has two students assigned to work as a team in preparing to advocate it. While some issues may lend themselves to three positions (and thus to groups of six), the complexity of synthesizing three positions and managing the interaction among six students is such that groups are typically limited to four. The more inexperienced students are in working cooperatively and engaging in controversy, the shorter the class period, and the more limited the materials, the more the size of the group should definitely be limited to four.

Assigning Students To Groups

In order to increase the potential for controversy, the heterogeneity of students within each learning group should be maximized so that students of different achievement levels in math, ethnic backgrounds, sexes, and social classes work together. The heterogeneity among group members increases the likelihood that different perspectives and viewpoints will naturally occur. In addition, heterogeneity among students typically increases performance in problem-solving and conceptual-learning tasks. When a student is isolated from his or her classmates, either because of shyness or because of being stigmatized as having a special learning problem or being from a minority group, teachers will want to plan carefully to ensure that the student is placed with outgoing, friendly, and accepting peers. When in doubt as to how to maximize heterogeneity, however, randomly assign students to groups.

Arranging The Room

Members of a learning group should sit close enough to each other so that they can share materials, talk to each other quietly, and maintain eye contact with all group members. Circles are usually best. The Teacher should have clear access lanes to every group. Students will have to move into pairs and then back into groups of four.

Planning Instructional Materials To Promote Interdependence And Controversy

Within controversies, materials are divided into pro and con so that each pair of students has part of the materials needed to complete the task. The following materials are typically prepared for each position:

1. A clear description of the group's task.

2. A description of the phases of the controversy procedure and the collaborative skills to be utilized during each phase.

3. A definition of the position to be advocated with a summary of the key arguments supporting the position.

4. A set of resource materials (including a bibliography) to provide evidence for and elaboration of the arguments supporting the position to be advocated.

A balanced presentation should be given for all sides of the controversy and the materials should be separated into packets containing articles, reports, or summaries supporting each position on the issue.

Assigning Roles

Inherent in the controversy procedure is assigning students to a pro or con advocacy pair. In effect, this is assigning students complementary roles which signal their positive interdependence within the controversy process. In addition, teachers may wish to assign students other roles related to working together cooperatively and engaging in intellectual arguments.

Explaining And Orchestrating The Academic Task, Cooperative Structure, And Controversy Procedure

Explaining The Academic Task

Teachers explain the academic task so that students are clear about the assignment and understand the objectives of the lesson. Direct teaching of concepts, principles, and strategies may take place at this point. Teachers may wish to answer any questions students have about the concepts or facts they are to learn or apply in the lesson. The task must be structured so that there are at least two well-documented positions (e.g., pro and con). The choice of topic depends on the interests of the teacher and the purposes of the course.

Structuring Positive Interdependence

Teachers communicate to students that they have a group goal and must work cooperatively. There are two group goals in a controversy:

1. The group is told to produce a single report and arrive at a consensus concerning what decision should be made. Students are responsible for ensuring that all group members participate in writing a quality group report and making a presentation to the class.

2. Students are informed that they are responsible for ensuring that all group members master all the information relevant to both sides of the issue (measured by a test which each student takes individually).

To supplement the effects of positive goal interdependence, the materials are jigsawed within the group (**resource interdependence**) and bonus points may be given if all group members score above a preset criterion on the test (**reward interdependence**).

Structuring The Controversy

The principal prerequisites for a successful structured controversy are a cooperative context, skillful group members, and heterogeneity of group membership. The cooperative context is established by:

1. **Assigning students to heterogeneous groups of four and dividing each group into two pairs.** A high reader and a low reader may be assigned to each pair. The responsibility of the pair is to get to know the information supporting its assigned position and prepare a presentation and a series of persuasive arguments to use in the discussion with the opposing pair.

2. **Assigning pro and con positions** to the pairs and giving students supporting materials to read and study. A bibliography of further sources of information may also be given. A section of resource materials may be set up in the library.

3. Structuring positive interdependence. This was discussed above.

Students will need to be taught the necessary conflict management skills. The skills may be taught simultaneously with having students participate in structured controversies. Heterogeneity among group members adds to the resources and the perspectives that may be contributed to spirited and constructive argumentation and increases the quality of the structured controversy experience.

More specifically, there are five stages involved in a controversy. The stages and the instructions given to students are as follows:

1. **Learning positions.** Meet with your partner and plan how to advocate your position effectively. Read the materials supporting your position. Find more information in the library and in reference books to support your position. Give the opposing pair any information found supporting the opposing position. Prepare a persuasive presentation to be given to the other pair. Prepare a series of persuasive arguments to be used in the discussion with the opposing pair. Plan with your partner how to advocate your position effectively. Make sure you and your partner master the information supporting your assigned position and present it in a persuasive and complete way so that the other group members will comprehend and learn the information.

2. **Presenting positions.** Present the best case for your position to ensure it gets a fair and complete hearing. Be forceful and persuasive in doing so. Use more than one media. Listen carefully to and learn the opposing position. Take notes and clarify anything you do not understand.

3. **Discussing the issue.** Openly discuss the issue by freely exchanging information and ideas. Argue forcefully and persuasively for your position, presenting as many facts as you can to support your point of view. Listen critically to the opposing pair's evidence and reasoning, probe and push the opposing pair's thinking, ask for data to support assertions, and then present counter arguments. Defend your position. Compare the strengths and weaknesses of the two positions. Refute the claims being made by the opposing pair, and rebut the attacks on your position. Follow the specific rules for constructive controversy. Take careful notes on and thoroughly learn the opposing position. Sometimes a "time-out" period will be provided so you can caucus with your partner and prepare new arguments. Your Teacher may encourage more spirited arguing, take sides when a pair is in trouble, play devil's advocate, ask one group to observe another group engaging in a spirited argument, and generally stir up the discussions. Remember, this is a complex issue and you need to know both sides to write a good report. Make sure you understand the facts that support both points of view.

4. **Reversing Perspectives.** Change chairs with the other pair. Present the opposing pair's position as if you were they. Use your notes to do so. Be as sincere and forceful as you can. Add any new facts you know of. Elaborate their position by relating it to other information you have previously learned.

5. **Reaching a decision.** Drop your advocacy of your assigned position. Summarize and synthesize the best arguments for both points of view. Reach consensus on a position that is supported by the facts. Change your mind only when the facts and rationale clearly indicate that you should do so.

a. Write a group report with the supporting evidence and rationale for the synthesis your group has agreed on. Often the resulting position is a third perspective or synthesis that is more rational than the two assigned. All group members sign the report when it is as good as they can make it, indicating that they agree with it, can explain its content, and consider it ready to be evaluated. Organize your report to present it to your entire class.

b. Take a test on both positions. If all members score above the preset criteria of excellence, each receives five bonus points.

c. Process how well the group functioned and how their performance may be improved during the next controversy. Teachers may wish to structure the group processing to highlight the specific conflict management skills students need to master.

In addition to explaining the procedure, you may wish to help the students "get in role" by presenting the issue to be decided in as interesting and dramatic a way as possible.

Structuring Individual Accountability

The purpose of the controversy is to make each member a stronger individual and, therefore, the level of each student's learning needs to be assessed. Individual accountability is structured by individually testing each student on the material studied and/or randomly choosing one member of each group to present their group's decision and its rationale to the class as a whole. Students should also be observed to ensure that each participates in each step of the controversy procedure.

Explaining Criteria For Success

Evaluations within cooperatively structured lessons (and controversies are no exception) need to be criteria-referenced. At the beginning of the lesson teachers need to explain clearly the criteria by which students' work will be evaluated.

Specifying Desired Behaviors

No matter how carefully teachers structure controversies, if students do not have the interpersonal and small group skills to manage conflicts constructively the controversy does not produce its potential effects. The **social skills** emphasized are those involved in systematically advocating an intellectual position and evaluating and criticizing the position advocated by others, as well as the skills involved in synthesis and consensual decision making. Students should be taught the following skills.

1. Emphasize the mutuality of the situation and avoid win-lose dynamics. Focus on coming to the best decision possible, not on winning.

2. Confirm others' competence while disagreeing with their positions and challenging their reasoning. Be critical of ideas, not people. Challenge and refute the ideas of the members of the opposing pair, but do not reject them personally.

3. Separate your personal worth from criticism of your ideas.

4. Listen to everyone's ideas, even if you do not agree with them.

5. First bring out the all the ideas and facts supporting both sides and then try to put them together in a way that makes sense. Be able to differentiate the differences between positions before attempting to integrate ideas.

6. Be able to take the opposing perspective in order to understand the opposing position. Try to understand both sides of the issue.

7. Change your mind when the evidence clearly indicates that you should.

8. Paraphrase what someone has said if it is not clear.

9. Emphasize rationality in seeking the best possible answer, given the available data.

10. Follow the golden rule of conflict. The golden rule is, act towards your opponents as you would have them act toward you. If you want people to listen to you, then listen to them. If you want others to include your ideas in their thinking, then include their ideas in your thinking. If you want others to take your perspective, then take their perspective.

Structuring Intergroup Cooperation

When preparing their positions, students can check with classmates in other groups who are also preparing the same position. Ideas as to how best to present and advocate the position can be shared. If one pair of students finds information that supports its position, members can share that information with other pairs who have the same position. The more conferring between pairs of students, the better. The positive outcomes found with a cooperative learning group can be extended throughout a whole class by structuring intergroup cooperation. Bonus points may be given if all members of a class reach a preset criteria of excellence. When a group finishes its work, the Teacher should encourage the members to go help other groups complete the assignment.

Monitoring And Intervening

Monitoring Students' Behavior

Teachers observe group members to see what problems they are having completing the assignment and skillfully engaging in the controversy procedure. Whenever possible, teachers should use a formal observation sheet where they count the number of times they observe appropriate behaviors being used by students. The more concrete the data, the more useful it is to their teacher and to students. Teachers should not try to count too many different behaviors at one time, especially when they first start formal observation. At first they may want just to keep track of who talks in each group to get a participation pattern for the groups. We have a chapter describing systematic observation of cooperative groups in **Learning Together and Alone** (1994) and our current list of behaviors (though rather long) includes: contributing ideas, asking questions, expressing feelings, active listening, expressing support and acceptance (toward ideas), expressing warmth and liking (toward group members and group), encouraging all members to participate, summarizing, checking for understanding, relieving tension by joking, and giving direction to group's work. All the behaviors we look for are positive behaviors which are to be praised when they are appropriately present and are a cause for discussion when they are missing. It is also a good idea for the teacher to collect notes on specific student behaviors so that the frequency data is extended. Especially useful are skillful interchanges that can be shared with students later as objective praise.

Providing Academic Assistance

In monitoring the learning groups as they work, teachers will wish to clarify instructions, review important concepts and strategies, answer questions, and teach academic skills as necessary. Students may need assistance at any stage of the controversy procedure, whether it is researching their position, advocating it, refuting the opposing position, defending their position from attack, reversing perspectives, or creatively syntheiszing.

Intervening To Teach Controversy Skills

While monitoring the learning groups, teachers will often find (a) students who do not have the necessary conflict skills and (b) groups where members are having problems in disagreeing effectively. In these cases, teachers intervene to suggest more effective procedures for working together and more effective behaviors. Basic interpersonal and small group skills may be directly taught (Johnson, 1993; Johnson & F. Johnson, 1994). Teachers may also wish to intervene and reinforce particularly effective and skillful behaviors that they notice. At times the teacher becomes a consultant to a group in order to help it function more effectively.

The best time to teach controversy skills is when the students need them.
Intervening should leave group members with new skills that will be useful in the future.
At a minimum:

1. Students need to recognize the need for the skill.

2. The skill must be defined clearly and specifically including what students should say
    when engaging in the skill.

3. **The practice of the skill must be encouraged.** Sometimes just the Teacher standing
    there with a clipboard and pencil will be enough to promote student enactment of the
    skill.

4. **Students should have the time and procedures for discussing how well they are
    using the skills.** Students should persevere in the practice until the skill is
    appropriately internalized. We never drop a skill, we only add on.

Evaluating And Processing

Providing Closure To Lesson

At the end of each instructional unit, students should be able to summarize what they
have learned. You may wish to summarize the major points in the lesson, ask students to
recall ideas or give examples, and answer any final questions students have.

Evaluating Students' Learning

Students' work is evaluated, their learning assessed, and feedback is given as to how
their work compares with the criteria of excellence. Qualitative as well as quantitative
aspects of performance should be addressed. Students receive a group grade on the
quality of their final report and receive an individual grade on their performance on the
test covering both sides of the issue.

Processing How Well The Group Functioned

When students have completed the assignment, or run out of time, they should have time
to describe what member actions were helpful (and unhelpful) in completing the group's
work and make decisions about what behaviors to continue or change. Group processing
occurs at two levels—in each learning group and in the class as a whole. In small group
processing members discuss how effectively they worked together and what could be
improved. In whole-class processing the teacher gives the class feedback and has
students share incidents that occurred in their groups. In structuring small group

processing teachers should avoid questions that can be answered "yes" or "no." Instead of saying, *"Did everyone help each other learn?"* the teacher should ask, *"How frequently did each member (a) explain how to solve a problem and (b) correct or clarify other member's explanations?* Feedback given to students should be descriptive and specific, not evaluative and general (see Johnson, 1993).

Discussing group functioning is essential. **A common teaching error is to provide too brief a time for students to process the quality of their cooperation and controversy**. Students do not learn from experiences that they do not reflect on. If the learning groups are to function better tomorrow than they did today, students must receive feedback, reflect on how their actions may be more effective, and plan how to be even more skillful during the next group session.

Summary

The teacher's role in implementing structured academic controversies is an extension of the teacher's role in using cooperative learning. It consists of specifying the learning and social skills objectives, making a number of preinstructional decisions, explaining and orchestrating the academic task and the controversy procedure, monitoring and intervening, and evaluating and processing. Academic controversies may be used in any subject area with any age student. Yet implementing structured academic controversies is not easy. It can take years to become an expert. Teachers may wish to start small by taking one subject area or one class and using controversy procedures until they feel comfortable, and then expand into other subject areas or other classes. Teachers are well-advised to pick out topics for which they are pretty sure a controversy will work, plan carefully, and do not rush the process. In order to implement academic controversies successfully, teachers will need to teach students the interpersonal and small group skills required to cooperate, engage in intellectual inquiry, intellectually challenge each other, see a situation from several perspective simultaneously, and synthesize a variety of positions into a new and creative decision. **The use of controversy is as productive for adults as it is for students**. When teachers work together in colleagial support groups or faculty committees, the decisions made are of higher quality and more creative when the teachers use the controversy procedure. Teachers will want to give some thought to their own use of the controversy procedure as they implement academic controversies in their classrooms (see Chapter 8).

In addition to understanding the overall teacher's role in conducting academic controversies, teachers must be able to manage each step of the controversy procedure. The first step is to have students research their assigned position and prepare to advocate it. This topic is addressed in the next chapter.

⤜⟨ CONTROVERSY CONTRACT ⟩⤛

Major Learnings	Implementation Plans

Date _____   Date of Progress Report Meeting _____

Participant's Signature _____

Signatures of Other Group Members _____ _____

_____ _____ _____

CHAPTER VOCABULARY

Working with a partner, learn the definitions of the following words.

1. Define each word in two ways.

   First, write down what you think the word means.

   Second, look it up in the book and write down its definition.

   Note the page on which the definition appears.

2. For each word write a sentence in which the word is used.

3. Make up a story in which all of the words are used.

4. Learn how to spell each word. They will be on your spelling test.

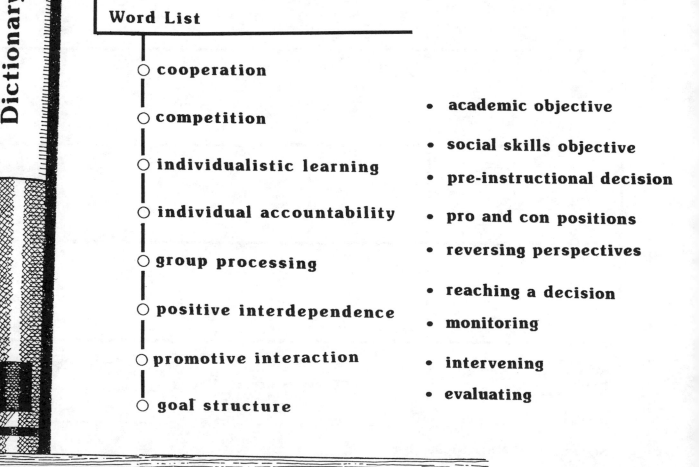

Word List

- ○ **cooperation**
- ○ **competition**
- ○ **individualistic learning**
- ○ **individual accountability**
- ○ **group processing**
- ○ **positive interdependence**
- ○ **promotive interaction**
- ○ **goal structure**

- • **academic objective**
- • **social skills objective**
- • **pre-instructional decision**
- • **pro and con positions**
- • **reversing perspectives**
- • **reaching a decision**
- • **monitoring**
- • **intervening**
- • **evaluating**

CONTEST OF THE CODES:
Who'll Be the Best?

Your **task** is to solve the following codes. You have a set of coded messages and the same messages decoded. Your task is to identify the pattern so that you are able to write a message with the code.

This is a **competitive** activity. Work by yourself. Try to break the codes faster and more accurately than the other students. At the end of this activity you will be ranked from best to worst in breaking codes.

NEHWEHTGNITTESSIEVITITEPMOCIMIWS

WHENTHESETTINGISCOMPETITIVEISWIM

DNAUOYKNISROIKNISDNAUOYMIWS.

ANDYOUSINKORISINKANDYOUSWIM.

The pattern for this code is _____.

VA N PBBCRENGVIR TEBHC, GUR ZBER FHPPRFFSHY LBH NER
IN A COOPERATIVE GROUP, THE MORE SUCCESSFUL YOU ARE

GUR ZBER V ORARSVG NAQ GUR ZBER FHPPRFFSHY V NZ.
THE MORE I BENEFIT AND THE MORE SUCCESSFUL I AM.

The pattern for this code is _____.

GM D H A 6 J   A 9 C   K 7 9 C6 A 10C 2   10H   MH K9 J
MY G O A L S   A R E   U N R E L A T E D   TO   Y O U R S

L 4 C 7   LC   LH 9 F   E 72 E 11E 2 KA6 E J10EBA66M
W H E N   WE   WORK   I N D I V I D U A L I S T I C A L L Y.

The pattern for this code is _____.

Conquering the Codes Together

Your **task** is to solve the following codes. You have a set of coded messages and the same messages decoded. Your task is to identify the pattern so that you are able to write a message with the code.

This is a **cooperative** activity. Work together. Encourage and assist each other's learning. Agree on one answer to each question. Every member must be able to explain what the code is and be able to write a message with the code.

---

18 5 13 5 13 2 5 18   20 8 1 20 9 14 1 3 15 15 16 5 18 1 20 9 22 5 7 18 15 21 16

R E M E M B E R   T H A T I N A C O O P E R A T I V E G R O U P

23 5 1 12 12 19 9 14 11 15 18 19 23 9 13 20 15 7 5 20 8 5 18

W E A L L S I N K O R S W I M T O G E T H E R.

The pattern for this code is _____.

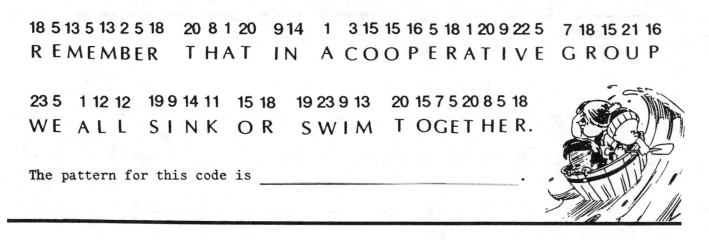

HDFK LQGLYLGXDU PXVQ EH DFFRXQWDEUH IRU KLV/KHU

EACH INDIVIDUAL MUST BE ACCOUNTABLE FOR HIS/HER

RZQ SHUIRUPDQFH ZKHQ ZRUNLQJ FRRSHUDWLYHOB.

OWN PERFORMANCE WHEN WORKING COOPERATIVELY.

The pattern for this code is _____.

WHN W WRK CPRTVLY, W HLP, SHR,

WHEN WE WORK COOPERATIVELY, WE HELP, SHARE,

ND NCRG CH THR T LRN.

AND ENCOURAGE EACH OTHER TO LEARN.

The pattern for this code is _____.

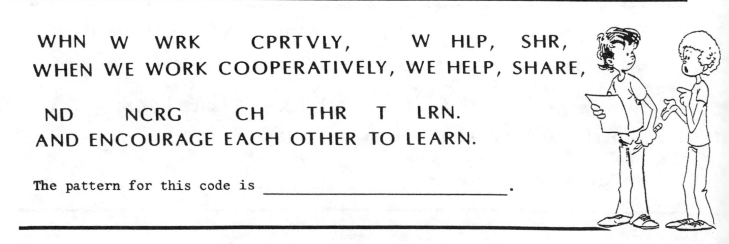

NATURAL CONTROVERSIES

Which pole is taller?

Connect all nine dots with four straight lines. Do not lift your pen. Do not retrace any line.

Divide the circle into 10 parts with 3 lines.

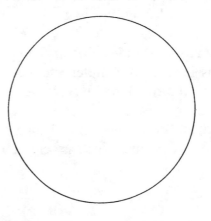

Are the black areas the tops or bottoms of the cubes?

There are 2 U.S. coins which total 55 cents in value. One is not a nickel. Please bear this in mind.
What are the two coins?

4:21

The Teacher's Role
in Controversy

Make Decisions

Specifying Academic and Controversy Skills Objectives. What academic and/or controversy skills do you want students to learn or practice in their groups? Start with something easy.

Decide on Group Size. Unless there are three or four sides to the issue (avoid more than two sides to an issue unless your students are highly experienced and skilled), use groups of four.

Assign Students To Groups. Heterogeneous groups are the most powerful, so mix abilities, sexes, cultural backgrounds, and task orientations. Assign students to groups randomly or select groups yourself.

Plan Materials. Divide materials into pro and con so that each pair of students has the materials needed to complete the task. This includes the position to be advocated, supporting information to be organized, and a guide to further resources.

Assign Roles. In addition to assigning pro and con roles, there are roles that will help students work together, such as perspective-taker, checker, accuracy coach, and elaborator.

Set The Lesson

Explain The Academic Task. Explain lesson objectives, define concepts, explain procedures, give examples, and ask questions to ensure that students understand what they are supposed to accomplish.

Structure Positive Interdependence. Students must believe that they need each other to complete the group's task, that they "sink or swim together." Use mutual goals, joint rewards, shared materials and information, and assigned roles to create a perception of mutuality.

Structure The Controversy. Students must understand the procedure and the time limits for preparing their position, presenting it, advocating it, reversing perspectives, and reaching a conclusion.

Structure Individual Accountability. Each student must believe he or she is responsible for learning the material and helping his or her groupmates. Frequent oral quizzing of group members picked at random and individual tests are two ways to ensure this.

Explain Criteria For Success. Student work should be evaluated on a criteria-referenced rather than on a norm- referenced basis. Make clear your criteria for evaluating the work of individual students and the entire group.

Specify Desired Behaviors. Clearly explain the constructive controversy rules.

Teach Controversy Skills. After students are familiar with the controversy procedures, pick one controversy skill, point out the need for it, define it by giving students specific phrases they can say to engage in the skill, observe for it, and give students feedback about their use of the skill. Encourage the use of the skill until students are performing it automatically.

Structure Intergroup Cooperation. Having students check with and help other groups and giving rewards or praise when all class members do well can extend the benefits of cooperation to the whole class.

Monitor And Intervene

Ensure All Students Present, Advocate, Criticize, And Synthesize. The beneficial educational outcomes of controversy are due to the oral interaction among students.

Monitor Students' Behavior. This is the fun part! While students are working, circulate to see whether they understand the assignment, the procedure, the material. Give immediate feedback and praise the appropriate use of controversy skills.

Provide Task Assistance. If students are having trouble with the academic material, you can clarify, reteach, or elaborate on what they need to know.

Intervene To Teach Controversy Skills. If students are having trouble with the controversy process, you can suggest more effective procedures for working together on more effective behaviors for them to engage in.

Provide Closure. To reinforce student learning, you may wish to have groups share answers or paper, summarize major points in the lesson, or review important facts.

Evaluate And Process

Evaluate Student Learning. Assess the quality of the group report and give students the individual test on the material being studied.

Process Group Functioning. In order to improve, students need time and procedures for reflecting on how well their group is functioning and how well they are using controversy skills. Processing can be done by individuals, small groups, or the whole class.

CONTROVERSY LESSON PLAN

Title _____

Your Name _____

School and District _____

Subject Area _____   **Grade Level** _____

Lesson Topic and Summary _____
_____
_____

Instructional Objectives _____
_____

Materials Needed

    Pro _____

    Con _____

Time Required _____   **Group Size** _____

Assignment to Groups _____
_____

Roles
(Name and _____
Explain) _____
_____
_____

The Lesson

Task _____
_____
_____
_____
_____

Positive Goal/Reward Interdependence _____
_____
_____

Controversy Procedures

Preparing Positions _____

_____

Presenting Positions _____

_____

Discussing the Issue _____

_____

Reversing Perspectives _____

_____

Reaching a Decision _____

_____

Individual Accountability _____

_____

_____

Criteria for Success _____

_____

_____

Expected Behaviors _____

_____

_____

Monitoring and Processing

Monitor for _____

_____

_____

Intervene if _____

_____

_____

Process by _____

_____

_____

End by _____

_____

(Attach any materials needed to run the lesson)

Controversy Lesson Plan Worksheet Explanation

Step One: Select The Topic

Choose an issue which has sufficient materials and resources for each side. Clearly define each perspective of the issue. Differentiate between the sides so they know how they differ from one another. To more clearly define sides, give each side a sticker or badge to distinguish it from the other side.

Step Two: Make Decisions

Group Size: Pairs of students representing each side help keep student involvement high. You want to insure that **one** person does not become the spokesperson for the pair.

Assignments to Groups: Try to get a mixture of students in each group and in each pair. Decide who will be partners in each group.

Room Arrangement: There should be space between groups and also space within groups so that the pairs can meet separately.

Materials: Resource materials can be given to the students or students can do the research. Some introductory articles could be given as well as requiring students to do research.

Step Three: Introduction to Controversy

Definition: It is important to define controversy to your students in language they understand. Stress the clash of opposing ideas but also that eventually there will be a mutual problem-solving situation within the groups.

Introductory Exercise: You may want to preteach necessary controversy skills before the actual controversy begins by using a mini-controversy. This introduction should stress that there are logical arguments in a controversy and it is not just a "fight."

Expected Behaviors: Specify the skills your students will need to learn to participate effectively in a controversy. Name the specific behaviors.

Step Four: The Controversy

Prepare Positions: Tell students how they have to prepare their arguments. If you will use badges or symbols representing each side hand them out now. Indicate whether materials will be made available by the teacher or will be found in the library.

Present Positions: Make sure to remind students that they will be changing sides later in the controversy. Opponents must listen carefully and take notes on the arguments of the other side.

Open Discussion: Requiring a product during this segment of the controversy can insure active listening--ask for a list of best arguments from both sides.

Perspective Reversal: Being able to unlock from the chosen position is essential. The perspective reversal can be dramatically illustrated by having sides exchange seats or badges or symbols.

Final Decision: A synthesis is necessary so that the best ideas and information on both sides are used. This also keeps the controversy from being a "win/lose" situation.

Step Five: Monitoring And Processing

Observing: To ensure active participation of all students, the teacher will be the observer. Students observers should also be used periodically.

Teacher Feedback: Give students feedback on effective behaviors and strategies practiced in the groups. Share the positive behaviors you noticed.

Student Processing: Decide on the questions you will ask to help students process about the behaviors they practiced during the controversy and **not** on the issues of the controversy. Asking open-ended questions rather than close-ended questions will help students really talk about their behaviors. Phrase the question so that they cannot answer merely yes or no.

Bonus Point System

While you are engaging in the open discussion of the issue the teacher will be systematically observing your actions. Given below are the skills you need to demonstrate in order for the discussion to go well. Your group will receive two points if the teacher sees you engage in a difficult skill and one point for each needed skill. Your group will lose one point for everytime the teacher observes you engagaing in a negative action.

Difficult / Important Skills: Plus Two Points

Reversing Perspectives
Criticizing Ideas, Not People
Creating A Synthesis Of Both Positions

Needed Skills: Plus One Point

Stating One's Position
Giving A Supporting Fact
Paraphrasing Other's Remarks
Summarizing Own Or Other's Position
Stating We "Sink Or Swim Together"
Changing Your Mind When You Are Logically Persuaded
Explaining Your Evidence And Reasoning

Negative Actions: Minus One Point

Insults
Unparliamentary Behavior
Discounting
Quietness

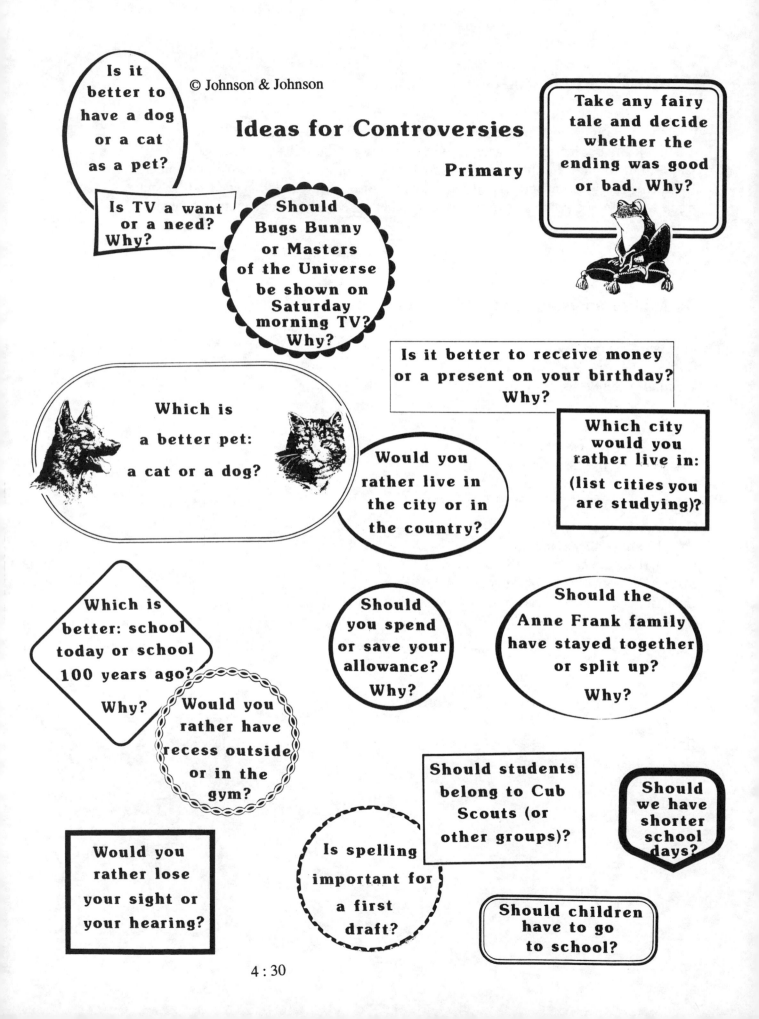

© Johnson & Johnson

Ideas for Controversies

Primary

Is it better to have a dog or a cat as a pet?

Is TV a want or a need? Why?

Should Bugs Bunny or Masters of the Universe be shown on Saturday morning TV? Why?

Take any fairy tale and decide whether the ending was good or bad. Why?

Which is a better pet: a cat or a dog?

Is it better to receive money or a present on your birthday? Why?

Would you rather live in the city or in the country?

Which city would you rather live in: (list cities you are studying)?

Which is better: school today or school 100 years ago? Why?

Should you spend or save your allowance? Why?

Should the Anne Frank family have stayed together or split up? Why?

Would you rather have recess outside or in the gym?

Should students belong to Cub Scouts (or other groups)?

Should we have shorter school days?

Would you rather lose your sight or your hearing?

Is spelling important for a first draft?

Should children have to go to school?

4 : 30

Should students wear uniforms to school?

Should we have recesses in elementary school?

Intermediate

Should students who misbehave in gym, music and other classes be allowed to go to these classes?

Primary

Which is better: Japanese or American education?

Why were the pyramids built? Were they a good idea?

Do you need math for daily living? Why/why not?

Is it better to live in a hot or a cold climate?

Would you rather be in school on a rainy or a sunny day?

Who was right: American Tories or American Revolutionaries?

(See My Brother Sam)

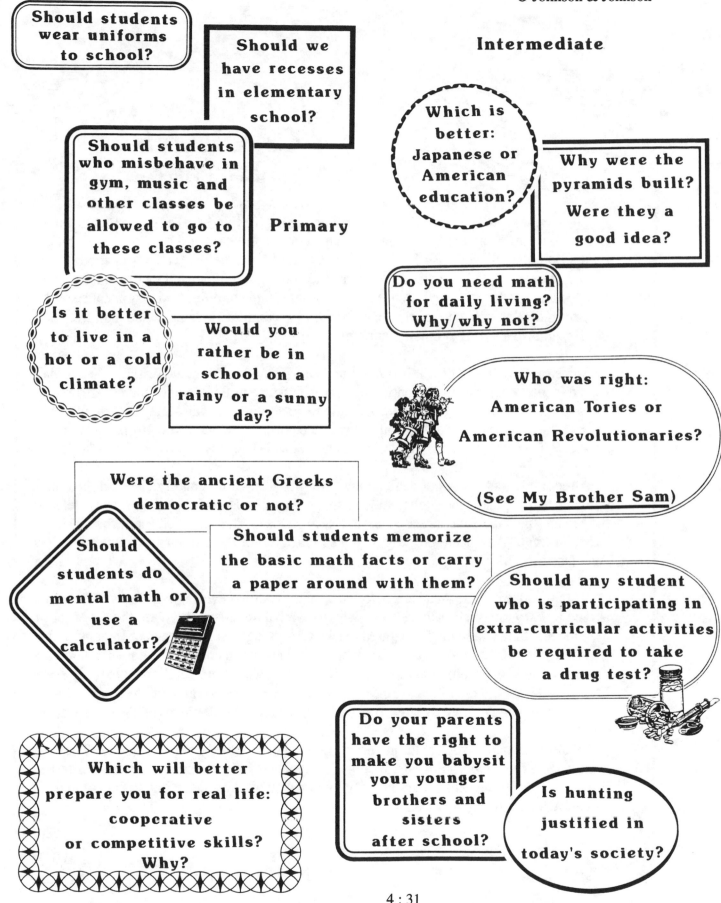

Were the ancient Greeks democratic or not?

Should students do mental math or use a calculator?

Should students memorize the basic math facts or carry a paper around with them?

Should any student who is participating in extra-curricular activities be required to take a drug test?

Do your parents have the right to make you babysit your younger brothers and sisters after school?

Which will better prepare you for real life: cooperative or competitive skills? Why?

Is hunting justified in today's society?

4:31

THE ACADIANS

Thomas Morton

They came from France to trade furs around the Bay of Fundy in the early 1600's, but in a few years Les Acadiens, the Acadians, had started to build dikes and carve out farmland on the rich, marshy soil. By 1755, the population of l'Acadie or Acadia was about 8,000 people. Long isolated from France by that date and highly influenced by the Indians, they had developed a life of independence and freedom. Yet the building and maintenance of the dikes required much cooperation and so with a common language and culture, they developed also a strong sense of community.

Since the Treaty of Utrecht in 1713, the Acadians had lived under British rule and had tried to remain neutral in the continuing conflicts between Britain and France. However, their farms lay in a strategic area between the British settlements at Annapolis Royal and at Halifax, the important naval base, and New France, which included New Brunswick, Prince Edward Island (Isle St. Jean), and Cape Breton Island (Isle Royale).

Although it was not yet official, another war between Britain and France and thus their colonies had begun. The English Lieutenant Governor at Halifax, Charles Lawrence, saw the French speaking Acadians as a possible security risk. This fear increased when in June, 1755, an Anglo-American force captured the French fort of Beausejour and found some 200 Acadians inside.

Britain had asked the Acadians before to swear loyalty to the English Crown. They had agreed in 1729, but their oath had been with the verbal understanding with the governor of the time that they would not be required to take up arms against the French or Indians. After Beauseiour's fall, Lawrence insisted that the Acadians give an unqualified oath of allegiance or be deported south to other British colonies. (They would not be allowed to go to New France as this would only increase the enemy's military power.) Again the Acadians tried to remain neutral and refused to agree to an oath that would oblige them to fight French armies.

In this controversy you are the governing council of the colony of Nova Scotia. The date is July 28, 1755. Do you decide to support Lawrence's plan to ship the Acadians to the English speaking colonies to the south or do you accept the Acadians' limited oath of loyalty and allow them to stay on their land?

❧ Against Deportation ❧

Your position is in opposition to Lieutenant-Governor Lawrence's plan to expel the Acadians. You feel that they will continue to remain neutral as they have for years and should be allowed to farm on their land in peace.

1. For over a century there have been repeated attacks and counterattacks and shifting control of Acadia from France to Britain. For the Acadians to commit to one side today may mean punishment from the other tomorrow. They are wise to stay neutral. They are no threat.

2. The Acadians already took an oath of loyalty to the Crown in 1729 and have kept their word. They are, therefore, British subjects and entitled to remain on their own land.

3. The French priest, Abbe le Loutre, at Fort Beauseiour threatened Acadian villages with attacks by Micmac Indians if the Acadians did not agree to join with the French in the fort. The Micmac even burned an Acadian village to the ground to force them to move. Thus it is hard to say if any of the 200 found at Beauseiour were truly in support of the French.

4. Why should 8,000 people lose their land for the supposed crime of 200 at Beauseiour? It is unjust to punish all Acadians because of the risk posed by a few.

5. The people of Acadia have built and maintained the dikes, cleared the land, and tilled the soil for over a century. To rip them from their homes and cast them into English colonies will destroy them as a people or leave them embittered against Britain and British justice. The previous British governor, Peregrine Hopson, firmly believed the Acadian claims to neutrality and was convinced that if they were treated fairly they would be loyal British subjects. Treat the Acadians fairly and their loyalty towards Britain will grow stronger.

EVANGELINE

A Tale of Acadie

This is the forest primeval. The murmur-
    ing pines and the hemlocks,
Bearded with moss, and in garments green,
    indistinct in the twilight,
Stand like Druids of eld, with voices sad
    and prophetic,
Stand like harpers hoar, with beards that
    rest on their bosoms.
Loud from its rocky caverns, the deep
    voiced neighboring ocean
Speaks, and in accents disconsolate answers
    the wail of the forest.

This is the forest primeval; but where
    are the hearts that beneath it
Leaped like the roe, when he hears in the
    woodland the voice of the hunts-
    man?
Where is the thatch-roofed village, the
    home of Acadian farmers, --
Men whose lives glided on like rivers that
    water the woodlands,
Darkened by shadows of earth, but reflect-
    ing an image of heaven?
Waste are those pleasant farms, and the
    farmers forever departed!
Scattered like dust and leaves, when the
    mighty blasts of October
Seize them, and whirl them aloft, and
    sprinkle them far o'er the ocean.

Ye who believe in affection that hopes,
    and endures, and is patient,
Ye who believe in the beauty and strength
    of woman's devotion,
List to the mournful tradition, still sung by
    the pines of the forest;
List to a Tale of Love in Acadie, home of
    the happy.

4 : 34

HENRY WADSWORTH LONGFELLOW

1847

❧ **For Deportation** ❧

Your position is in favor of Lieutenant Governor Lawrence's plan to force the 8,000 Acadians from their land and deport them to the 13 colonies to the south. Britain has been fair to the Acadians and yet they have chosen to refuse unqualified loyalty. They are a threat to British lives and must leave.

1. War with France is certain and the French are powerful. The mighty fortress of Louisbourg lies just to the north. Nova Scotia is on the frontlines. It would be suicide for the British to fight a war while thousands of people of doubtful loyalty are in their midst. Britain does not wish to force anything on anyone, but the survival of Nova Scotia is at stake.

2. Governor Lawrence has stated that the Acadians "have continually furnished the French and Indians with intelligence, quarters, provisions and assistance in annoying the Government...and 300 of them were found in arms at the French Fort at Beauseiour." The Acadians are not neutral.

3. Britain has been tolerant towards the Acadians for years. Although the Acadians were a conquered people, the British let them keep their land, practice their religion, and generally live as they please. Until the present threat, they have even been allowed to refuse to defend the colony. The Acadians must now repay this kindness or accept the consequence.

4. The obligation to fight to defend one's government is an essential duty of a citizen. To keep the rights of citizens, such as ownership of property, the Acadians must fulfill the duties of citizens. The Lieutenant-Governor has given Acadians a clear choice between full citizenship and deportation. They have chosen not to be full citizens.

5. Deportation is a harsh measure, but it is not death. The Acadians can start anew elsewhere. However, if they were in Nova Scotia, British settlers and soldiers might die.

Which Books Do We Take?

Task: Scientists have suddenly discovered that a large comet is going to strike the Earth. All life, if not the earth itself, will be destroyed. Your group (four members) has been picked to move from Earth to a new planet. The conditions on the new planet will be harsh and difficult. You will be starting life over, trying to develop a farming and technological society at the same time. Because of limited room in the spaceship, you can only bring three books. *Think carefully,* the captain says. *You will never return to Earth. You will never be able to get more books from Earth.* Write a report on the issue, **"Which books should we take?"** The report should present a position and the reasons why the position is valid.

Cooperative: Write one report for the group, everyone has to agree, and everyone has to be able to explain the choice made and the reasons why the choice is a good one.

Procedure:

1. **Research And Prepare Your Position:** Your group of four has been divided into two pairs. Each pair is to (a) make a list of three books to take, (B) plan how to present the best case possible for your to the other pair.

2. **Present And Advocate Your Position:** Forcefully and persuasively present the best case for your list to the opposing pair. Be as convincing as possible. Take notes and clarify anything you do not understand when the opposing pair presents.

3. **Open Discussion:** Argue forcefully and persuasively for your list. Critically evaluate and challenge the opposing pair's list and reasoning, and defend your reasoning from attack.

4. **Reverse Perspectives:** Reverse perspectives and present the best case for the opposing list. The opposing pair will do the same. Strive to see the issue from both perspectives simultaneously.

5. **Synthesis:** Drop all advocacy. Synthesize and integrate the best evidence and reasoning from both sides into a joint list that all members can agree to. Then (a) finalize the group report, (b) present your conclusions to the class, and (c) process how well you worked together as a group and how you could be even more effective next time.

Chapter Five: Preparing Positions

Introduction

He that wrestles with us strengthens our nerves, and sharpens our skill. Our antagonist is our helper.

Edmund Burke, Reflection of the Revolution in France

In 1982 a B-737 crashed into the 14th Street Bridge while taking off from National Airport in Washington, D.C. The crash was traced to a mechanical problem. The pilot, misled by an ice-jammed thrust indicator, had set the engine thrust too low to achieve a safe takeoff. But faulty group decision making also contributed to the crash. During the takeoff the copilot noticed that the plane was not reacting properly, and he repeatedly advised the captain. The copilot's warnings, however, were so subtle that the captain ignored them (Foushee, 1984). In 1978 a DC-8 crashed because the crew, while checking a malfunctioning instrument, ignored their dangerously low level of fuel. The flight engineer reported the low fuel to the captain, but he dismissed the warning. The problem of poor cockpit-crew decision making is a significant one. It literally means life or death, not only for the crew themselves, but for the passengers as well. Estimates suggest that between 65 percent and 80 percent of all airplane transport crashes that occurred in the United States between 1969 and 1979 resulted from faulty group decision making rather than mechanical problems (Cooper, White, & Lauber, 1979). Poor decision making by the cockpit-crew most often occurs when the crew members have no procedure for disagreeing with each other in a constructive way.

Whether the organization is a business, an industry, a government agency, a hospital, a law firm, a family, or a school, people are disagreeing with each other as decisions are made and problems are solved. In almost every meeting room within every organization, people are disagreeing with each other. Involved participation in such situations means that different ideas, opinions, beliefs, and information will surface and clash, i.e., **controversy**. Most groups waste the benefits of such disputes, but every effective decision-making situation thrives on what controversy has to offer. Decisions are by their very nature controversial, as alternative solutions are suggested and considered before agreement is reached. When a decision is made, the controversy ends and participants commit themselves to a common course of action.

Students, just like engineers, executives, politicians, and judges, have to make decisions to solve problems in every class they take. Participating in academic controversies is just as powerful as (and wonderful preparation for) the controversies involved in decision making within business, industry, government, and other similar settings.

Figure 5.1 Preparing A Position

Researching Position

    Organizing Results Into Conceptual Structure

      Leaping To A Conclusion

        Preparing To Present Position

Preparing Positions

"Was the Boston Tea Party an act of heroic patriotism? Or was it a needless criminal act that did not help America achieve its freedom? What do you think? Convince me you are right." To harness the power of academic controversy, the teacher assigns students to groups of four and asks them to prepare a report on the Boston Tea Party. There is to be one report from the group representing the members' best reasoned judgment about the issue. The groups are then divided into two-person advocacy teams. One team is given the position that the Boston Tea Party was an act of heroic patriotism and the other team is given the position that the Boston Tea Party was a useless criminal act. Both advocacy teams are given articles and materials supporting their assigned position. They are then given time to read and discuss the materials with their partner and to plan how best to advocate their assigned position so that they (a) learn the information and perspective, (b) convince the opposing team of the soundness of the team's position, and (c) teach the members of the opposing team the material contained in the resources. In order to engage in a controversy students:

- **Research (Look):** Gather evidence to support the assigned position.

- **Conceptualize (Think):** Organize the evidence into a logical structure that provides a rationale for the position.

- **Leap To Conclusion:** Once the evidence is gathered and organized into a logical sequence, students must reach a tentative conclusion based on their current understanding of the issue.

- **Present (Tell):** Plan how to advocate it forcefully and persuasively.

As they research, conceptualize, conclude, and tell, students (a) seek as complete an intellectual understanding of the issue as current knowledge allows and (b) use a set of social and cognitive skills.

Researching A Position (Finding Relevant Information)

Researching a position involves gathering and collecting of all facts, information, experiences, and other evidence relevant to the assigned position. Students take their assigned thesis statement or claim and, working in preparation pairs, engage in these activities:

1. Read the textbook and the materials provided by the teacher

2. Do library research to find facts, information, experiences, and other evidence to support the validity of the position. Students search the library and find books and

© Johnson & Johnson

Author:
Date of Publication:
Title of Article:

Title of Book or Journal:

City and State Where Published:

Publisher:
Pages Used:

articles on the topic. Their research can include computer searches and interviewing knowledgeable individuals.

3. List resources, writing down all the information needed to list the resource in your bibliography on an index card.

4. List and detail the facts, information, experiences, and other evidence that relate to the thesis statement. Each piece of relevant information may be listed on an index card.

5. Sort the evidence into supporting and nonsupporting categories. All the nonsupporting evidence is given to the opposing pair.

6. Select the most important evidence to include in the rationale by:

   a. Dividing the information supporting the thesis statement into three categories:

      1. Most important.

      2. Moderately important.

      3. Least important for the claim being made.

   b. Using the criteria of:

      1. Recency.

      2. Quantity of evidence.

      3. Quality of evidence.

      4. Consistency of evidence.

The more recent the evidence, the greater the amount, the more reliable and valid it is, and the more consistent it is, the better.

Differentiating Between Fact And Belief (Opinion)

In constructing the rationale for your position, you should stay as close to the facts as possible. This means you need to know the differences among fact and belief. **Facts** refer to things, states, or events that are provable by experience. Facts are verifiable by (a) the senses (measuring, weighing, and counting) or (b) inferences from physical data so strong as to allow no other explanation. Examples of facts are: Roger weighs 150 pounds, Edythe is over five feet tall, Abraham Lincoln was President of the United States. **Beliefs**, on the other hand, are things thought to be true but yet beyond the reach of verification through our senses, for example, it cannot be measured, weighted, or counted). Many people believe that world peace is possible, even though they cannot prove it. You may believe that life exists on other planets in the universe, that Atlantis will someday be discovered, and that an earthquake will destroy Los Angeles. But you cannot prove any of these things. Beliefs can be presented as part of a persuasive argument, as long as you do **not** assume that (a) you have proved them or (b) your beliefs prove your claim. In using beliefs as part of your argument remember the medieval saying, *De gustibus non est disputandum*—tastes are not to be disputed. You may believe that Chinese food tastes better than Italian food, but you should not argue about it.

It is often advisable to expand on your major points with examples, stories, and anecdotes. Facts that are merely stated before moving on are often missed by the audience. It may be best to make a point, make it again in different words, illustrate the point with an example or anecdote, and then make it once more in order for the point to be clearly understood.

Appeal To Authority

In gathering your information you are setting up an appeal to authority. You first appeal to the theory and research as the major authority. What do we now know is an important question in any controversy. You second appeal to the beliefs of great theorists or researchers as authorities, even though the critical research and theorizing may not be done in the authority.

An appeal to an authority to prove your point is actually an appeal beyond logic (but not necessarily beyond reason). *"Freud said..."* can silence many an objection. Appeals to Einstein, Shakespeare, Eleanor Roosevelt, Adam Smith, or Gandhi can authenticate many a claim since such people have often proved themselves to be right. Appeals to authority, however, risk four common fallacies. The more eminent the authority, the easier it is to make one of the fallacies. The fallacies are:

1. Appealing to an authority outside of his or her field. Freud had a brilliant mind, but he did not know a great deal about mass media. Ask, *"Am I citing the authority outside of his or her field?"*

2. Misunderstanding or misrepresenting what the authority really said. Ask, *"Am I presenting his or her views accurately?"*

3. Assuming that one quote from an authority represents his or her conclusions accurately. Ask, *"Is this instance really representative?"*

4. Not knowing that the authority is outdated. Ask, *"Is he or she still fully authoritative?"*

Appeal To Longevity Of Conclusion

Related to appeals to authority are **appeals to the longevity of a conclusion**. You can say, *"Because this belief has persisted, it must be true,"* but no one should agree with you. For hundreds of years people believed the ancient Greek Philosophers who concluded, *"There are four basic elements in the physical world—air, earth, fire, and water."* Because the belief lasted hundreds of years did not make it true.

Organizing What Is Known Into A Reasoned Position

When the research is completed, the information has to be organized into a persuasive argument. The aim of a persuasive argument is to lead listeners **step-by-step** from lack of knowledge to an informed conclusion that agrees with their thesis statement. A **persuasive argument** begins with a thesis statement or claim and presents a rationale that leads the audience to a clearly defined conclusion that is the same as the thesis statement. In other words, a persuasive argument has three parts:

1. A **thesis statement or claim** that asserts something is "true." " *George Washington was the greatest president the United States has ever had."*

2. A rationale that arranges the supporting facts, information, experiences, and other evidence into a coherent, reasoned, valid, and logical sequence that leads the audience to the clearly-defined conclusion that the claim is *"true."* *"Because George Washington militarily won our independence from England, was a unifying symbol for all thirteen colonies, was the role model for subsequent presidents, and provided a stable government during our country's formative years, then..."*

3. A **conclusion** that is the same as the original thesis statement. *"...George Washington was the greatest President the United States has ever had."*

Students organize or conceptualize what is known into a reasoned position by arranging the information into:

1. A conceptual framework.

2. A logical order.

Creating A Conceptual Framework

To learn, students first need to form or be aware of concepts and second organize the concepts into a structure that relates them in some meaningful way. This process of conceptualizing promotes understanding of what is being studied and long-term retention of what is being learned.

First, students form concepts. A **concept** names a person, place, thing, or event that has certain characteristics. A golden retriever, for example, is a dog, bred to hunt and retrieve birds, friendly, loyal, motivated to please its owner, and motivated to use its terrific sense of smell. All this information helps define the concept, "golden retriever." A **concept pattern** exists when all the information presented relates to a single word or phrase.

An important aspect of defining and understanding concepts is differentiating a concept from other concepts. The **similarity** or **dissimilarity** between concepts may be identified. For example, two dogs may be seen as very similar. They both have four legs. They both have big teeth. They both wag their tails. The same two dogs may be seen as very different. One is big and one is small. One is brown and one is black. One is fast and one is slow. A **similarity and dissimilarity pattern** exists when two or more concepts are compared and their similarities and dissimilarities are noted.

Second, concepts must be organized into a structure that relates them in some meaningful way. Concepts have to be organized into a rationale to support the assigned position. Four of the methods of doing so are an outline, a web network, a hierarchy, or a causal network. These ways of organizing concepts provide students with a means of summarizing and integrating important information.

Constructing An Outline

To build a coherent position out of isolated facts, students must arrange the evidence into a sequence. To do so they construct an outline to put their ideas together in an orderly manner and organize their presentation into a logical form so that it will make sense to listeners. Four types of outlines are simple, persuasive, AIDA, and PPP. A simple outline consists of:

Major Idea
    Supporting Idea   _____
    Supporting Idea   _____
    Supporting Idea   _____
                            _____

The topic may be broken down into subcomponents and all the information gathered about the issue is grouped into categories. Indentation is used to suggest subordination. In stating that the wolf should be a protected species, for example, information about the wolf may be separated into categories such as the wolf as a predator, the family life of the wolf, how wolves communicate with one another, and the dominance patterns within a wolf pack.

A more complex, persuasive outline is commonly divided into three parts: opening, body, and conclusion.

1. The **opening** of the presentation contains the thesis statement. Essentially, the opening is a clear, detailed, and to the point statement of the thesis statement. The opening should catch the listeners' immediate attention and arouse their interest in what is being presented. The opening may begin with a question, a visual display, or a generalization that is attention getting.

2. The **body** of the presentation is the evidence that provides a rationale for the thesis statement. The rationale consists of four to six points arranged in a logical progression that leads listeners, step-by-step, to the conclusion. Under each point an example, anecdote, or explanation is listed that helps persuade listeners to accept the point as valid. Facts, descriptions, expert opinions, statistics, and other concrete details are used, as a presentation that contains only vague generalizations is boring. More specifically, the body may consist of:

   a. Your first argument and supporting evidence and examples.

   b. Your second argument and supporting evidence and examples.

   c. Your third argument and supporting evidence and examples.

   d. Your fourth argument and supporting evidence and examples.

3. The **conclusion** summarizes the points made and draws the conclusion (i.e., thesis statement) forcefully, with confidence, and, sometimes, with drama.

Two other common types of outlines are as follows. The **AIDA outline** is:

> **A** Win their **attention**.
>
> **I** Arouse their **interest**.
>
> **D** Create a **desire**.
>
> **A** Stimulate **action** or **agreement**.

The past-present-future outline is:

> **Past** There was a time when...

Present But today, things have changed...

Future As we look into the future...

Like all written products, outlines go through several drafts. Students write a preliminary outline using the thesis statement as a guide. They start by arranging their evidence in the order they think best suited to the purpose of their presentation. They then experiment with the order. It helps if each piece of evidence is on a 3x5 card. Students can group the evidence into major categories, then sort each major category into subcategories. They can imagine themselves making the presentation to ensure that the order of the evidence is logical. Once they are satisfied with the order, they finalize it while keeping an open mind so they can learn and consider the opposing evidence.

Web Networks

A **web network** is a wheel in which a main idea, important fact, or conclusion is in the center, with supporting ideas and information radiating from it. The purpose of the web network is to clarify what students know about a concept. In the center of the wheel, for example, students may place the concept "Paul Revere." Radiating from the center the students then write down words that describe Paul Revere, such as patriot, American, man, revolutionary, silver smith, and brave. Doing so helps clarify their conception of Paul Revere.

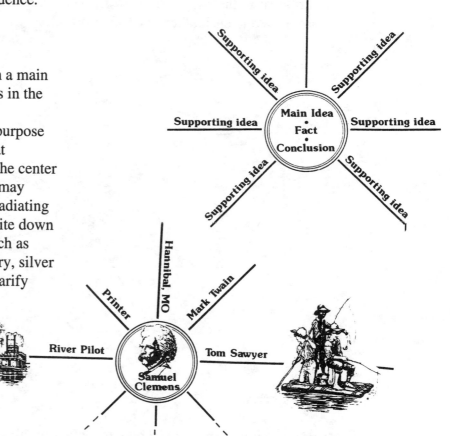

The web network may be taken one step further and used as a tool for clarifying relationships among concepts. This is done by constructing a mind map. A **mind map** is an expanded web network that has four major features: (a) key idea, (b) sub-ideas, (c) supporting ideas, and (d) connectors that show relationships. The purpose of a mind map is to help clarify the relationships among various ideas. Mind maps may be used for (a) note taking in a lecture or from a reading assignment, (b) exploring new ideas, (c) planning a course of action, or (d) generating and organizing the ideas to be contained in a written essay or report. Students, for example, could make web networks for the

American revolution, Paul Revere, the Battle of Concord, the Boston Massacre, and the Boston Tea Party. Then they could construct a mind map by writting out the:

~ **Key Idea:** Write "The American Revolutionary War" in the center circle.

~ **Sub-Ideas:** Write "Paul Revere," "The Battle of Lexington and Concord," "The Boston Massacre," and "The Boston Tea Party" in circles clustered around the center circle.

~ **Supporting Ideas:** For each of the sub-ideas write several supporting ideas in circles clustered around the appropriate circle.

~ **Connectors:** Draw lines from the key idea to the sub-ideas. Draw lines from the sub-ideas to their supporting ideas. Then draw lines from any supporting ideas that are related to each other or to other sub-ideas.

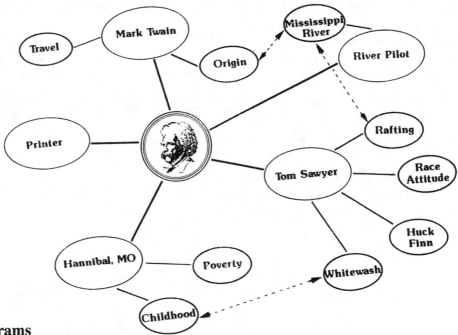

Venn Diagrams

Many times it is helpful to list how two ideas or things are similar and dissimilar. A comparison, for example, may be made between golden retrievers and toy poodles. There are ways these two types of dogs are similar. They both have four legs. They both have teeth. They both wag their tails. There are other ways these two types of dogs are different. One is big and one is small. One is brown and one is white or black. One has a high voice and one has a deep voice. Such comparisons may be facilitated by using Venn Diagrams. A **Venn Diagram** is two or more overlapping circles within which students list what is similar and what is different about two (or more) concepts. The purpose of a Venn Diagram is to show how two or more concepts are alike and different. To make a Venn Diagram students:

1. Draw two overlapping circles. Each circle represents one concept. For example, one circle could represent "Hamlet" and the other circle could represent "Macbeth."

2. List the characteristics that are similar between two concepts in the overlapping section. The characteristics Hamlet and Macbeth share in common are that they are both characters in plays by Shakespeare, they are both royalty, they are both men, and so forth.

3. In the separate parts they list characteristics of the concept being described but not true of the other concept. Hamlet for example was young, a prince, unmarried, and Danish. Macbeth was old, a king, married, and Scottish.

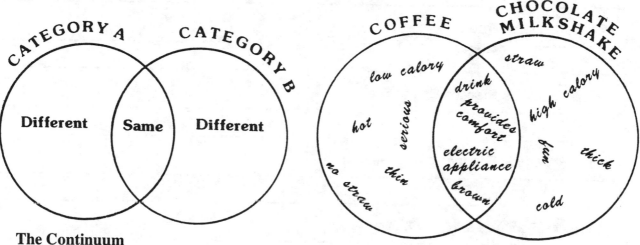

The Continuum

You have students use a **continuum** for tasks that require a ranking or ordering according to given criteria. A science class could use a continuum to rank the life spans of various animals, birds, or insects. You would give them a list of animals and a blank continuum and ask students to rank the animals' life spans from longest to shortest. You could follow this up with asking students to rank the quality of each animal's life from highest to lowest. Students specify the criteria for quality of life. Then they rank each animal according to those criteria.

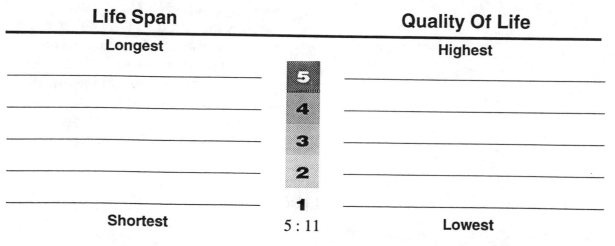

The Chain Diagram

To record stages of a process or steps in a procedure, you can use a **chain diagram**. Presenting the steps in teaching a skill is an example. You then present students with a series of behaviors and have them classify each according to the step it belongs in. The stages of evolution, the steps in baking a cake, the procedure for driving a golf ball and many, many other things can all be put in chain diagrams to give a visual organizer for what is being learned.

Teaching A Skill

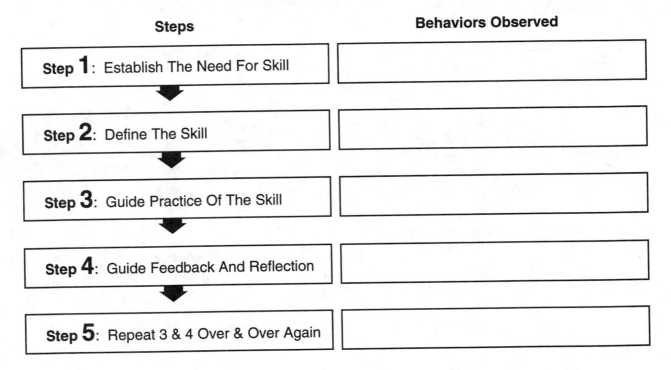

Steps	Behaviors Observed
Step **1**: Establish The Need For Skill	
Step **2**: Define The Skill	
Step **3**: Guide Practice Of The Skill	
Step **4**: Guide Feedback And Reflection	
Step **5**: Repeat 3 & 4 Over & Over Again	

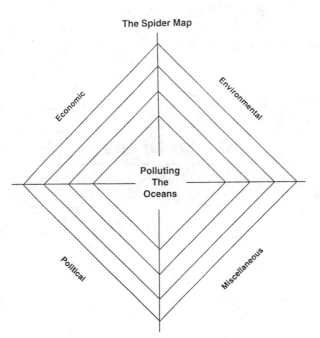

The Spider Map

Economic

Environmental

Polluting The Oceans

Political

Miscellaneous

The Spider Diagram

A spider diagram is used to create supporting details for a central idea. You give students a central idea, such as black holes in the universe, and have them generate a set of categories on which to evaluate it. Under each category they list their ideas. You may, for example, ask students to focus on the effects of polluting the oceans. The group may decide to use the criteria of economic, environmental, political, and miscellaneous effects. Under each criterion students list relevant factors.

The Chart

A **chart** is used to formulate a conclusion and then justify it with specific facts. Charts are used to compare or contrast ideas, events, styles, or people in any subject area. You could, for example, give your students the task of making three critical decisions leading up to the Revolutionary War. To do so they must (a) research each position, (b) formulate a personal decision based on the information they gather, and (c) justify the quality of the decision by referencing the facts. This format of asking for judgments and justification can be applied in a wide range of academic subject areas and disciplines. Students can evaluate any historical or literary event by this method.

Chart 1: Decisions Leading Up To The Revolutionary War

Decision Made	Student Decision	Justification
Boston Tea Party		
Demonstration Leading To Boston Massacre		
Armed Resistance At Lexington And Concord		

Another form of this procedure is to have students evaluate historical figures. Have students examine primary and secondary resources on the individuals being studied. Students then give each leader a "grade" on the basis of the criteria specified. After using such a chart several times, students will be able to generate their own criteria to evaluate historical or literature figures.

Chart 2: Comparison Of Historical Figures

Teddy Roosevelt	Grade	Reasons
Issues Focused On		
Leadership		
Personal Values		

Hierarchies

There are two types of hierarchies. The first is **part-to-whole hierarchies**. The whole may be broken down into parts. A tree, for example, may be conceptualized as a division of labor in which the roots anchor the tree and transport water and nutrients up to the sapwood, the sapwood carries the water and nutrients from the roots up to the leaves, the leaves make food for the tree by combining carbon dioxide from the air and water from the soil in the presence of sunlight to form sugar, the inner bark then carries the sugar made in the leaves down to the branches, trunk, and roots where it is converted to other substances vital for the tree's growth, the outer bark protects the tree from insect and disease attack, excessive heat and cold, and other injuries, and finally the heartwood gives the tree strength and stiffness. This division of labor ensures that the tree lives, grows, and produces. Breaking the concept "tree" down into parts allows for better understanding of what a tree actually is.

The second type of hierarchy is **class or category hierarchies**. Concepts can be classified from generic to specific. Trees, for example, may be divided into deciduous and coniferous. Deciduous trees may be divided into a variety of species, such as oak, maple, or apple. Oak trees may be further divided into red oak, white oak, and burr oak. Coniferous trees may be divided into a variety of species, such as pine, spruce, or fur. Pine trees may be divided into white pine, red pine, and ponderosa pine.

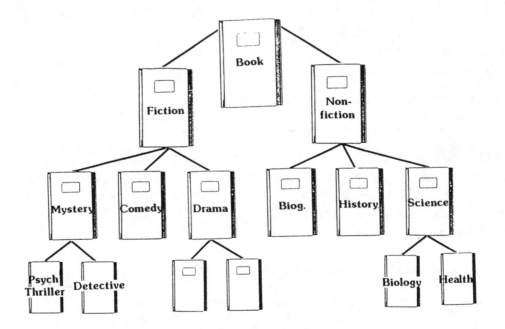

Causal Networks

A **causal network** organizes information in sequence so that one or more events are shown to have caused another. The message communicated is, "if a, b, and c occur, then d will follow." An example is, "If a thunderstorm is occurring, you are standing at the highest point around, and you are holding a metal golf club above your head, then you are likely to be struck by lighting." An example is that if you drop a 20 pound can of paint on your foot, pain will result. If you jump in a lake, you end up wet. If you shoot an arrow in the air, the force of gravity will bring it down. The world is full of cause-and-effect relationships.

Summary

The importance of information changes according to the pattern in which it is placed. Different patterns can be used to organize the same information, and some information may be important for one pattern but not for another. For any issue, the relevant information must be assembled and organized into a pattern. Which information is selected to be used and presented depends on the pattern students use.

Creating A Logical Sequence

A logical sequence is created through the combined use of inductive and deductive logic. Inductive and deductive logic go hand in hand. Inductive logic is used to establish general principles. Deductive logic is used to apply a general principle to a specific case. In creating a persuasive argument, both are used.

Inductive Reasoning

"Has anything escaped me?" I asked with some self- importance. "I trust there is nothing of consequence that I have overlooked?"

"I'm afraid, my dear Watson, that most of your conclusions were erroneous. When I said that you stimulated me I meant, to be frank, that in noting your fallacies I was occasionally guided towards the truth."

From **The Hound of the Baskervilles** by Sir Arthur Conan Doyle

After an issue has been conceptually analyzed and all known information about the issue has been grouped into categories, it is placed into a logical structure and involves both inductive and deductive reasoning. Induction and deduction are the two ways to reason. Induction is "leading into" (**in + ducere** = to lead) a conclusion while deduction is "leading away from" a general conclusion to its particular parts and consequences.

In 1620, Sir Francis Bacon described inductive reasoning in his famous **Novum Organum, sive indicia vera de interpretatione naturae** ("The New Instrument, or true evidence concerning the interpretation of nature"). His new instrument changed the entire course of thought. Bacon believed that deductive reasoning was too rigid to measure nature's subtlety. He wanted two things, for observed facts to create doubt about old ideas and for theories to replace "truths." Before Bacon, scholars had deduced the consequences of general ideas. After Bacon, scholars looked around and induced new generalizations from what they saw. Unfortunately, Bacon died from a cold caught while stuffing a chicken's carcass with snow for an inductive test of refrigeration.

Inductive reasoning is taking known facts, information, experiences, and evidence and making a "likely" conclusion. It involves thinking through the evidence to some general conclusion. Induction is called the scientific form of reasoning, for it is the process that all scientists use to develop theories. Scientists collect the facts and see what they come to. It may also be called human reasoning because the human brain operates on induction. You can not help but reason inductively. You collect evidence and come to a conclusion. Your whole life is spent reasoning inductively and, therefore, it is of great importance to do so skillfully. Whenever you are deciding, constructing a conclusion to summarize the known facts, or explaining something, you are engaging in inductive reasoning.

Inductive reasoning may be seen as addition, as a leap, and as an arrow. First, thinking inductively is very akin to the process of addition. In math class students add 2, 4, 8, and 10 to arrive at a conclusion of 24. In court a jury may add up 16 bits of evidence to arrive at a conclusion of not guilty. When you observe that 10 of the 12 most popular students in your school are athletes, you add it up to make a conclusion. "So what does it add up to?" is a question you are always asking in a controversy.

When you start to add up instances to arrive at a conclusion there is an inductive leap when you "jump" to a conclusion. This is risky! You might be wrong! In inductive reasoning, a person leaps from one ledge (known facts) over a chasm (the unknown) to the ledge on the other side (the conclusion). All inductive conclusions are uncertain (not 100 percent sure). You can never be absolutely sure your conclusion is valid. No amount of evidence can logically prove an assertion because one and some can never equal all. Because the sun has risen on every morning so far in the history of the world does not prove logically that it will do so tomorrow. There is a very small probability that something catastrophic will happen to the earth or the sun during the night.

Within inductive reasoning the evidence "points" like an arrow toward the conclusion. There is a sense of multiple strands converging, like multiple streams coming together to form a large river. Inductive reasoning is a process by which many facts, experiences, and pieces of information converge to point towards a single conclusion.

Inductive reasoning results in **tentative conclusions** that are stated as probabilities, not certainties. Your current tentative conclusion is the "truth" as you understand it, but with new learning and new understanding you will revise it. You should be willing to be led to whatever conclusion the facts direct you, while remembering that all decisions are temporary, tentative, and always open to modification on the basis of new evidence.

The inductive leap is always risky because **all** the evidence cannot be known. **Remember, one and some never equal all!** There is never enough evidence for certitude. You can never be 100 percent sure. No matter how many the facts, or how carefully they are weighted, a time comes when a person must abandon the consideration of evidence and leap to a conclusion. The inductive leap is always based on probabilities. The major lesson of induction is that **nothing** can be proved, except as a probability. The best that can be managed is a **hypothesis**. One must, of course, keep an open mind to new facts that might disprove what we currently conclude. The lesson of induction, therefore, is the lesson of caution. The beauty of induction is that it keeps our minds open for new hypotheses. The danger lies in thinking our conclusions are absolute.

Since more than one conclusion may be drawn from the same evidence, the leap may also be in the wrong direction. Conclusions must always be checked by asking if any other conclusion might not be just as valid. To justify a leap three conditions must be met:

1. Are the samples reasonably numerous?

2. Are the samples truly typical?

3. Are exceptions explainable, and demonstrably not typical?

When you add up what you know and the evidence points like an arrow to a conclusion and you are about to make "the leap" by tentatively adopting the conclusion, you have just engaged in the process of synthesizing. **Synthesizing** occurs when you integrate a number of different ideas and facts into a single position. Putting things together is synthesis. All the facts, information, and experiences gathered have to be synthesized into one or a set of conclusions. Synthesizing often results in seeing relationships and patterns that at first were not apparent. This often results from creative insight and improved understanding. From the consideration of all the information, you are pointed towards a new conclusion that is a synthesis of everything you presently know about the issue.

Some guidelines for inductive reasoning are:

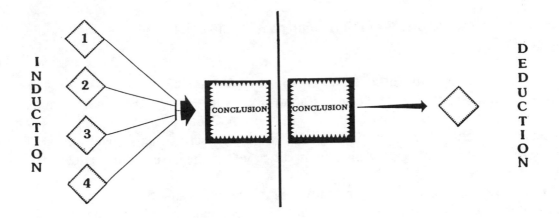

1. Do not jump too quickly to your conclusion. Take your time in formulating your conclusions.

2. Obtain enough instances before you formulate your conclusion. Try not to make conclusions on incomplete information.

3. Rank order your facts from the most important to the least important before you decide. Remember that not all facts are created equal. Some are more important than others.

4. Is the conclusion based on "all," "most," "some," or "few"? How qualified do you want to be in your conclusions? Avoid exaggerating.

5. Formulate optional hypotheses. Do not decide on one hypothesis unless you have seriously considered at least one other. Always choose among competing hypotheses.

6. Avoid unnecessary complexity. The simpler your conclusion the better.

7. Control bias. Do not let your preconceived ideas push you to formulate conclusions that are not substantiated by the data.

Deductive Reasoning

Some men see things as they are and say why? I dream things that never were and say "Why not?"

George Bernard Shaw

In addition to inductive reasoning there is deductive reasoning. While induction goes from specific instances to a conclusion, deduction leads away from a general statement or conclusion to specific instances. **Deductive reasoning** may be defined as applying a generalization to specific instances. Deduction and induction move back and forth in much of our reasoning, complementing and supplementing each other. Inductive reasoning results in a conclusion or general statement based on a number of specific instances, deductive reasoning then takes that conclusion or general statement and applies it to additional specific instances.

When Roger discovers that Edythe was just admitted into Holubec College, he deduces, "she must have made very good grades in high school." In deductive reasoning a general statement is applied to a specific case in order to make a conclusion. In the case of Roger, the reasoning is:

General Statement (Major Premise): Only students with high grade-point averages in high school are admitted into Holubec college.

Specific Case (Minor Premise): Edythe was admitted into Holubec college.

Conclusion: Edythe had a high grade-point average in high school.

Deductive reasoning is carried on in syllogisms, a word that originates from the Greek **syllogismos**—which is a combination of **syn**, meaning "together," and **logismos**, meaning "logical discourse." The word **synthesis**, an intellectual bringing together of ideas and facts, also originates from syllogismos. A **syllogism** is a bringing together of two statements to arrive at a conclusion. Of the two statements, one is a generalization (major premise) and the second is a specific factual statement (minor premise) related to the general statement. A syllogism brings together two "knowns" into a new assertion (the conclusion). Another example is:

> **General Statement:** All Americans believe in freedom of speech.
> **Specific Case:** Roger is an American.
> **Conclusion:** Therefore, Roger believes in freedom of speech.

The general structure is:

> All A are B.
> C is A.
> Therefore, C is B.

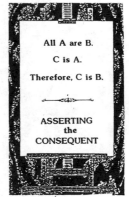

People use deduction constantly whether they realize it or not. Deduction is embedded in public speeches, editorials, essays, literature, drama, and especially advertising. It is beyond the scope of this chapter to discuss the rules of logic, but there are two simple and most common errors of deductive reasoning that (a) should be avoided and (b) should be recognized when someone is using them to persuade you. The first is known as **asserting the consequent.** It goes like this:

All A are B.
C is B.
Therefore, C is A.

While all A's are B's, not all B's are A's. This is known as **guilt by association**. When applied to straightforward matters of fact, the fallacy is usually obvious:

All mammals are warm-blooded.
A robin is warm-blooded.
Therefore a robin is a mammal.

But when applied to more ambiguous situations, the fallacy may be harder to spot:

All wars are preceded by arms build-ups.
We have had an arms build-up.
Therefore, we will have a war.

Advertising uses asserting the consequent frequently:

All handsome men use brand x.
If you use brand x,
Then you will be a handsome man.

The second simple and common fallacy in deductive reasoning is **denying the antecedent**. It goes like this:

All A are B.
C is not A.
Therefore, C is not B.

Again, while all A are B, not all B are A and, therefore, it is possible to be B without being A. When applied to straightforward matters of fact, this fallacy is also easy to spot:

All creatures who argue are human beings.
An infant does not argue.
Therefore, an infant is not a human being.

This fallacy can be harder to spot when it is used with more ambiguous assertions:

All proponents of school prayer are Christians.
Jones is not a proponent of school prayer.
Therefore, Jones is not a Christian.

The more quickly you recognize when someone is asserting the consequent or denying the antecedent the less likely you are to be persuaded to accept an invalid conclusion.

Leaping To A Conclusion

"And what is important as knowledge?" asked the mind.
"Caring and seeing with the heart," answered the soul.

Jeremy Campbell

In a controversy students are assigned (a) a position and (b) the tasks of preparing and presenting the best case possible for the position. In preparing the best case possible for the assigned position, students research the issue and organize the evidence into a conceptual framework and a logical sequence that lead the audience step-by-step to conclude that the position is valid and correct. Conclusions, however, are never completely proved because we never know everything there is to know about a thesis or claim. There are three parts to reaching a conclusion:

- What is known.

- What is unknown or yet to be discovered.

- The conclusion that the thesis or claim is (a) valid and correct or (b) invalid and incorrect.

The audience must leap from what is known, across the chasm of what is unknown, to a conclusion about the thesis or claim. There is always a leap of faith in reaching a conclusion that what we know outweighs what we do not know.

In leaping to a conclusion, there are three levels of reasoning that students may use (Davison et al., 1987—based on the theorizing of John Dewey, William Perry, and Karl Popper):

- **Dualistic thinking** in which students see the world in dualistic terms of right or wrong and accept the opinion of authority without question. This is the most common type of thinking among elementary, middle school, high school, and many college students.

- **Relativistic thinking** in which authorities and experts are seen as only sometimes being right, and anyone's view of right or wrong is as valid as anyone's else's on most questions. Clear distinctions between facts and beliefs are not made.

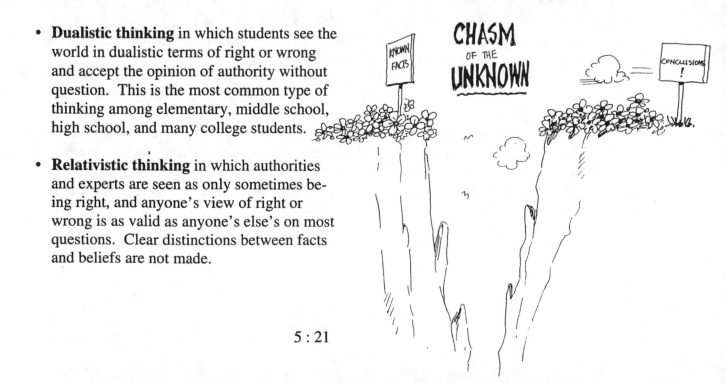

- **Probabilistic thinking** in which students accept the available knowledge only in degrees of certainty. Students appreciate the knowledge of experts, but do not defer to it automatically. Expert opinion, evidence, and personal experience are melded or integrated into a fairly noncontradictory view of knowledge. Students are willing to (a) assess which conclusions are more probable than others, (b) stand behind their own judgments, and (c) reformulate their point of view on the basis of new evidence. They are comfortable expressing degrees of certainty in discussing what they know.

The controversy procedure teaches students to think in probabilistic terms. To analyze information critically, students must be aware of what they do and do not know, the strength of the evidence on both sides of an issue, and the need to keep conclusions tentative so that they may derive an even more reasoned position in the future. A more reasoned position is derived by (a) incorporating new information into conceptual frameworks and (b) changing positions when the evidence indicates it is appropriate to do so.

Preparing To Present Your Position

Quickly, bring me a beaker of wine so that I may wet my brain and say something clever.

Aristophanes

Once the evidence has been gathered and organized into a compelling rationale, students must plan how to present their assigned position and its rationale with vigor, sincerity, and persuasiveness while keeping an open mind. In doing so students will want to understand the audience's perspective, use more than one modality, and practice the presentation before delivering it for real.

Perspective Taking

The first duty of a wise advocate is to convince his opponents that he understands their arguments and sympathizes with their just feelings.

Samuel Taylor Coleridge (1772-1834)

In order to persuade the proponents of the opposing position to accept your evidence and adopt your position, you must speak from their perspective. Other people are motivated only by what they want, not by what you want. As you organize your presentation, put yourself in your audience's shoes. Analyze what it will take to motivate your audience to agree with you, understand you, or take action on your behalf; and then develop your ideas to best supply that motivation.

Using More Than One Modality

You will want to use more than the auditory modality in presenting your position. The easiest modality to add is visual. People believe what they see before believing what they hear, and they better remember what they both see and hear. **Visual displays** are used to clarify, reinforce, or support points during your presentation. Visuals should be prepared in advance. They should be large enough so that listeners can see them easily. They should be colorful. They should be introduced and explained. They should be presented at the appropriate time. They should convey the meaning of and dramatize the points being made. They should be so simple that listeners will easily understand the ideas presented. Finally, know how and when you will use the visual, and practice until you can do it smoothly. Anticipate all possible problems, especially when machines are involved.

Practice Pairs

Students need to practice their presentation, preferably with the aid of someone who will give helpful feedback. After preparing their presentation, therefore, students are paired with a classmate who has the same position as they but is a member of another group. They practice their presentations using their visual aids. After both have presented, the two discuss how to improve each other's presentation. They are to take the best aspects from both presentations. At the very least, they are to take something from the other presentation and use it to improve their own.

Required Social / Cognitive Skills

There are a set of social and cognitive skills needed to work with a partner to formulate a rationale for an assigned position. These skills provide the mental processes needed to build deeper level understanding of the material being studied, to stimulate the use of higher quality reasoning strategies, and to maximize mastery and retention of the material supporting both the student's assigned position and the opposing position. These **formulating skills** include:

- Seeking mastery by **summarizing out loud** what has just been read, heard, or discussed as completely as possible without referring to notes or to the original material. All the important ideas and facts should be included in the summary. Every member of the group must summarize from memory both their own and the opposing position often if their learning is to be maximized.

- Seeking accuracy by **correcting a member's summary**, adding important information he or she did not include, and pointing out the ideas or facts that were summarized incorrectly.

- **Seeking elaboration** by asking other members to relate the material being learned to earlier material and to other things they know.

- **Seeking clever ways of remembering** the important ideas and facts by using drawings, mental pictures, and other memory aids.

- **Making implicit reasoning overt and thus open to correction and discussion** by asking other group members to vocalize what their reasoning was in arriving at their conclusions.

- **Planning how to teach material to others** by asking other members to plan out loud how they would **teach another** student the material being studied. Planning how best to communicate the material can have important effects on quality of reasoning strategies and retention.

- **Generating additional alternative answers** by going beyond the first answer or conclusion and producing a number of plausible answers to choose from.

Summary

As the first step in structuring academic controversy students are assigned to a cooperative learning group of four members. An academic issue is presented that has both pro and con points of view. To ensure that both sides of the issue are given fair and complete consideration, the cooperative group is divided into two pairs and each pair is given one side of the issue to represent.

Pairs of students then prepare the best case possible for their assigned position on the issue. To do so they must research the issue to collect all the evidence they can find to support their assigned position (Research or Look), organize the evidence into a conceptual framework that logically leads the audience to conclude that the position presented is valid and correct (Conceptualize or Think), leap to the conclusion that their assigned position is valid, and present the position and its rationale to the opposing pair (Present or Tell).

Students research the issue by finding facts, information, experiences, and evidence to support their assigned position. Students examine the text and course materials, do library and computer searches, list relevant information and sort it into supporting and nonsupporting and categorize the supporting evidence into most important to least important on the basis of criteria such as recency, quantity, quality, and consistency of evidence. In categorizing the supporting information they must differentiate between facts (provable by experience) and beliefs (thought to be true but unverifiable). In gathering information students are setting up an appeal to authority. The most powerful appeal is to the relevant theory and research. A less powerful but frequently used appeal is to the beliefs of great theorists or researchers as authorities. An appeal to longevity is tempting, but invalid.

When the research is completed, students organize the information into a persuasive argument. A persuasive argument needs a beginning (a thesis statement or claim that asserts something is true), a rationale that consists of a conceptual framework in which the information is arranged in a logical order, and an ending (a conclusion). Because it is a persuasive argument (as opposed to a story or poem), the opening and the conclusion are the same. To build a coherent position out of isolated bits of information, students must arrange the evidence into a sequence. Four of the ways of doing so are an outline, a hierarchy, a causal network, or a web network. The most common and useful is an outline, which may be a major idea with supporting ideas (simple), a thesis statement, body, and conclusion (persuasive), aimed at gaining the listener's attention, interest, desire to achieve a goal, and action (AIDA), or present the past, present, and future (PPP). These outlines are aimed at putting their ideas together in an orderly manner and organizing their presentation into a logical form so that it will make sense to listeners. There are two types of hierarchies: part-to-whole and category. In addition, there are a number of ways students can organize evidence into patterns.

Once the evidence is gathered and organized, logic is used to derive conclusions. **Inductive reasoning** is the taking of known facts, information, experiences, and evidence and making a "likely" conclusion about a general principle. **Deductive reasoning** may be defined as applying a general principle to specific instances. Deduction and induction move back and forth in much of our reasoning, complementing and supplementing each other. Inductive reasoning results in a conclusion or general statement based on a number of specific instances, deductive reasoning then takes that conclusion or general statement and applies it to additional specific instances. The use of inductive logic especially leads students past dualistic and relativistic thinking to probabilistic thinking in which students accept knowledge as available only in degrees of certainty. Based on a probability, students take the leap to a conclusion and use the social and cognitive formulating skills to prepare their positions.

Students now have a plan for presenting that position with vigor, sincerity, and persuasiveness while keeping an open mind. Presenting their position is the topic of the next chapter.

⚔ CONTROVERSY CONTRACT ⚔

Major Learnings	Implementation Plans

Date _____   **Date of Progress Report Meeting** _____

Participant's Signature _____

Signatures of Other Group Members _____ _____

_____ _____ _____

VOCABULARY SHEET

Working with a partner, learn the definitions of the words below.

1. Define each word in two ways.

   First, write down what you think the word means.

   Second, look it up in the book and write down its definition.

   Note the page on which the definition appears.

2. For each word write a sentence in which the word is used.

3. Make up a story in which all of the words are used.

4. Learn how to spell each word. They will be on your spelling test.

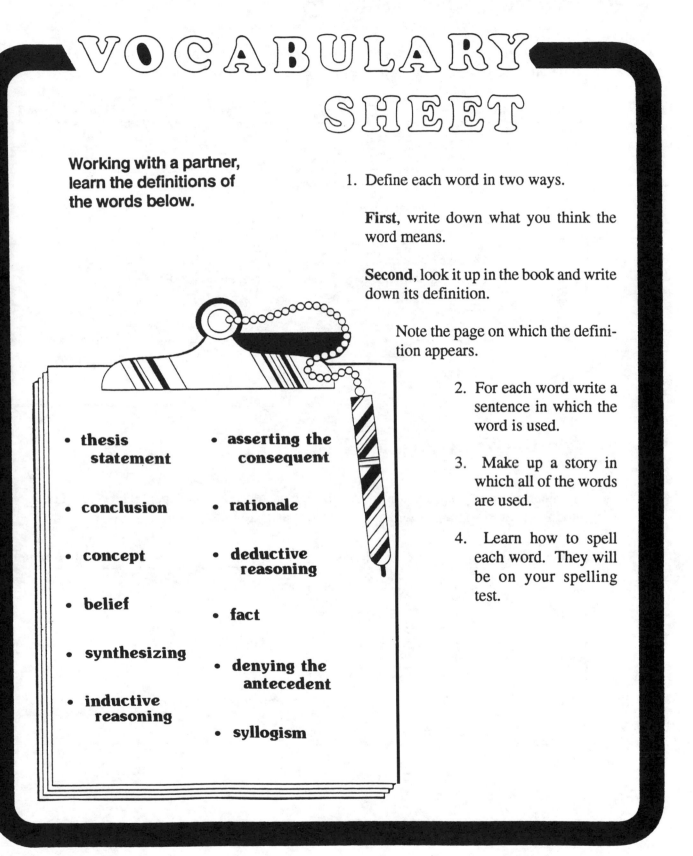

- **thesis statement**

- **conclusion**

- **concept**

- **belief**

- **synthesizing**

- **inductive reasoning**

- **asserting the consequent**

- **rationale**

- **deductive reasoning**

- **fact**

- **denying the antecedent**

- **syllogism**

☯ Preparing Your Position ☯

You are required to prepare your assigned position on the issue being studied. Your preparation of your position will be evaluated on the following criteria:

Points Possible	Criteria	Points Earned
100	Notes from at least four sources, including an encyclopedia and a book	
100	A bibliography listing the sources from which the notes were taken.	
100	An outline of the position.	
25	A visual aid to help present a persuasive case for your position.	
100	A position paper.	
425	**Total**	

Writing Your Position Paper

In preparing your position, you are required to write a position paper. The criteria on which your position paper will be evaluated is as follows.

Points Possible	Criteria	Points Earned
20	Begin With A Position Statement	
10	Indent Each Paragraph	
10	Begin Each Paragraph With A Topic Sentence	
20	Include Persuasive Supporting Sentences	
20	Capitalization, Appearance, Punctuation, Spelling	
20	Include A Title And Conclusion	
100	**Total**	

Listing and Sorting Your Evidence

As you search the resource materials for support for your thesis statement or claim, you list each piece of relevant information on an index card. When you have finished gathering your information:

1. Sort the evidence into supporting and nonsupporting categories. Give all the nonsupporting evidence to the opposing pair.

2. Divide the supporting evidence into three categories: **3 = Most Important, 2 = Moderately Important, 1 = Least Important**. Importance is determined by recency, quantity, quality, and consistency of the evidence.

Supporting Evidence	Rating	Nonsupporting Evidence

ORGANIZING A POSITION

A position consists of three parts: thesis statement, rationale, and conclusion. Your **thesis statement** is, "The Boston Tea Party was an act of heroic patriotism."

From the statements given below choose the three that best provide a rationale for your position:

1. The participants risked prison and even death to stand up for their belief in independence for America.

2. The participants had nothing to gain personally from their actions; they were motivated by their commitment to and love for America.

3. The participants broke the law; they hurt the American companies who were going to sell the tea more than they hurt the British government.

4. The participants gave hope to many Americans by showing that British rule could be resisted and overthrown.

5. The participants disguised themselves as Indians so they would not be recognized.

Place your three statements in a sequence that leads to your conclusion.

Boston Tea Riot

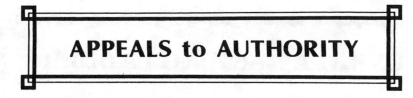

APPEALS to AUTHORITY

Each of the following statements contains at least one fallacious citation to authority. Identify it, and explain how it involves one or several of these mistakes: *Outside Field*, *Not Accurately Presented*, *Not Representative*, or *Out of Date*.

1. Karl Marx proved that war between the working class and the upper class is inevitable.

2. Einstein stated that everything is relative.

3. If he were alive today, Frances Bacon would recommend drinking a glass of red wine with dinner.

4. Walt Disney was in favor of controlling the power of the federal government.

5. Aristotle proved that the four basic elements are air, earth, fire, and water.

6. Freud once said that psychotherapy is a waste of time.

USING A RANKING LADDER

One way to conceptualize information about an issue is to rank order what you know. **Rank order** means to place in order on the basis of a criterion such as importance, value, or size. A **criterion** is a standard by which things are judged. Your **task** is to rank a number of items in each question. Work **cooperatively** with a partner. Both of you need to agree on the order of the ranking and both of you need to be able to explain why you ranked each item as you did.

Rank order your pets (a horse, a dog, and a cat) from largest (1) to smallest (3):

1. _____

2. _____

3. _____

You have a house, a car, a chair, and a desk. Rank order them from most valuable (1) to least valuable (4).

1. _____

2. _____

3. _____

4. _____

Rank order the following characteristics from most important for success (1) to least important for success (5). The characteristics are luck, hard work, intelligence, social skills, and money.

1. _____

2. _____

3. _____

4. _____

5. _____

Friends are loyal (stick by you), supportive (help in difficult situations), caring (like you as you are), and truthful (give you honest feedback when you ask for it). Rank order these characteristics from most important (1) to least important (4) in being a friend.

1. _____

2. _____

3. _____

4. _____

Making a Web Network into a Mind Map

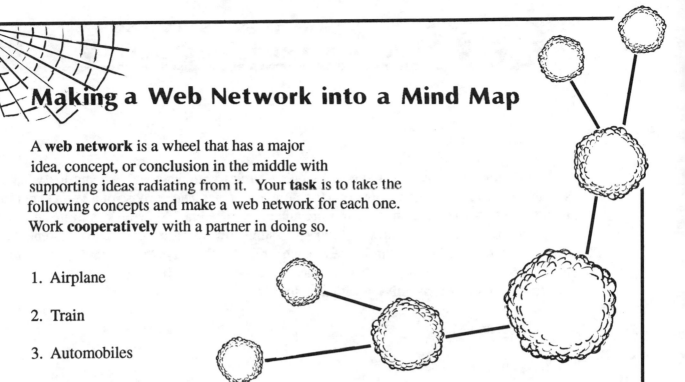

A **web network** is a wheel that has a major idea, concept, or conclusion in the middle with supporting ideas radiating from it. Your **task** is to take the following concepts and make a web network for each one. Work **cooperatively** with a partner in doing so.

1. Airplane

2. Train

3. Automobiles

4. Walking

You are now ready to take the web network one step further and use it as a tool for clarifying relationships among concepts. This is done by constructing a mind map. A **mind map** is an expanded web network that has four major features: (a) key idea, (b) sub-ideas, (c) supporting ideas, and (d) connectors that show relationships. Your **task** is to construct a mind map by completing the following steps:

1. **Key Idea:** Draw a circle in the center of a sheet of paper. Write "transportation" in that circle.

2. **Sub-Ideas:** Draw four circles around the key-idea circle. Connect each to the key idea circle with a line. Write "airplanes" in one, "trains" in another, "automobiles" in the third, and "walking" in the fourth.

3. **Supporting Ideas:** Draw several circles around each of the sub-ideas circles. Connect each to the appropriate sub-idea circle with a line. Write in the supporting ideas for each of the modes of transportation.

4. **Connectors:** Check on the connections among the ideas. Draw a line between any two ideas that should be connected. You may wish to use different colored lines to show major and minor connections.

Your next **task** is to read a story or a chapter in a textbook. Form a pair with a classmate who has read the same material. Working **cooperatively**, make a mind map of what you have read.

Making a Venn Diagram

A **Venn Diagram** is two or more overlapping circles within which students list what is similar and what is different about two (or more) concepts. The purpose of a Venn Diagram is to show how two or more concepts are alike and different. Your **task** is to make Venn Diagrams to compare the following things by noting how they are similar and different. For each, draw two overlapping circles, label each circle, list the ways the two things are similar in the overlapping section, and list the ways they are different in the two separate parts of the circles. Work **cooperatively** with a partner.

1. Earth and Mars.

2. China and India.

3. Automobiles and boats.

4. Poems and short stories.

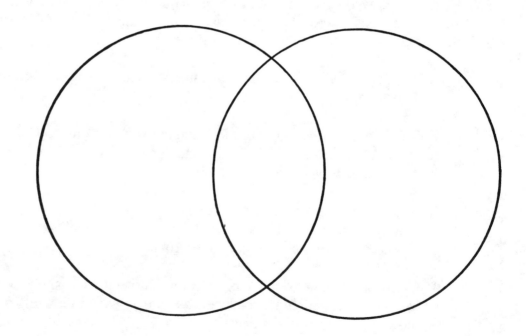

● INDUCTIVE and DEDUCTIVE REASONING ●

Identify whether individuals are using inductive or deductive reasoning or both in the following questions. If the answer is inductive, identify the evidence used to arrive at the conclusion. If the answer is deductive, explain the syllogism.

Meg has a golden retriever pet dog who is very friendly. Her friend Sarah has a black laborador pet dog who is very friendly. Meg sees a strange dog. "It will be friendly," she says.

_____ **Deductive**   **Inductive** _____

Evidence or Syllogism _____

_____

Roger was conducting a science class. His students discovered that paper clips and thumb tacks were attracted to magnets and pieces of paper and plastic bottles were not attracted to magnets. They concluded that only metal objects were attracted to magnets. If magnets attract all metal objects, the class decides, then knife blades will be attracted to magnets.

_____ **Deductive**   **Inductive** _____

Evidence or Syllogism _____

_____

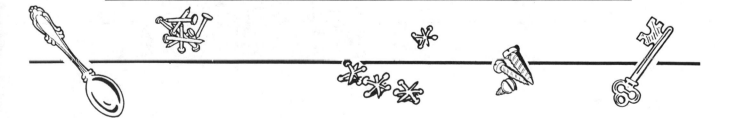

"The way you tell that an object in the night sky is a star, not a planet," Roger tells
class, "is that stars twinkle." "That object is twinkling," said Keith. "I conclude it
star."

_____ **Deductive**   **Inductive** _____

Evidence or Syllogism _____

_____

I read **Oliver Twist** and liked it. I read **Great Expectations** and liked it. I think I wo
like any book by Charles Dickens.

_____ **Deductive**   **Inductive** _____

Evidence or Syllogism _____

_____

DEDUCTIVE REASONING

Supply the missing terms for the following valid syllogisms. Work cooperatively with a partner. Make sure you both agree on the answers and can explain why your answers are correct.

No human being is always happy.
College professors are human beings.
Therefore, no college professor is

_____ .

Human beings know right from wrong.
Criminals are _____ .
Therefore, criminals know right from wrong.

All socialists believe in Marx.
Some post office workers believe in Marx.
Therefore, some _____

are _____ .

No fish are mammals.
Some _____ are sea creatures.
Therefore, some _____ are not fish.

U.S. MAIL

No _____ is a fighter pilot.
All _____ are teenagers.
Therefore, no fourteen-year-old is a fighter pilot.

A pessimist is a disillusioned idealist.
_____ is a

_____ .

Therefore, Keith is a disillusioned idealist.

CAN I TRICK YOU WITH THESE?

Given below are several examples of deductive reasoning. Identify the general statement, the specific case, and the conclusion for each example. Then decide which of the examples use valid deductive reasoning and which use invalid deductive reasoning. If the reasoning is invalid, identify whether the mistake is asserting the consequence or denying the antecedent.

1. "I know that on musical instruments, the shorter the string the higher the sound. When you put your finger there, you shorten the string. You're going to get a high sound."

General Statement: _____

Specific Case: _____

Conclusion: _____

Valid Or Invalid And Why: _____

2. All Americans believe in freedom. You believe in freedom. You're an American!

General Statement: _____

Specific Case: _____

Conclusion: _____

Valid Or Invalid And Why: _____

3. That mother monkey is nursing her baby. That means monkeys are mammals!

General Statement: _____

Specific Case: _____

Conclusion: _____

Valid Or Invalid And Why: _____

© Johnson & Johnson

4. All ecologists advocate clear air. You are not advocating clean air. You are not an ecologist!

General Statement: _____
Specific Case: _____
Conclusion: _____

Valid Or Invalid And Why:_____

———∞———

5. All Johnsons have inferiority complexes. You have an inferiority complex. You have to be a Johnson.

General Statement: _____
Specific Case: _____
Conclusion: _____

Valid Or Invalid And Why:_____

———∞———

6. Heavy round objects sink in water. That ball-bearing is a heavy round object. It will sink.

General Statement: _____
Specific Case: _____
Conclusion: _____

Valid Or Invalid And Why:_____

———∞———

7. Pick an issue you are studying. Construct a valid syllogism. Then change it to assert the consequence. Then change it to denying the antecedent.

———∞———

JAMES WOLFE: A True ^OR a False Hero?

Thomas Morton

For years English-Canadian children have grown up on the legend of the brave, young general, James Wolfe, the victor at Quebec in 1759. Until the second world war, the unofficial national anthem of English Canada was **The Maple Leaf Forever** which began with the words *From England's shore, Wolfe, the undaunted hero, came....*

When the British fleet that carried Wolfe and his army set anchor off Isle d'Orleans on June 26 in 1759, Quebec looked impossible to conquer. Surrounded by a wall, the government palaces, cathedral, convent, and other buildings along with General Montcalm's army sat on top of a 60 foot high limestone cliff.

Against this seemingly secure citadel, General Wolfe tried various tactics throughout the summer to lure the French outside the walls into open battle against his larger army of British regulars. But General Montcalm with his army of French regulars, Canadiens, and Indians stayed behind his defenses. Finally, late in the summer, on September 12, Wolfe launched a daring plan. Under cover of night the British managed to slip past a French sentry and climb a trail up from the Anse au Foulon (Wolfe's cove), not far from the city. In the early hours of September 13 on the Plains of Abraham next to Quebec, Wolfe led his men into battle. Montcalm rushed his troops to the attack. In less than a half-hour of fierce fighting victory went to the British, although both Wolfe and Montcalm were shot and killed.

The victory was a turning point in Canadian history. It meant the fall of New France and the beginning of British control of Canada. The victorious general was soon to be the hero of song, story, and painting.

However, there is another very different story about Wolfe. In French Canada, the fall of Quebec was a defeat and not a victory. The emphasis of French and Quebec historians has been on French mistakes as causes of the defeat. In addition, the devastation of the countryside by the British army during the siege left the Canadiens, the common people, bitter. Even on the British side, before the battle and Wolfe was hailed as a hero, his officers had intensely disliked him. One of them, George Townshend, had even taken to drawing and circulating insulting cartoons of Wolfe during the summer campaign.

You will take the role of historians arguing this question: Does James Wolfe deserve his reputation as a hero or was he a false hero--a disagreeable, cruel man who got lucky?

WOLFE

THE HERO

Your position is that Wolfe, though he had faults, clearly deserves his reputation as a hero both for his personal qualities and his great accomplishments.

1. A hero succeeds despite obstacles. James Wolfe lacked the money or aristocratic family that so often meant promotion in the British army in the 18th century. Instead he advanced because of his bravery and intelligence. At Louisbourg in 1757, he led his troops ashore in stormy weather, with boat after boat overturning, to seize the French fort. Prime Minister Pitt recognized his heroism with the rank of Major General when Wolfe was just 32. He was to lead 8,600 of the finest British soldiers against Montcalm at Quebec.

2. A hero has honorable personal qualities. Wolfe neither drank nor gambled, common vices among officers of the day. He showed his concern for his men when he left L2,000, a huge sum for that time, in his will to be distributed amongst his army.

3. Although during the siege of the summer of 1759, the British army destroyed the countryside around Quebec, it was common wartime practice at that date and Wolfe tried to stop the worst of it. He issued an order that "strictly (forbade) the inhuman practice of scalping, except when the enemy are Indians, or Canadiens dressed as Indians."

4. Wolfe listened to the advice of his officers. It was they who proposed landing troops upstream from Quebec. He then added his own brilliant twist, to attack much closer to the city by climbing the cliffs up to the Plains of Abraham. He had listened to others, but like a hero, he was willing to risk boldness.

5. A hero is brave. On the morning of September 13, Wolfe led his troops into battle. He ordered them to lie down while he stood in his red uniform, exposed to sharpshooters. He was shot first in the wrist, then the stomach, but he walked on. Eventually, a third bullet tore into his chest. At the moment of victory, General Wolfe died, a hero.

6. A hero achieves great things. Wolfe's victory changed the course of Canadian history. Canada was to become British.

WOLFE
A FALSE HERO

Your position is that Wolfe was a false hero. He was cruel, suspicious, and showed poor judgment during the campaign. His success was due mainly to French errors and luck. It was the circumstances of history that made people hail him as a hero.

1. Wolfe had few honorable personal qualities. Wolfe often spoke with contempt and even hatred against Indians, Scots, and Americans, even though the latter two were part of his army. He called the American rangers "the dirtiest, most contemptible cowardly dogs."

2. Wolfe was cruel. Throughout the summer of 1759, his cannons bombarded civilian buildings. As the siege advanced, he ordered the looting and burning of the countryside for 60 miles around Quebec. He did little to stop scalping, and at St. Joachin, Wolfe's soldiers scalped a priest and 30 men. The church was then burned. The British troops also suffered savage discipline and Wolfe was little concerned for their welfare. He once said that he would risk the loss of 1,000 men in order to raise the reputation of his country.

3. Until the Plains of Abraham, Wolfe's campaign was a failure. On July 23, he ordered an attack at Beauport to the east of Quebec, even though the beach was within easy range of French guns. The British suffered heavy losses and retreated. The fault was his plan.

4. Wolfe was highly suspicious. Although it was common practice of the day to consult with officers, Wolfe did not do so until very late in the campaign. It was the officers who suggested the concentrated attack upstream from Quebec. Wolfe changed the location of the landing and then refused to tell anyone until the very night of the attack.

5. Wolfe's plans succeeded because of luck. Anse au Foulon was easy to defend, but the Comte de Bougainville forgot to post enough of his 3,000 men to defend the cove properly. It was luck that a French-speaking Scot in Wolfe's army was able to fool the French sentry who challenged him, and so no warning was given of the landing.

6. Wolfe also succeeded because of French errors. When the French commanders at Beauport heard that British troops were on the Plains of Abraham, they refused to believe it and did not send reinforcements right away. Montcalm could have sent an order and awaited the Beauport troops. He could also have waited for Bougainville's soldiers. His Indian and Canadien sharpshooters hidden in the woods were already taking a terrible toll of the British troops on the plains. Instead, despite being outnumbered, Montcalm attacked and the French lost. Montcalm's error made Wolfe appear brilliant.

Chapter Six: Advocating Positions

Introduction

...instead of looking on discussion as a stumbling-block in the way of action, we think it an indispensable preliminary to any wise action at all.

Pericles

We live in a society that values highly the notion that truth is more likely to be approximated if opposing views can be freely and openly expressed. **Rooted in the ancient Athenian tradition of the democratic, open society, we encourage rather than suppress the expression of opposing views.** We labor in the faith that truth will spring from the uninhibited clash of opposing views. Such clashes begin with researching a topic, organizing and conceptualizing the evidence, taking the leap to a conclusion, and then advocating that conclusion to the best of one's ability. **Advocacy** is the presenting of a position and providing reasons why others should adopt it. Advocacy is essential for (a) ensuring that the assigned position gets a complete and fair hearing and (b) teaching the opposing students the information one is presenting. In advocating their assigned positions, students:

- Keep in mind that the overall goal is for the group to make a reasoned judgment about the issue. Members, therefore, must learn the evidence and reasoning contained in both sides of the issue in order to create a synthesis or integration that is insightful and illuminating.

- Present and advocate the position with the intent of (a) persuading the other group members of its validity, (b) ensuring that it gets a fair and complete hearing, and (c) teaching the information to the opposing students.

- Learn the opposing position and perspective in order to better understand and refute it.

- Refute the (a) evidence supporting the opposing position and (b) reasoning used to organize that evidence. Critical analysis subjects each position to a "trial-by-fire" in which the opposition challenges the strength of one's evidence and the validity of one's reasoning.

- Rebut the opposition's attacks on the validity of the evidence and reasoning contained in one's own position.

- Search for further evidence and a better conceptualization.

- Use the social and cognitive skills for challenging and defending.

Table 6.1: Advocating Your Assigned Position

Advocates Of Position A	Advocates Of Position B
Present Position A Persuasively	Present Position B Persuasively
Learn Position B	Learn Position A
Refute Position B	Refute Position A
Rebut Attacks On Position A	Rebut Attacks On Position B
Search For Further Information	Search For Further Information
Reconceptualize Understanding Of Issue	Reconceptualize Understanding Of Issue

Presenting Your Position

Alfred Sloan, a former chairman of General Motors, once stated at an executive meeting in which a major decision was being considered (cited in Drucker, 1974, p. 472): *I take it we are all in complete agreement on the decision here. . . . Then I propose we postpone further discussion until our next meeting to give ourselves time to develop disagreement and perhaps gain some understanding of what the decision is all about.*

Within a controversy participants present and advocate positions to others who, in turn, are advocating opposing positions. In essence, the student's responsibility is to say, *Here is the best case for my assigned position. I am going to ensure that it receives a fair hearing and full consideration.* The format for presenting positions is:

1. Person "A" presents his or her position as sincerely and thoroughly as he or she can. Person "B" listens carefully and takes notes.

2. The students reverse presenting/listening roles.

The guidelines for making a persuasive presentation are:

1. **The presentation should begin with (a) a thesis statement or claim and (b) a strong, sincere, and enthusiastic appeal for the listeners to agree with the thesis or claim.** Both the position being taken on the issue and the presenters' conviction and enthusiasm should be clear.

2. **The rationale for the thesis or claim should be presented.**

   a. The rationale should consist of a conceptual framework containing several points of evidence arranged in a logical sequence. Evidence to support the validity of the thesis or claim should be presented within a well-conceptualized framework.

b. To ensure that the important points are not missed by the audience, each major point included in the rationale should be (1) clearly stated, (2) stated again in different words, (3) illustrated with an example, story, anecdote, or visual display, and (4) stated once more.

3. **The presentation should end with a conclusion that is the same as the thesis or claim and a strong note of appeal.**

4. **The presentation should be delivered with enthusiasm, conviction, and sincerity.** Students should give a presentation that is an appeal, a call for action to consider their viewpoint. Unless the presenter has convictions and can illustrate them in a well conceptualized and logical form, the presenter has nothing to say. The first sentence should wake opponents up and make them listen. The conclusion should wind up on a strong note of appeal. The presenter has to convince the listeners to listen and consider the position open-mindedly.

5. **The presenters should not to try to cover too much in their initial presentations.** They should save some of their evidence for the open discussion. During the initial presentation, it may be best for students to select a few major points, four or five at the most, and expand on them by use of examples, illustrations, stories, and anecdotes.

6. **The presenters should make eye contact with opponents.** They should first look directly at one person for a few seconds, then look at the other so no one feels left out of their presentation.

7. **The presentation should be conducted within the time limits.**

8. **The presentation should contain more than one media.** Visual aides help students present their positions convincingly and clearly.

9. **The presentation should be practiced.** Practice makes perfect. Students should practice their presentation until they are comfortable delivering it and can do so naturally.

In presenting the rationale for your position, it is important to present the best evidence available organized into well-conceptualized and logically valid frameworks. As a joke, or to see if your opponent is awake, however, you may wish to use one of the "tricks of the trade" in arguing.

Tricks Of The Trade: Fallacies In Arguing Commonly Used To Win

Arguing with skill is an art. Students have to disagree without being disagreeable, improve their understanding of the other's position and reasoning, represent their ideas with a delicate blend of vigor and restraint, and extract from their own and the other's arguments a sound synthesis of the two positions. In doing so there are a number of fallacies to avoid and look out for. Occasionally you may wish to slip one of these fallacies into your presentation as a joke.

Ignoratio elenchi is missing the point. It is an attempt to discredit the opponent's position by disproving an assertion that the opponent has not actually made. It is often used intentionally and deviously either to force the opponent to defend the indefensible, or to escape a tight spot where one might otherwise be forced to yield to the opponent's arguments. An example is when one person argues against the building of nuclear weapons and the opponent accuses him or her of being naive about other countries' military aggressiveness.

The two simplest and most common errors of deductive reasoning are asserting the consequent and denying the antecedent. **Asserting the consequent** goes like this: All A are B. C is B. Therefore, C is A. An example is: All wars are preceded by arms buildups. We have had an arms buildup. Therefore, we will have a war. **Denying the antecedent** goes like this: All A are B. C is not A. Therefore, C is not B. An example is: All cowboys ride horses. Pecos Bill is not riding a horse. Therefore, Pecos Bill is not a cowboy.

Arguing from analogy happens when the outcome of a proposed course of action is predicted by citing the outcome of some previous similar course of action. Arguments from analogy are always deductively fallacious for the simple reason that no two situations are exactly alike. Nevertheless, some analogies are better than others. Almost any argument from a single analogy can be undermined by pointing out the differences in the situations, since between any two situations there are apt to be as many differences as similarities. The arguer's hope, therefore, is to cite not just one but many roughly similar situations, all of which resulted in the outcome he or she is predicting for the proposed course of action. When enough even remotely plausible analogies are combined, their individual weaknesses become nearly irrelevant, and they can topple the strongest proposals.

There are three sneaky ways questions can be used. **A rhetorical question** is a statement (usually a broad or exaggerated one) expressed as a question to which there can be only

one answer, in the hope that the listener will draw the desired conclusion on his or her own. *"Do you want a President who cares nothing about the poor in our society?"* is an example. The **fallacy of many questions** consists of asking a series of questions all at once rather than asking only one question at a time. The **fallacy of a question with a presupposition** is a question that cannot be given any answer without the answer conceding a point that is in dispute (*"Do you still beat your wife?"* or *"How do you explain the deterioration of the*

6 : 4

Never answer such a question.

economy?"). All such questions are fallacious, mainly because they are rhetorical questions posing as genuine inquiries. Never answer such a question.

Reduction ad absurdum consists of directly challenging the assumptions on which the other's arguments are based by suggesting that if the assumptions were uniformly applied they would lead to absurd conclusions. Within most arguments a general principle is stated or inferred (Killing is wrong. Liberty is an unalienable right of humans. Freedom of speech is desirable.) and facts are presented to prove that the principle applies to the case at hand. The principle can then be identified and challenged on the basis that it leads to absurd conclusions if applied in **every** case.

Finally, **argumentum ad hominem** consists of directing arguments at the opponent rather than at his or her ideas. There are three ways in which such arguments can be made. The **genetic fallacy** is an attempt to discredit an argument by questioning the motives of the arguer. **Argumentum ad personam** is an appeal to personal interest (he wants x because it will benefit him). **Accusing the opponent of inconsistency** is probably the most common form of argumentum ad hominem.

Most individuals have failed to learn the joys of recreational arguments. The above sneaky ways of attempting to disprove arguments may add humor and enjoyment to your arguing. At the very least you should be able to recognize them and avoid being trapped by opponents using them.

Learning Opposing Positions And Perspectives

...it is critical that one seek to understand (other peoples') perceptions if one is to understand the circumstances under which their behavior might change.

Harold J. Leavitt

Two of the primary purposes of the controversy procedure are for students to (a) teach what they know to their opponents and (b) learn the opposing evidence and perspective. There are at least two reasons for learning the position and perspective of the opposition. The **first** is personal achievement. The opposing position and perspective must be thoroughly understood in order to (a) create a synthesis based on the best reasoning by both sides and (b) do well on a test covering both sides of the issue. Individuals engaging in controversy tend to be motivated to know others' positions and to develop understanding and appreciation of them (Tjosvold & Johnson, 1977, 1978; Tjosvold, Johnson, & Fabrey, 1980; Tjosvold, Johnson, & Lerner, 1981). In addition, individuals involved in a controversy develop a more accurate understanding of other positions than do persons involved in noncontroversial discussions, concurrence-seeking discussions, and individualistic efforts (Smith, Johnson, & Johnson, 1981; Tjosvold & Johnson, 1977, 1978; Tjosvold, Johnson, & Fabrey, 1980).

The **second** is to be able to refute the opposing position. The better the opposing position is understood, the more devastating the attack on it can be. Refutation requires finding and highlighting where the evidence and reasoning are faulty.

To learn the opposing position students must learn both the information being presented and the perspective from which the issue is viewed. Learning the opposing information and perspective (position) may be facilitated by:

1. Listening carefully to the opposing presentation.

2. Asking for additional evidence (facts and information).

3. Clarifying anything that is not understood through paraphrasing. **Paraphrasing** is restating, in one's own words, what another person says, feels, and means. Paraphrasing is an invitation for clarification or correction to make sure the speaker's understanding is accurate. Paraphrasing also helps students get into the other person's shoes and see the issue from his or her perspective. It is discussed in more depth in the chapter on perspective-taking.

4. Taking notes detailing the information and evidence being presented. In doing so it is helpful to classify the information being presented by taking notes in two columns. Write down the strong points being presented in the first column and the weak points being presented in the second column. The information in the strong column can then be ranked from most important to least important.

5. Drawing a picture of the information and evidence being presented. Identify the conceptual structure of the opposing position by placing the information being presented in an outline, hierarchy, or cause-and-effect diagram.

6. Think of other supporting evidence that the opposing students did not present but would strengthen their position. Add it to your notes.

Open Discussion Of Issue

When two men in business always agree, one of them is unnecessary.

William Wrigley, Jr.

Once the issue is researched and the positions are presented, an open (free-for-all) discussion takes place. The goals of the discussion are (a) to ensure all group members understand both sides of the issue thoroughly and completely, (b) for students to continue to advocate the best case for their assigned position, (c) to subject each position to a *"trial-by-fire"* in which the opposition critically analyzes and challenges the strength of the evidence and the validity of the reasoning, (d) for students to defend their assigned position and rebut the attacks being made on it, and (e) for the uncertainty created by the critical analyses and challenges to motivate a search for additional information and a reconceptualization of the issue. The procedure is as follows:

1. Students present arguments forcefully and persuasively emphasizing evidence and reasoning.

2. Students listen critically to the opposing position, trying to find flaws in evidence and reasoning. They ask for facts and rationale to clarify their understanding.

3. Students attack the opposing position, pointing out the weaknesses, flaws, and mistakes in evidence and reasoning.

4. Students defend their position from the opponent's attacks, presenting counter-arguments, clarifications, and extensions.

Students keep in mind that the overall goal is to make a reasoned judgment about the issue and, therefore, they must learn the evidence and reasoning contained in the opposing position. Reasoned judgment requires a thorough understanding of all sides of the issue. Students prepare themselves to make a reasoned judgment by ensuring that each position (a) gets a fair and complete hearing (by having classmates advocate it strongly) and (b) is examined critically (by having classmates attempt to refute it).

Continued Advocating

During the open discussion students are responsible for a continued advocacy of their assigned position to ensure that it gets a complete and fair hearing and the opposing students learn the information presented. In continuing to advocate their position, students present arguments forcefully and persuasively emphasizing facts and evidence. The more persistently, consistently, and confidently positions are presented, the more credible the positions are perceived to be (Nemeth, Swedlund, & Kanki, 1974; Nemeth & Wachter, 1983). Advocacy, furthermore, tends to increase learning. The process of argument and counter-argument aimed at persuading others to adopt, modify, or drop positions requires students to contribute information, repeat information, elaborate on the material being discussed, critically evaluate the validity and correctness of claims, critically evaluate evidence, and use higher-level reasoning processes.

Refuting The Opposing Position

...the noise could be heard all over the city. Our fights over words were furious, blasphemous, and frequent, but even in their hottest moments we both knew that we were arguing academically and not personally.

Richard Rogers (recalling his work with lyricist Larry Hart)

Refutation means to attack another person's position in an attempt to weaken or even destroy it. Refutation is an attempt to cast significant doubt on and/or show the inadequacies of the opposition's evidence and reasoning so that they (or interested other people) will be willing to change their minds. Students listen critically to the opposing position, trying to find flaws in evidence and reasoning. They ask for facts and rationale to clarify their understanding. They attack the opposing position, attempting to find the weaknesses, flaws, and mistakes in its evidence and reasoning. Charging the opposition with having faulty evidence or using faulty reasoning are standard refutation practices.

Refuting Opponent's Evidence

Imagine that your students are involved in a controversy over the play **Hamlet**. Within each cooperative group, two students advocate the position that Hamlet was indecisive. Two students advocate the position that Hamlet was very decisive, but had bad luck, never catching his step-father at the right moment. One pair may say, *"Hamlet was indecisive. Trust us on this one. We are right."* The other pair asks for evidence, *"We know your opinion, where are your facts? Show us the passages in the play that support your thesis."*

In a controversy, students do not blindly believe each other's opinions. They differentiate between fact and opinion. A **fact** is a thing, state, or event that is verifiable by (a) the senses (measuring, weighing, and counting) or (b) making an inference from physical data so strong as to allow no other explanation. An **opinion** is an unproven belief or judgment. *"Columbus reached American in 1492,"* is a fact. *"Columbus was a great man,"* is an opinion. If you are not sure whether a statement is a fact or an opinion, treat it as an opinion.

In a controversy students also ask for evidence, which they critically examine to determine if it is valid or faulty. Evidence may be faulty for a number of reasons. The procedure for evaluating evidence is as follows.

1. **Determine if the claim can be supported by evidence.** A **supportable claim** is a claim that can be supported by evidence in the form it is stated. Claims that cannot be supported by evidence in the form they are stated require clarification. They are:

    a. **Vague claims** that are impossible to support because they convey no distinct meaning (their interpretation is too open). Examples of vague claims are, *This house is a pig pen! Teachers are lazy!* These statements are open to many interpretations and, therefore, are too vague to support.

    b. **Ambiguous claims** that can be interpreted in two or more very different ways. An example is, *The shooting of the police was justifiable* (did the police shoot or were they shot?).

   c. **Meaningless claims** that use contrived terms intended to promote a false impression, such as *Our product is new and improved* or *This is light butter.*

   d. **Euphemisms** that substitute a mild expression for a blunt one in order to soften the meaning of certain information. Euphemisms employ vague words that are insupportable as claims, such as *The cat had an accident,* or *The horse should be put to sleep.*

2. **Determine if there is sufficient evidence to validate their claim.** The evidence presented may be of insufficient quantity if (a) there is not enough of it or (b) only some of it is presented (key evidence is omitted).

3. **Determine if the evidence presented is of sufficient quality.** Evidence lacks quality when it is (a) inaccurate, (b) outdated, (c) biased, or (d) irrelevant to the claim. Evidence also lacks quality if the presenter is not qualified to make the judgments being presented.

4. **Determine if the evidence is reliable.** The evidence is unreliable if the presenter:

   a. **Oversimplifies causal relationships** by presenting information that is partially true while excluding a great deal of necessary other information. Ignoring the complexity and number of causes for an event distorts reality. For example, *The cause of the civil war was slavery in the southern states.* This statement is not totally incorrect but it oversimplifies why the Civil War took place. Such errors are common and students should be able to recognize them.

   b. **Lacks a credible source.** When the information originates from a source of insufficient credibility, it is unreliable.

   c. **Slants the information.** Evidence is unreliable if it is based on slanted or biased information.

   d. **Appeals to emotion.** When the intent is simply to stir up emotion (rather than inform), the evidence is unreliable.

If the claim can be supported by evidence that is of sufficient quantity, quality, and reliability, then the claim is substantiated.

Refuting Opponent's Reasoning

Our...advantage was that we had evolved unstated but fruitful methods of collaboration. If either of us suggested a new idea, the other, while taking it seriously, would attempt to demolish it in a candid but nonhostile manner.

Francis Crick, Nobel Prize Winner (codiscoverer of the double helix)

Not only may the evidence presented to support a position be faulty, but the reasoning used to organize the evidence may be faulty. The procedure for evaluating reasoning is as follows:

1. **Determine if there are errors of perception based on a limited or inadequate perspective. Errors of perception** are faulty ways of seeing reality, preventing persons from being open-minded even before they begin to think. Some common errors of perception are (a) "mine is better" competitive orientation, (b) selective perception (including perceiving evidence that supports current ideas and rejecting anything that challenges them), (c) pretensions of knowing (when they do not), (d) resistance to change, and (e) either/or dualistic thinking (taking extreme positions on an issue when other positions are possible).

2. **Determine if there are errors of judgment. Errors of judgment** are flaws in reasoning that occur in the process of sorting out and assessing evidence. Some common errors of judgment are:

   a. **Overgeneralizing** by making conclusions that far exceed the available evidence. Examples are, "Nothing can be worse than losing the championship game," "Everyone from Edina is a rich snob." Faulty generalizations may also result from the opposition being too hasty, using an insufficient number of instances, using the wrong qualifier, exaggerating the evidence, using untypical or biased instances, and not considering plausible alternative explanations. One important type of overgeneralizing is the use of **stereotypes** that prevent students from seeing important differences among individual people, places, and things.

   b. **Making unwarranted assumptions. Assumptions** are ideas taken for granted. They are usually implied rather than expressed and, therefore, are often hard to detect. **Unwarranted assumptions** occur when a person takes too much for granted and, therefore, does not ask useful questions and explore possibilities. Students should consider what the presenter has taken for granted and make a judgment about whether it is warranted or not.

   c. **Failing to make distinctions. Distinctions** are subtle differences among things. Care in making distinctions helps individuals overcome confusion and deal with complex issues effectively. Important distinctions are between (a) the person and the idea (judge an idea on its own merits, not on who presented it), (b) assertion and evidence (judge ideas on how well supported—and supportable—they are), (c) familiarity and validity (hearing an assertion often does not make it true), and (d) "always" and "often," or "never" and "seldom."

3. **Determine if there are errors of reaction. Errors of reaction** are defensive ways to preserve a self-image. They occur when one person expresses a position and another person reacts negatively. Some common errors of reaction are:

a. **Explaining away.** If students explain away challenges to their ideas, they will not succeed in altering reality; they will just postpone dealing with it. The longer the postponement, the more painful the experience. It is better to face unpleasant ideas directly and honestly.

b. **Shifting the burden of proof** to the challenger. Accepting the burden of proof means supporting one's assertions with evidence. The burden of proof falls on the person who makes the assertion. The more the assertions challenge accepted wisdom, the greater the burden of proof. If students make an assertion and find that they can not defend it, they should not shift the burden of proof on the challenger. Instead, they should withdraw the assertion.

c. **Attacking the person.** When the message is unpleasant or disturbing, there is a tendency to attack the messenger.

4. **Determine if there are errors in the way ideas are interrelated.** In listening to persuasive arguments, there are key words to listen for. These words tell the listener what type of relationship among ideas is being presented. The three main **relationships** in persuasive arguments are:

a. **And** relationships signal that what follows **adds** to what preceded. "And," for example, may signal that more evidence is being offered to support an assertion. "And" words include "also, in addition, next, further, moreover, besides, another, finally."

b. **But** relationships signal that what follows **contrasts** with what preceded. "But," for example, may signal that an exception or qualification is to follow. "But" words include "however, nevertheless, yet, in contrast."

c. **Therefore** relationships signal that a conclusion is being made about the preceding evidence. "Therefore" words include "so, consequently, accordingly, thus, it-follows-that.

5. **Determine if there are errors of logic. Errors of logic** occur when students use faulty inductive or deductive reasoning (such as asserting the consequent or denying the antecedent).

In critically evaluating and refuting the opposing evidence and reasoning, students will wish to punch and counter-punch with various *"tricks of the trade."* The commonly used tricks used to win arguments are discussed next.

© Johnson & Johnson

Rebutting Attacks On Own Position

When the opposing pair point out faulty evidence and reasoning, students can give up and agree with the opposing pair or they can defend their position and its rationale. Students, of course, defend their position from the opponent's attacks, presenting counter-arguments, clarifications, and extensions. In other words, students rebut the attacks on their position. **Rebuttal**, or resubstantiation, is the rebuilding of one's case that has been attacked by the opponent. Students clarify their evidence and reasoning and present further evidence. The fire of the refutation tempers and strengthens the rationales and students' understanding of the issue being studied. It also creates uncertainty, conceptual conflict, and disequilibrium. Within structured academic controversies, refutation and rebuttal constantly go on.

Students should summarize the opposing position frequently and concisely for at least three reasons. **First**, a summary is an excellent way for students to increase their understanding of the opposing position. **Second**, a summary helps illuminate the inadequacies of the opposing position by reviewing how evidence and reasoning has been unraveled and refuted. **Third**, a summary clarifies what students agree and disagree on and what is "true" and "untrue." When positions are complex they may be broken down into sub-issues and a spreadsheet constructed to help analyze the validity of the evidence and reasoning for each sub-issue. An effective summary is expressed in the student's own words, emphasizes the key points, and is accurate.

In order to arrive at a synthesis that is acceptable to all group members, the issue must be viewed from all perspectives. Understanding the statements of other members is not enough. The perspective from which the member is speaking must also be clearly understood. In order to ensure that all perspectives are understood, students are encouraged to present their position and its rationale clearly and concisely, paraphrase accurately the position and rationale of other group members, and demonstrate understanding by presenting the other point of view fairly and persuasively during the perspective-reversal stage. Taking a variety of perspectives in viewing the issue teaches students about the subjective nature of knowledge. The importance of information depends on the perspective from which it is seen. In synthesizing information from a variety of perspectives certain pieces of information will be highlighted as important, but if you look at the same information from a different perspective, other pieces of information will be highlighted as important.

Caucus With Practice Partner

In the middle of the open discussion, students should caucus with their partner and compare notes on how they think they are doing. Students should discuss (a) the arguments the other side is making and plan how to refute them and (b) discuss the attacks the other side is making on their position and plan how to rebut them.

Searching For Further Evidence And A Better Conceptualization

The more the opposition challenges students' evidence and reasoning, unravels students' arguments, and points out students' errors of perception, judgment, and reaction, the more uncertain students become. Conceptual conflict, uncertainty, and disequilibrium tend to result when students hear other alternatives being advocated, having their position criticized and refuted, and are challenged by information that is incompatible with and does not fit with their conclusions (Johnson & Johnson, 1979, 1989). Uncertainty tends to motivate an active search for more information in hopes of resolving the conceptual conflict. Indices of epistemic curiosity include individuals' actively (a) searching for more information, (b) seeking to understand opposing positions and rationales, and (c) attempting to view the situation from numerous perspectives. The uncertainty is heightened by the students knowing that they have to learn (and pass a test on) the information being presented by the opposing pair. The more uncertain students become, the more they should be encouraged to seek out further information about the issue and use the new information in reconceptualizing the rationale for their position.

Using Social And Cognitive Skills For Challenging And Defending

The social and cognitive skills involved in challenging groupmates' conclusions and evidence and defending one's own position from attack are called **fermenting skills**. Some of the most important aspects of learning take place when group members skillfully challenge each other's conclusions and reasoning. Academic controversies cause group members to "dig deeper" into the material, to assemble a rationale for their conclusions, to think more divergently about the issue, to find more information to support their positions, and to argue constructively about alternative solutions or decisions. Some of the fermenting skills are:

1. **Group members should be critical of ideas, not of persons.** Arguments should concern ideas, not personality traits. There should be nothing personal in disagreement. Members should be highly critical of each other's ideas while affirming each other's competence. They should look each other in the eye and say, *I can see why you think that from your perspective; I see it differently.* Or, *I have great respect for your intelligence and, therefore, I am taking what you say very seriously; right now I have a different opinion.* When disagreeing with another member, students should criticize his or her ideas

and conclusions while communicating respect and appreciation for him or her as a person. Any inference of incompetence or weakness and any hint of rejecting another member should be avoided. The focus is on the position and its rationale, not on the person. Defensiveness should not be provoked through attacks on the person. *"I appreciate you, I am interested in your ideas; I disagree with your current position"* should be communicated rather than, *"You are stupid and ignorant."*

2. **Group members should not take personally other members' disagreements with and rejection of their ideas.** Students should take disagreement with their ideas and conclusions as an interesting opportunity to learn something new, not as a personal attack, rejection, or disrespect. Students should always separate the quality of their rationale from their competence and worth as a person.

3. **Group members should remember that the ultimate goal is to formulate a joint position everyone agrees with.** The controversy is taking place within a cooperative learning group. At the end of the unit a group report is required and every group member will take a test covering all sides of the issue being studied. While the immediate task is to evaluate critically and challenge the opposing position and its rationale, the long-term goal is to ensure that members learn the opposing rationale and teach their evidence to the opposing pair.

4. **Members should ensure that there are several cycles of differentiation** (bringing out differences in positions) **and integration** (combining several positions into one new, creative position) before a final consensus is reached. Differentiation must come before integration is attempted. More specifically:

    a. **Differentiation** involves seeking out and clarifying differences among members' ideas, information, conclusions, theories, and opinions. It involves highlighting the differences among members' reasoning and seeking to understand fully what the different positions and perspectives are. All different points of view must be presented and explored thoroughly before new, creative solutions are sought.

    b. **Integration/synthesis** involves combining the information, reasoning, theories, and conclusions of the group members into a single position that satisfies them all. After it has differentiated positions, the group needs to seek a new, creative position that synthesizes the thinking of all the members.

    c. The group members should never try to integrate different positions before adequate differentiation has taken place. The potential for integration is never greater than the adequacy of the differentiation already achieved. Most controversies go through a series of differentiations and integrations before a final consensus is reached.

5. An important aspect of differentiation is the **asking for justification why the member's conclusion or answer is the correct or appropriate one.** Students

should say, *"Why do you think that way?"* "What is the evidence that supports your position?" *"Prove to me that what you are saying is correct."* Students should clarify and seek other's rationale by questioning. Students should probe by asking questions that lead to deeper understanding or analysis, such as, *"Would it work in this situation...?"* *"What else makes you believe...?"*.

6. **Group members should try to refute each other's evidence or reasoning.** To do so requires conceptually taking the opposing rationale apart to determine if the evidence or the reasoning is faulty.

7. **Group members should change their minds when they are logically persuaded to do so.** All conclusions are tentative based on current evidence. As students learn more about the issue, they should change their minds (as long as they have subjected the new evidence to the fire of critical analysis).

Primary and preschool students will need simplified versions of the skills. It is important that teachers translate controversy skills into language and images that their students can understand and identify with. For example, the fermenting skills could be simplified to skills such as adding an idea, asking for proof, and seeing the idea from the other person's perspectives.

Summary

After researching their position and constructing a convincing rationale, students are ready to advocate their assigned positions. During the discussion they critically analyze the opposing position and point out its shortcomings while defending their own position from the attacks of the opposing pair. Students do so by (a) presenting their position to the opposing pair and (b) engaging in an open discussion of the issue being studied.

Presenting Your Position

Advocacy begins with students presenting their positions as sincerely and thoroughly as they can while the opposition listens carefully and takes notes. More specifically, students:

1. Present (and advocate) their position to the opposition with the intent of persuading the other group members of its validity. Students should be as sincere and thorough as they can in their presentation.

2. Listen carefully to the presentation of the opposing position, take notes, and learn the opposing position as well as their own for at least two reasons:

a. To be able to (1) write a group report that synthesizes both positions and (2) pass an individual test covering all sides of the issue.

b. To be able to refute more incisively the opposing position. If students do not know the opposing position, they cannot challenge it effectively.

Open Discussion That Includes Refutation And Rebuttal

After both sides have presented, an open (free-for-all) discussion of the issue being studied takes place. Students:

1. **Continue to advocate their position.** They present their arguments forcefully and persuasively; emphasize facts, evidence, and rationale; and try out the "tricks of the trade" to see if they can (a) win with fallacious arguments and (b) add humor and interest to the discussion. Common tactics are **ignoratio elenchi** (missing the point), arguing from analogy, sneaky ways of using questions, **reduction ad absurdum**, and **argumetum ad hominem**.

2. **Learn the evidence and information contained in the opposing position.** Students keep in mind that the overall goal is to make a reasoned judgment about the issue. They need to know both sides thoroughly. Students listen critically to the opposing position and analyze it to find flaws in logic and evidence.

3. **Critically analyze the evidence used by the opposition.** Then students **refute** it by attacking its weaknesses, flaws, and mistakes. This involves:

    a. Differentiating between facts and opinions.

    b. Determining if the evidence supports the claim. If the claims are vague, ambiguous, or meaningless, or if euphemisms are used, then the claim is not supportable.

    c. Determining if the evidence is of sufficient quantity and quality to validate the claim.

    d. Determining if the evidence is reliable enough to support the claim. If the opponent overgeneralizes, oversimplifies, does not cite credible sources, slants information, or appeals to emotion, then the evidence is not reliable.

4. **Critically analyze the reasoning used by the opposition.** Then students **refute** it by attacking its weaknesses, flaws, and mistakes. This involves looking for erroneous reasoning based on errors of perception (faulty ways of seeing reality), judgment (flaws in reasoning such as overgeneralizing, hasty conclusions, unwarranted assumptions, and failure to make distinctions), and reaction (defensively explaining away, shifting the burden of proof, or attacking the other person). It also involves

examining the ways in which evidence is interrelated (and, but, or therefore relationships) and looking for errors in the use of inductive and deductive reasoning.

5. **Defend their position by rebutting the attacks of the opposition.** Students present counter-arguments, clarifications, and extensions. They rebuild their case. They clarify their evidence and reasoning and present further evidence.

6. **Reduce their uncertainty by seeking further evidence and reconceptualizing the issue.** The fire of the refutation not only tempers and strengthens the evidence being considered, it creates uncertainty, conceptual conflict, and disequilibrium. Uncertainty tends to motivate an active search for more information (often called **epistemic curiosity**) in hopes of resolving the conceptual conflict.

7. **Use necessary social and cognitive skills.** Refutation and rebuttal require the use of a number of social and cognitive skills, including criticizing ideas (not people) and clarifying differences between the two positions.

⊷⊶⟨ CONTROVERSY CONTRACT ⟩⊷⊶

Major Learnings	Implementation Plans

Date _____   Date of Progress Report Meeting _____

Participant's Signature   _____

Signatures of Other Group Members   _____   _____

_____   _____   _____

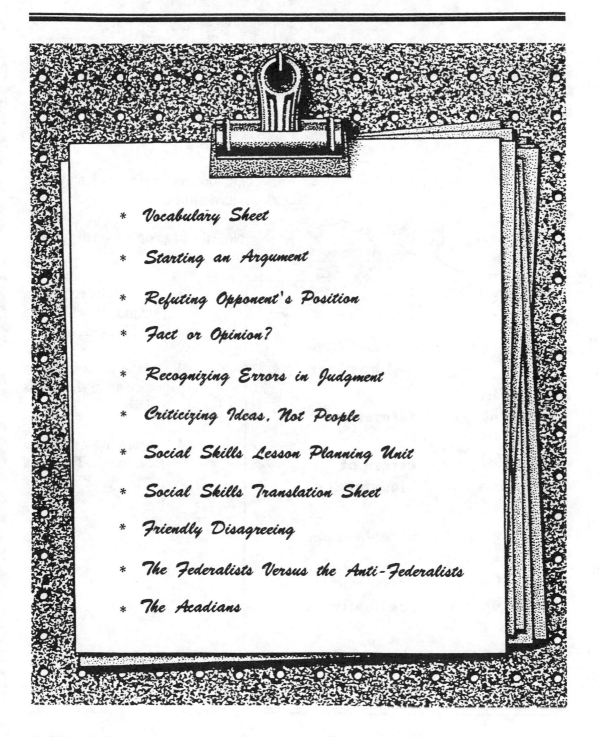

EXERCISE MATERIALS

* *Vocabulary Sheet*

* *Starting an Argument*

* *Refuting Opponent's Position*

* *Fact or Opinion?*

* *Recognizing Errors in Judgment*

* *Criticizing Ideas, Not People*

* *Social Skills Lesson Planning Unit*

* *Social Skills Translation Sheet*

* *Friendly Disagreeing*

* *The Federalists Versus the Anti-Federalists*

* *The Acadians*

VOCABULARY SHEET

Working with a partner, learn the definitions of the words below.

1. Define each word in two ways.

   First, write down what you think the word means.

   Second, look it up in the book and write down its definition.

   Note the page on which the definition appears.

2. For each word write a sentence in which the word is used.

3. Make up a story in which all of the words are used.

4. Learn how to spell each word. They will be on your spelling test.

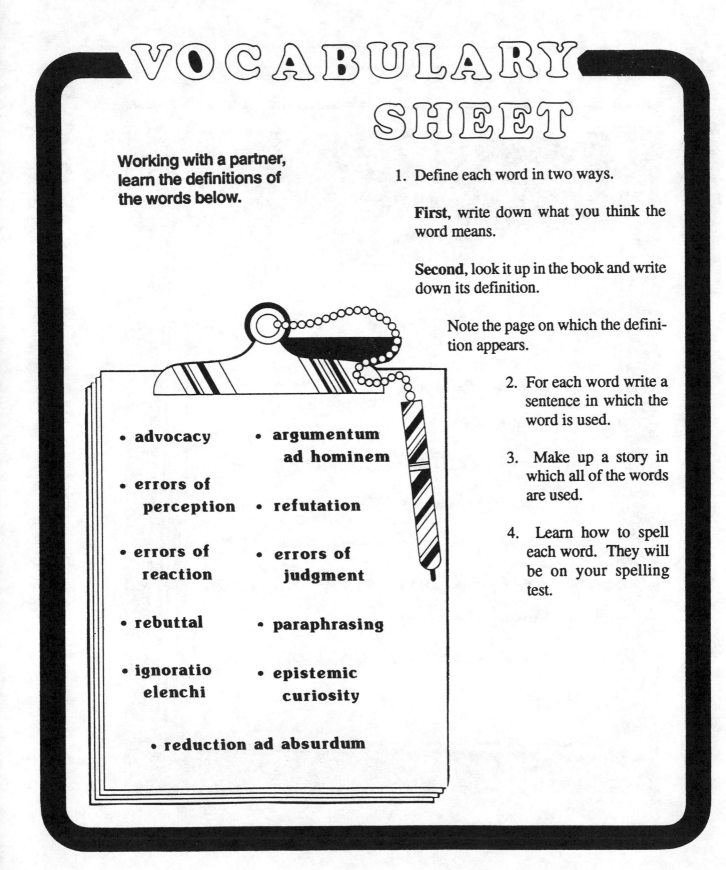

- advocacy

- errors of perception

- errors of reaction

- rebuttal

- ignoratio elenchi

- argumentum ad hominem

- refutation

- errors of judgment

- paraphrasing

- epistemic curiosity

- reduction ad absurdum

STARTING AN ARGUMENT

1. The purpose of this exercise is to "warm up" members of your class so they are ready to engage in spirited arguments. Pair up with the person next to you.

2. Your **task** is to contradict every statement made by your partner. Say the opposite very forcefully. Start softly, get louder and louder, and then bring the volume back down to soft again. Decide who is going to make the first statement. The other states the opposite. The only rule is that you cannot use either the words "I" or "you." Use hand motions to emphasize your words. Remember, start soft, gradually increase your volume until it is quite loud (with matching gestures), and then gradually lower your volume until it is soft again.

3. Reverse roles and repeat the procedure.

4. Make up with your partner. Tell your partner you did not really mean it. Apologize and forgive.

Refuting Opponent's Position

Refuting is attacking another person's position in an attempt to weaken or even destroy it. It is an attempt to cast significant doubt on and/or show the inadequacies of their arguments so that the person (or interested other people) will be willing to change his or her mind.

There are a number of ways to refute your opponent's position:

1. Challenge the quantity of the supporting evidence.

2. Challenge the quality of the supporting evidence.

3. Challenge the logic of the argument.

4. Challenge the assumptions underlying the position.

5. Challenge the perspective (do they see the whole picture).

Write out a phrase for each approach to refutation. For example, the quantity of evidence may be expressed in the statement, "You have only two facts; that is not enough to be convincing."

Form a pair. For each statement, share your phrase, listen carefully to your partner's phrase, then jointly create a new one that is better than either original one.

FACT

OR OPINION ?

What is fact? What is opinion? Given below are a series of statements. Identify which are fact and which are opinion. Work cooperatively with a partner in doing so.

1. Linda is eating lunch.

2. Abraham Lincoln was a great man.

3. Harry Truman authorized the use of atomic bombs on Japan.

4. Abraham Lincoln was President during the Civil War.

5. Linda is a wonderful person.

6. Harry Truman would do anything to end World War II.

If you are not sure whether a statement is a fact or an opinion, treat it as an opinion.

Working with your partner, choose a topic you are studying. Write out three facts and three opinions about the topic.

Recognizing Errors in Judgment

Errors of judgment are flaws in reasoning that occur in the process of sorting out and assessing evidence. Some common errors of judgment are (a) overgeneralizing or stereotyping, (b) hasty conclusions, (c) unwarranted assumptions, (d) failure to make a distinction, and (d) oversimplification.

Read the examples below. Label the error of judgment in each example.

1. My French teacher makes us rewrite any assignment that contains more than four errors in grammar or usage. I have had to rewrite three assignments this week. I think she dislikes me.

2. Mr. Jackson smokes. I bet most of our teachers have addictive personalities.

3. I saw a woman in the grocery store using food stamps. I hate people who go on welfare because they are too lazy to work.

4. Teachers have it easy. They get off work at three o'clock every day and only work nine months of the year.

5. Everyone says that John Smith would make a good senator. That's who I'm going to vote for.

6. I wouldn't believe anything that Ralph said.

7. Everyone on welfare is cheating.

8. I just read that job discrimination against women is a thing of the past. That's a relief.

9. My jacket is missing. I bet my roommate stole it!

10. All teenagers are self-centered and rebellious.

Criticizing Ideas, Not People

One of the most critical skills in conflict resolution is being able to criticize a person's ideas while confirming their competence as a person. The activity below is designed to emphasize that strategy.

The first step is to make a sign that says **ME** and attach it to yourself. Then build three others which say **MY IDEA** (or simply write the phrase on sheets of 8 1/2 by 11 paper).

ROUND I

Person 1: *This is me* (pointing to himself). *This is my idea* (picking up one of the sheets and putting it down on the table; the card or sheet must be physically separated from the owner and he must obviously let it go).

Person 2: *I like you.* (Reaches across, picks up idea card and tears it in half) *I don't like your idea* or *I don't agree with your idea.*

To complete Round 1, participants swap roles and repeat the process.

ROUND II

Person 1: *This is me. This is my idea.* (Again, the card is placed on the table, separate and apart from Person 1.)

Person 2: *I like you, but there are parts of your idea I don't like* or *I don't agree with.* (She reaches over and tears off one fourth of the card.)

As in Round 1, participants trade roles and repeat the process.

ROUND III

Person 1: *This is me. This is my idea.*

Person 2: *I like you and I would like to add to your idea.* (She takes one of her idea cards and lays it down, overlapping Person 1's idea card.)

Person 1 and 2 exchange roles and repeat Round 3.

The exercise above models the three stages of this process:

Round I = Complete Disagreement

Round II = Partial Disagreement

Round III = Integration

Step 2: How Are You Going To Define The Skill?

1. Phrases (list 3):

   a. _____

   b. _____

   c. _____

2. Behaviors (list 3):

   a. _____

   b. _____

   c. _____

3. How will you explain and model each social skill?

   _____ a. Demonstrate the skill, explain each step of engaging in skill, and then redemonstrate the skill.

   _____ b. Use a videotape or film to demonstrate and explain the skill.

   _____ c. Ask each group to plan a role-play demonstration of the skill to present to the entire class.

   _____ d. Make a "T-Chart."

   e. Other(s): _____

Step 3: How Will You Ensure That Students Practice The Skill?

_____ 1. Assign specific roles to group members ensuring practice of the skills.

_____ 2. Announce that you will observe for the skills.

_____ 3. Give bonus points, stars, or stickers to groups in which the skills are being used.

_____ 4. Have specific practice sessions involving nonacademic tasks.

_____ 5. Other(s): _____

Step 4: How Will You Ensure Students Receive Feedback And Process Their Use Of The Skills?

Teacher Monitoring:

_____ 1. Structured observation with the social skills observation sheet, focusing on each learning group an equal amount of time (30 minutes, 6 groups, each group is observed for 5 minutes).

_____ 2. Structured observation with the social skills observation sheet, focusing only on the learning groups in which target students (emotional/behavior problem students, handicapped students, low achieving students, and so forth) are members. '

_____ 3. Anecdotal observation (eavesdropping) to record the significant, specific events involving students engaging in social skills with each other.

_____ 4. Give bonus points, complements, stickers, or stars to groups when you hear members using the targetted skills.

_____ 5. Other(s): _____

Teacher Intervening:

1. If the social skills are not being used in a cooperative group, I will:

_____ a. Prompt group members to use the skill.

_____ b. Ask the group what it has done so far and what it plans to try next to increase the use of the social skills.

_____ c. Other: _____

Social Skills Lesson Planning Unit

David W. Johnson and Roger T. Johnson

What Are The Social Skills You Are Going To Teach?

1. _____

2. _____

3. _____

4. _____

    Pick one skill and complete the rest of this unit. Then repeat the unit for the second skill. Repeat untill a plan is completed for all skills identified.

Step 1: How Are You Going To Communicate The Need For The Collaborative Skills?

_____ 1. Room displays, posters, bulletin boards, and so forth.

_____ 2. Telling students why the skills are needed.

_____ 3. Jigsawing materials on the need for the skills.

_____ 4. Have groups work on a task and then ask students to brainstorm what skills are needed to help the group argue constructively.

_____ 5. Giving bonus points or a separate grade for the competent use of the skills.

_____ 6. Other(s): _____

_____

_____

2. If the social skills are being used in a cooperative group, I will:

_____ a. Interrupt the group, call attention to the use of the skills, and compliment the group.

_____ b. Note it on the observation sheet or anecdotal record and come back to the group during the processing time, call attention to the use of the skills, and compliment the group.

_____ c. Call attention to the use of the skill during the whole-class processing.

_____ d. Other: _____

Student Observers:

1. Student observers will be selected by: _____

2. Student observers will be trained by: _____

3. Time for the student observers to give group members feedback will be provided by:_____
_____

During the group processing time:

1. Feedback given by:

_____ a. Other group members.

_____ b. Student observer.

_____ c. Teacher.

_____ d. Visiting observer.

2. Assessing skill use:

_____ a. Individuals: How well did I use the skill?

_____ b. Groups: How well did we use the skill?

_____ c. Class: How well did our class use the skill?

  3. Refining skill use by making plans to better use the skills tomorrow:

_____ a. Individual plan.

_____ b. Group plan.

_____ c. Class plan.

Step 5: Ensure That Students Persevere In Practicing The Skills

I will provide continued opportunity for students to practice and repractice the collaborative skills by:

_____ 1. Assigning the social skills to the groups as a whole with all members being responsible for their use.

_____ 2. Assigning the social skills to individual group members.

_____ 3. Asking another teacher, an aide, or a parent volunteer to tutor and coach target students in the use of the skill.

_____ 4. Asking the groups to process how well each member is using the skills.

_____ 5. Intermittently spend a class session on training students to use the skill.

_____ 6. Intermittently give any group whose members use the skill above a certain criterion a reward of _____.

_____ 7. Other: _____

_____

Social Skills Translation Sheet

What is the targeted social skill? _____

How will the skill be introduced so that each student sees a need to develop it?

_____
_____
_____

How is the skill defined?

1. Specific phrases (sounds like):

_____
_____
_____

2. Specific behaviors (looks like):

_____
_____
_____

How will the skill be practiced?

1. Teacher encouragement strategies:

_____
_____

2. Peer encouragement strategies:

_____
_____

3. Parent encouragement strategies:

_____
_____

How will the use of the skill be processed?

1. Whole class:

_____

_____

2. Group:

_____

_____

3. Individual:

_____

_____

How is perseverance in using the skill encouraged?

_____

_____

_____

How is refinement in using the skill encouraged?

_____

_____

_____

Friendly Disagreeing

DAN BREWSTER

Snohomish,
WA

Subject Area: Any

Grade Level: Intermediate and Secondary

Lesson Summary: Students work on a task while practicing "friendly disagreeing." Use of the skill is then discussed.

**Instructional
Objectives:**   Students will leaqrn to disagree in friendly ways while maintaining effective working relationships within their group.

Materials:

Item	Number Needed
Survival Worksheet	One per group
Observation Sheet	One per group

Time Required: One hour

6:33

≈ Decisions ≈

Group Size:	Four
Assignment To Groups:	Teacher assigns students to groups to maximize heterogeneity
Roles:	

1. **Monitor:** Records each time a student "friendly disagrees"
2. **Praiser:** Praises other members for their use of the skill
3. **Recorder:** Writes the group's decisions on the worksheet
4. **Encourager:** Encourages all to participate and makes sure everyone shares their opinions

≈ The Lesson ≈

Controversy Skill:

There are five basic ways to disagree in a pleasant manner:

1. Ask for different opinions to start disagreements.

   "Why do you think that is best? "What is your opinion?"
   "What is your answer?"

2. Ask others to explain their reasoning.

   "Explain your thinking." "Explain that last part."
   "Show me how that would work." "How will that solve the problem?"

3. Add on or modify.

   "Could we expand on that answer?" "How about if we added this?"
   "How about if we changed . . ."

4. Offer alternative answers.

   "What do you think about . . ." "Wouldn't this also
   work?" "Here is a different way of looking at things."

6:34

5. State disagreement.

"I have a different idea." "My answer is different."
"Here is my explanation."

Instructional Task:

1. Read the wilderness survival exercise. Read the list of items. Decide on which item is most important (useful) to your survival and give it a rank of **"1."** Then give the rank of **"2"** to the next most important item. Continue until all the items are ranked.
2. Practice "friendly disagreeing."

Positive Interdependence:

The group members decide by consensus as to how each item should be ranked. There should be one ranking from the group, all members must agree, all members must be able to explain the reasons they ranked the items as they did.

Individual Accountability:

One member of each group will be picked at random to explain why a selected item was considered more important than another.

Criteria for Success:

1. If the group gets a score of 0 - 20 on their ranking, all members will receive 15 minutes of free time on Friday afternoon.
2. If all members of the group use "friendly disagreeing" at least 10 times each, the group will receive 15 minutes of free time on Friday afternoon.

∾ Monitoring and Processing ∾

Monitoring: 1. Each group will have a monitor to record the frequency with which members use constructive disagreement phrases.

2. Each group member will write down several instances of their use of "friendly disagreeing."

3. The teacher will be observing the groups to make sure the skill of "friendly disagreeing" is being practiced.

Intervening: If there are groups that are not appropriately applying the skill, intervene by reviewing the phrases for "friendly disagreeing." If necessary, model the skill for the group as they proceed with the activity.

Processing: Provide ample time for the monitors to give feedback and for students to discuss their use of "friendly disagreeing." Have them make specific plans.

Author's Note: This lesson was originally used in conjunction with a math lesson. It was felt it would be most effective to first teach the skill with a less academic task such as Wilderness Survival. The lesson, however, should be followed up with an academic lesson incorporating this same skill as soon as possible.

OBSERVATION FORM

	1	2	3	4	TOTAL
Asks for Opinions					
Asks for Explanations					
Add on or Modify					
Suggest Alternatives					
Disagree					
TOTAL					

The Federalists Versus the Anti-Federalists

Getting the Constitution approved by the States was a struggle. The supporters of the Constitution, called the Federalists, had a plan to get it ratified. The Anti-Federalists, the opponents of the Constitution, argued that the new plan of government should not be approved. Your **tasks** are to learn (a) the differences between the arguments of the Federalists and the Anti-Federalists, (b) the process of the Constitution's ratification, and (c) the definitions of the following words (ratified, ratifying conventions, Anti-Federalists, Federalists, **The Federalist**, and the Bill of Rights). Work **cooperatively** and ensure that all members of your group successfully complete the three learning tasks.

The Federalists wrote the Constitution of the United States in secret because many leaders in Congress and the state governments were against it. Because the Constitution was written in secret, the Anti-Federalists have not had time to prepare all their arguments against it. James Madison developed a plan for ratifying the Constitution. He was certain that if the Constitution were presented to either the Congress or the state legislatures for ratification, it would be rejected. He recommended, therefore, to present the Constitution directly to the eligible voters of each state at special **Ratifying Conventions** to be held in each state. The delegates to these conventions would be elected by popular vote of the people for the sole purpose of approving the Constitution.

Madison based his plan on the idea contained in the Preamble to the Constitution, which says, "We the People...do ordain and establish this Constitution...." The people who were to be governed by the new national government were asked to consent to its creation and to agree to obey its decisions. Thus, the Constitution can be considered a social contract.

The Framers at the Convention approved Madison's plan and made a few additions. They decided that the Constitution would be ratified nationally if nine of the thirteen states ratified it. They did this because they feared that requiring all thirteen states to ratify would result in its defeat. They also decided to encourage the states to organize and elect delegates to the state ratifying conventions as quickly as possible. They knew that the opposition had not had much time to prepare their arguments. By contrast, the supporters of the Constitution had worked on it for almost four months. They knew the arguments for and against it. They thought if the state conventions acted quickly, the Constitution would be ratified before its opponents, the Anti-Federalists, could organize.

In spite of the strategy adopted by the Federalists, the Anti-Federalists were able to put up a strong fight. The political struggle over ratification in the states was intense, sometimes bitter, and lasted ten months. In New York the fight was especially difficult. To help the Federalist cause, Alexander Hamilton, James Madison, and John Jay wrote a series of articles supporting ratification for a New York newspaper. These articles are now called **The Federalist**. The articles were also used in the Virginia ratification debates.

There were many leaders of the Anti-Federalist movement, most of whom wrote pamphlets explaining why they were against the Constitution. George Mason, Edmund Randolph, and Elbridge Gerry had attended the Philadelphia Convention but refused to sign the document. John Hancock, Samuel Adams, and Richard Henry Lee, all leading revolutionaries and signers of the Declaration of Independence, fought against ratification of the Constitution. Mercy Otis Warren, a playwright, also opposed ratification. Patrick Henry, who had always opposed the idea of a strong national government, became a leading Anti-Federalist at the Virginia ratifying convention.

The arguments for and against the Constitution focused on three basic questions:

1. Will the new Constitution maintain a republican form of government?

2. Will the national government would have too much power?

3. Is a bill of rights needed?

James Madison   Federalist   John Hancock   Anti-Federalist

The Federalists . . .

You represent the Federalist perspective. Your position is that the Constitution must be ratified. In preparing your position write several slogans for the ratification of the Constitution. Also make at least one visual to help you present a persuasive case for ratification.

1. **Without controls on factions gaining control of government for their personal gain a republic will not work.** History proves that all the small republics in the past were destroyed by special interests. The citizens' civic virtue was not enough to prevent them from seeking their own selfish interests rather than the common welfare. Special interests can be more easily controlled in a large republic where (a) the government is organized on the basis of checks and balances and (b) power is divided between the national and the state governments.

2. **Loyalty will be gained through results.** The national government will protect the rights of the people so well that they will soon give it their loyalty and support. The central government can not become a tyrant because of the limitations placed on it by the system of checks and balances and separation of powers.

3. **The power of the central government is limited.** The Constitution will give the national government greater power than it has under the Articles of Confederation. But its powers are limited to dealing with tasks that face the entire nation such as trade, currency, and defense. A stronger national government is needed to deal with these problems. The Constitution provides adequate protections for the state governments.

4. **The powers given to the central government are necessary.** The necessary and proper and general welfare clauses are necessary if the national government is to accomplish the things it is responsible for doing.

5. **A national balance of power protects the states.** The powers of the national government are separated and balanced among the three branches so no one can dominate the others. A strong executive branch is necessary for the national government to be able to fulfill its responsibilities. The Constitution gives Congress and the Supreme Court ways to check the use of power by the executive branch so it cannot become a monarchy.

6. **It is better to keep individual rights ambiguous.** A national bill of rights could give the impression that the people would only be given protection for those rights that were actually listed.

You represent the Anti-Federalist perspective. Your position is that the Constitution must not be ratified. In preparing your position write several slogans against the ratification of the Constitution. Also make at least one visual to help you present a persuasive case against ratification.

1. **It will not work in a large country.** Throughout history, the only places where republican governments have worked have been small communities where the people have been about equal in wealth and have held the same values. Thus, it was possible for them to possess civic virtue and to agree upon what was best for their common welfare.

2. **A federal government will resort to tyranny to keep its power.** Free government requires the active participation of the people. The national government provided by the Constitution would be located too far from most people's communities to allow them to participate. As a result, the only way the government would be able to rule would be through the use of military force. The result would be a tyranny.

3. **The state governments will be destroyed.** The Constitution gives the national government too much power at the expense of the state governments. It gives the government the power to tax citizens and to raise and keep an army. The supremacy clause means all of the national government's laws are superior to laws made by the states. As a result, it would only be a matter of time until the state governments are destroyed.

4. **The limits to the federal government's power are not clear.** The necessary and proper clause is too general and, as a result, gives too much power to the national government. It is dangerous not to list the powers of the government in order to put clear limits on them.

5. **The President will become a monarch.** The Constitution gives too much power to the executive branch of government. It could soon become a monarchy.

6. **The freedom of individuals is not protected.** The Constitution does not include a bill of rights which is essential for protecting individuals against the power of the national government.

WHAT HAPPENED?

One of the results of the debates between the Federalists and the Anti-Federalists was the addition of the **Bill of Rights**. In order to get enough support for the Constitution to be ratified, a compromise was reached on the issue of a bill of rights. The Federalists agreed that when the first Congress was held, it would draft a bill of rights, listing those rights of citizens that were not to be violated by the national government. But the Federalists insisted that the bill of rights include a statement saying that the list of rights should not be interpreted to mean that these were the only rights the people had. The Bill of Rights was not a useless addition. It has been vitally important to the protection of the basic rights of the American people.

WHAT DID YOU LEARN?

As a result of your controversy, be sure all your group members can correctly answer the following questions.

1. Who were the Federalists? Who were the Anti-Federalists?

2. Why did the Federalists not want the Constitution submitted to the existing Congress or state governments for ratification?

3. How did the Federalists answer the criticism that the Constitution gave the federal government too much power?

4. The Anti-Federalists lost their battle to prevent the adoption of the Constitution. Their struggle, however, left a permanent impact on the Constitution. What was their impact? How was it accomplished?

5. Would you have voted to ratify the Constitution as written in 1787? Explain your answer.

Chapter Seven: Making The Decision

Introduction

If there is any secret of success, it lies in the ability to get the other person's point of view and see things from his angle as well as from your own.

Henry Ford

The Neanderthals represent a high point in human history. Their lineage goes back to the earliest members of the genus **Homo**. And they were the original pioneers. Over thousands of years Neanderthals moved out of Africa by way of the Near East into India and China and Malaysia, and into southern Europe. In recent times, 150,000 or so years ago, they pioneered glacial landscapes, becoming the first humans to cope with climates hospitable only to woolly mammoths and reindeer. Neanderthals were quite remarkable physically. There is no doubt whatever that they were our physical superiors. Their strongest individuals could probably lift weights of half a ton or so. Physically, we are quite puny in comparison. And there is no anatomical evidence that the Neanderthals were inferior to us (the Cro-Magnons) cerebrally. If anything, their brains were larger than ours. But even though they were much stronger and probably just as smart, we have never been proud of our extinct predecessors, partly because of their looks. We consider them ugly.

What happened to the Neanderthals? Where are they now? In recent human history there have been two major groups: the Neanderthals and the Cro-Magnons (or homo sapiens sapiens). We are Cro-Magnons. Our origins are linked with the fate of the Neanderthals. We gradually replaced the Neanderthals during an overlapping period of a few thousand years. As the glaciers from Scandinavia advanced, northern populations of Neanderthals moved south while our ancestors were moving north out of Africa. We met in Europe about 35,000 years ago. They vanished about 30,000 years ago.

Why did they vanish? Where did they go? What happened to them? There are numerous explanations for the disappearance of the Neanderthals. Perhaps they evolved into us. Perhaps we intermarried and merged. The most interesting hypotheses, however, are the two that revolve around social interdependence. **The first is that we replaced the Neanderthals because we are better competitors.** Perhaps there was a competition for food, with the Neanderthals unable to meet our challenge, and they died off in marginal areas. **The second hypothesis is that we replaced the Neanderthals because we are better cooperators.** Perhaps the Neanderthals were too set in their ways and were unable to evolve and refine better ways to cooperate while we were continually organizing better cooperative efforts to cope with changing climatic conditions.

The teacher asks, "*What do you believe? Which hypothesis is most reasonable? Did we, the Cro-Magnons, replace Neanderthals because we are better competitors or because we are better cooperators?*" The teacher assigns students to groups of four and asks them to prepare a report entitled, "*Why we are here and the Neanderthals are not.*" Work cooperatively. There is to be one report from the group representing the members' best analysis of the issue. The teacher divides each group into two-person advocacy teams. One team is given the position that "*We are better competitors than the Neanderthals*" and the other team is given the position that "*We are better cooperators than the Neanderthals.*" Both advocacy teams are given articles and materials supporting their assigned position. They are then given time to read and discuss the material with their partner and to plan how best to advocate their assigned position so that: (1) they learn the information and perspective within the articles and books, (2) the opposing team is convinced of the soundness of the team's position, and (3) the members of the opposing team learn the material contained within the articles and technical reports. To do so, students proceed through five steps.

First, students research the issue (mastering the provided the material and searching the library for additional information), organize their information into a conceptual framework that presents the evidence in a logical sequence, and prepare their positions. **Second**, members of the two advocacy teams actively present and advocate their positions and reasoning to the opposition, thereby engaging in considerable cognitive rehearsal and elaboration of their position and its rationale. When the other team presents, students' reasoning and conclusions are challenged by the opposing view and they experience conceptual conflict and uncertainty. **Third**, students engage in a general discussion in which they advocate their position, rebut attacks on their position, refute the opposing position, and seek to learn both positions. The group discusses the issue, critically evaluates the opposing position and its rationale, defends positions, and compares the strengths and weaknesses of the two positions. When students are challenged by conclusions and information that are incompatible and do not fit with their reasoning and conclusions, conceptual conflict, uncertainty, and disequilibrium result. As a result of their uncertainty, students experience epistemic curiosity and, therefore, students actively (1) search for more information and experiences to support their position and (2) seek to understand the opposing position and its supporting rationale. During this time students' uncertainty and information search are encouraged and promoted by the teacher.

Up to this point, the teacher focuses on getting students "in role" so that they adopt the perspective of their assigned position and present the best case possible for it. The next issue for the teacher is to get students "out of role" so that they can see the issue from both points of view and create a synthesis or integration that is superior to either position. The **fourth step** in the controversy procedure, therefore is to have students reverse perspectives and present the opposing position. Each advocacy pair presents the best case possible for the opposing position. This sets up the **fifth step** in which the group of four reaches a consensus about a synthesis or integration of the two positions and prepares a group report. The emphasis during this instructional period is on students reconceptualizing their positions and synthesizing the best information and reasoning from both sides. Group members' ability to do so rests on their ability to hold both perspectives on the issue in mind at the same time. The group's report should reflect group members' colllective best reasoned judgment. Each group member then individually takes an examination on the factual information contained in the reading materials.

Table 7.1 Reversing Perspectives And Creating Synthesis Of Opposing Positions

Advocate Of Position A	Advocate Of Position B
Summarize Person B's Position And Rationale	Summarize Person A's Position And Rationale
Paraphrase Person B's Position And Rationale	Paraphrase Person A's Position And Rationale
Present B's Position As If You Were He/She	Present A's Position As If You Were He/She
Hold Both Perspectives At Same Time	Hold Both Perspectives At Same Time
Drop All Advocacy	Drop All Advocacy
Identify Best Evidence From Both Sides	Identify Best Evidence From Both Sides
Integrate Into New Position	Integrate Into New Position
Create Synthesis That Subsumes All Positions	Create Synthesis That Subsumes All Positions
Write It, Present It, Learn It	Write It, Present It, Learn It

Reversing Perspectives

The test of a first-rate intelligence is the ability to hold two opposed ideas in the mind at the same time, and still retain the ability to function.

F. Scott Fitzgerald

The position has been researched and a persuasive argument prepared, presented, and advocated. Students have critically evaluated the opposing position, unraveled it, examined it for faulty evidence and reasoning, and checked it for reasoning errors. In doing so students have learned the information contained in the opposing pair's arguments. To complete the controversy sequence, students must step-back and see the

issue from both perspectives simultaneously. To help students move beyond the perspective of their assigned position, they are required to present the opposing position (rationale and perspective) to the opposing students' satisfaction. Group members can then drop all advocacy and reach a consensus on the issue. A group report is then completed and students individually take a test on both sides of the issue.

In a controversy, students are asked to adopt a specific perspective that is different from the perspectives of others. A **perspective** is a way of viewing the world and his or her relation to it. **Perspective taking** is the ability to understand how a situation appears to another person and how that person is reacting cognitively and emotionally to the situation. More specifically, a **cognitive perspective** consists of (a) the cognitive organization being used to give meaning to a person's knowledge, and (b) the structure of a person's reasoning. The opposite of perspective taking is **egocentrism** or being unaware that other perspectives exist and that one's own view of the issue is incomplete and limited. Different people have different perspectives. Each person may have different perspectives at different times. On any issue being studied, there are always a variety of perspectives from which it may be viewed.

Students flush out and embellish their assigned perspective as they research the issue and prepare their position. The more they advocate the position, the more completely they adopt the assigned perspective. The members of the opposing pair likewise become more and more committed and locked into their assigned perspective. Adopting the assigned perspective is necessary to make sure that the position being represented receives a fair and complete hearing.

Understanding one's assigned perspective is not enough to create a thoughtful and insightful synthesis. To create a wise synthesis, students must have a clear understanding of **all** sides of the issue, an accurate assessment of their validity and relative merits, and the ability to think creatively to integrate the best reasoning from both sides and come up with potential syntheses. In other words, comprehending the information opponents present is not enough. The cognitive perspective the opponent is using to organize and intrepret the information must also be clearly understood. Creating a synthesis is then based on students (a) seeing the issue from both their own and the opposing perspective and (b) keeping both perspectives in mind at the same time.

In order to free students from their assigned perspective and to increase their understanding of the opposing perspective, students engage in a perspective reversal. **Perspective reversal** is taking the opposing pair's position and sincerely and completely presenting their position as if it were one's own. The procedure for taking each other's perspectives in a controversy is as follows:

~ **Person A presents Person's B position.** Students are to present the opposing position as if it were theirs. They are to be forceful and persuasive, adding new arguments, facts, and rationale when it is possible. Everything the students did to present a convincing case for their original position should be done during perspective reversal to ensure that students can in fact see the issue from the opposing perspective. Person B corrects errors in A's presentation and notes omissions.

~ **Person B presents Person's A position.** Person A corrects errors in B's presentation and notes omissions.

An important issue for synthesizing is to keep both your own and the other person's perspective in mind simultaneously. There are a number of reasons why such perspective taking is absolutely essential within conflict situations (see Johnson [1971] and Johnson & Johnson [1989] for a complete review of the research).

First, perspective taking improves communication and reduces misunderstandings and distortions by influencing how messages are phrased and received. Misunderstandings often occur because people assume that everyone sees the world through their perspective. **The better you understand the other person's perspective, the more able you are to phrase messages so the other person can easily understand them.** If a person does not know what snow is, for example, you do not refer to "corn snow" or "fresh powder." In addition, **understanding the other person's perspective helps you accurately understand the messages you are receiving from that person.** If the other person says, "That's just great!", for example, the meaning reverses if you know the person is frustrated. You must be able to stand in the sender's shoes to understand accurately the meaning of the messages that person is sending you.

Second, perspective taking is essential for a realistic assessment of the validity of evidence and reasoning. To propose workable syntheses you must understand how the other person sees the problem.

Third, the more able you are to take the other person's perspective, the broader the picture you get of the issue. Out of a mass of detailed information, people tend to pick out and focus on those facts that confirm their prior perceptions and to disregard or misinterpret those that call their perceptions into question. Each side tends to see only the merits of its case, and only the faults of the other side. It is not enough to logically understand how the other person views the problem. **If you want to influence the other person, you also need to understand empathetically the power of his/her point of view and to feel the emotional force with which he or she believes in it.**

Fourth, engaging in perspective taking tends to improve the relationship with the other person. You are more liked and respected when the other person realizes that you are seeing his or her perspective accurately and using it to create potential agreements that benefit both sides equally.

There is nothing more important to resolving conflicts constructively than understanding how the conflict appears from the other person's perspective. More information, both personal and impersonal, is disclosed when one is interacting with a person engaging in perspective-taking behaviors. Perspective-taking ability increases one's capacity to phrase messages so that they are easily understood by others and to comprehend accurately the messages of others. Engaging in perspective taking in conflict situations tends to increase understanding and retention of the opponent's information and perspective; facilitate the achievement of creative, high quality problem solving; and promote more positive perceptions of the information-exchange process, fellow group members, and the group's work (Falk & Johnson, 1977; Johnson, 1971, 1977). The greater the clarity of group members' understanding of all sides of the issues and the more accurate the assessment of their validity and relative merits, the more creative the synthesis of all positions in a controversy tends to be.

Taking a variety of perspectives in viewing the issue teaches students about the subjective nature of knowledge. The importance of information depends on the perspective from which it is seen. In synthesizing information from a variety of perspectives certain pieces of information will be highlighted as important, but if you look at the same information from a different perspective, other pieces of information will be highlighted as important.

Seeing a situation from just your own point of view gives you a partial understanding. Your limited perspective ensures that you can see only part of the picture. In order to see the whole picture, you have to see the situation from all perspectives simultaneously. An essential aspect of making informed decisions is creating a synthesis that springs from seeing the whole picture. An essential aspect of gaining true insight into the nature of a problem or the essence of a phenomena is through continually striving to see the whole picture. We should all remember what Harper Lee stated in **To Kill A Mockingbird**, *First of all,* he said, *if you can learn a simple trick, Scout, you'll get along a lot better with all kinds of folks. You never really understand a person until you consider things from his point of view..." "Sir?" "...until you climb into his skin and walk around in it.*

Integrating And Synthesizing

The need to be right is a sign of a vulgar mind.

Albert Camus

Controversies are resolved constructively when students create a synthesis based on the best evidence and reasoning from both sides of the issue. The **procedure** for this final stage of the controversy process involves six steps. Students are to:

~ Drop all advocacy.

~ Summarize and synthesize the best evidence and reasoning from all sides of the issue into a joint position that all members can agree to.

~ Write a joint report that (a) explains the group's synthesis and (b) is based on a group consensus supported by evidence.

~ Present the group's conclusions to the class.

~ Individually take the test covering both sides of the issue.

~ Process how well members worked together as a group and how they could be even more effective next time.

Drop All Advocacy

In the final step of structured academic controversy, students are to drop all advocacy, step back to achieve some objectivity, and try to view the issue from a variety of perspectives simultaneously. Students should strive to see new patterns within a body of evidence and generate a number of optional ways of integrating the evidence. By creating a number of operational syntheses, students help each other go beyond (a) the original positions advocated and (b) the first reasonable synthesis suggested. The more alternatives suggested, the less group members will be "frozen" to their original positions. Students unfreeze other member's fixation on their position by suggesting alternatives. The alternatives are then considered on their merits. Sometimes a member may be assigned the role of "generator" to ensure that additional positions are formulated. In generating possible syntheses students may wish to follow the DOVE procedure:

Defer judgment, any idea should be stated.

Opt for original, different ideas.

Vast numbers of ideas are needed.

Expand the list by piggybacking on other member's ideas.

Synthesize

We must learn to explore all the options and possibilities that confront us in a complex and rapidly changing world. We must learn to welcome and not fear the voices of dissent.

J. W. Fulbright

Students are to summarize and synthesize the best arguments and evidence from other sides into a joint position that all group members can agree to. **Synthesis** occurs when students create a new position that subsumes the previous two. Often, for example, there is a thesis, a counter-thesis, and then a synthesis that combines both. A synthesis is a new position that unifies the previous ones, brings them into harmony, and unites their best features at a higher level. The previous positions are seen as parts to be combined into a whole. A synthesis of the two positions, *"We, the Cro-Magnons, replaced Neanderthals because we were better competitors,"* and *"We, the Cro-Magnons, replaced Neanderthals because we were better cooperators,"* for example, is *"We, the Cro-Magnons, replaced Neanderthals because we had deeper emotional commitments (both positive and negative) to each other."* If a synthesis that is acceptable from all perspectives cannot be created, then probably not enough differentiation of and critical thinking about the original two positions has taken place.

Synthesis requires students to see new patterns within a body of evidence, view the issue from a variety of perspectives, and generate a number of optional alternative positions that subsume the evidence supporting the orginal two. The dual purposes of synthesis are to (a) arrive at the best possible position on the issue and (b) find a position that all group members can agree and commit themselves to. In achieving these purposes, students should (a) avoid the dualistic trap of choosing which position is "right" and which is "wrong," (b) avoid the relativistic trap of stating that both positions are correct, depending on your perspective, and (c) think probabilistically in formulating a synthesis that everyone can agree to.

In trying to create a synthesis, it is sometimes helpful to summarize the two original positions into a few words. Organizing large blocks of information into an abbreviated form often (a) clarifies the underlying nature of the positions and (b) illuminates the relationships and patterns in the evidence gathered by both sides, both of which help generate the creative insights necessary to synthesize the two positions.

Write Report

Students are expected to write a report that (a) explains the group's synthesis and (b) is based on a group consensus supported by evidence. The report should include:

~ A title page.

~ An introduction and statement of the issue.

~ The group's synthesis or new position.

~ The supporting evidence organized to lead the reader step-by-step to a conclusion. Diagrams, pictures, and charts should be included to help the reader understand your paper and make it more interesting.

~ A conclusion that is the same as the group's synthesis.

~ A listing of the references from which the evidence was gathered.

Neatness and style do count. All of the material on planning a position is relevant to writing the final report.

Present Conclusions To Class

Each group has to be ready to present its conclusions to the whole class. All the guidelines for making a good presentation included in Chapter 5 should be followed in planning the group's presentation.

Individually Take Test

Each student will individually take a test covering both sides of the issue. The group will receive bonus points if all members score above a preset criterion of excellence.

Group Processing

The final step is for each group to process how well members worked together and how they could be even more effective next time. Celebrate the group's success.

Summary

In a controversy, students are asked to adopt a specific **perspective** (a way of viewing the world and his or her relation to it) in preparing the best case for a position on an issue being studied. From preparing a rationale for the position and advocating the position to groupmates, students become embedded in the perspective. Adopting the assigned perspective is necessary to make sure that the position being represented receives a fair and complete hearing.

In order to free students from their perspective and to increase their understanding of the opposing perspective, students engage in a perspective reversal. Each pair presents the best case for the opposing position, being as sincere and enthusiastic as if the position were their own. After the students step back and see the issue from both perspectives, they drop all advocacy and seek to create a synthesis that subsumes the two positions or an integration of the best information and logic from both sides. Students attempt to see new patterns in the information by viewing the issue from a variety of perspectives and generating a number of optional ways of synthesizing or integrating the evidence so that they can (a) arrive at the best possible position on the issue and (b) find a position that all group members can agree and commit themselves to. In achieving these purposes, students need to (a) avoid the dualistic trap of choosing which position is "right" and which is "wrong," (b) avoid the relativistic trap of stating that both positions are correct, depending on your perspective, and (c) think probabilistically in formulating a synthesis that everyone can agree to.

Final Note

During the time we (the Cro-Magnons) overlapped with the Neanderthals our ancestors developed highly sophisticated cooperative effects characterized by social organization, group hunting procedures, creative experimentation with a variety of materials, sharing of knowledge, divisions of labor, trade, and transportation systems. We sent out scouts to monitor the movements of herds of animals we preyed on. The Neanderthals probably did not. We cached supplies and first aid materials to aid hunting parties far away from our home bases. The Neanderthals did not. Neanderthals apparently engaged their prey chiefly in direct combat. We learned more efficient ways of hunting, such as driving animals over cliffs. This changed fundamentally our relationship with the rest of the animal kingdom. Instead of behaving like lions and other carnivores, going after young and old and sick animals to weed out the less fit, large-scale game drives wiped out entire herds and perhaps entire species. We developed more sophisticated tools and weapons to kill from a distance such as the spear-thrower and the bow and arrow. The Neanderthals used local materials to develop tools. We were more selective, often obtaining special fine-grained and colorful flints from quarries as far as 250 miles away. This took a level of cooperation and organization that Neanderthals did not develop. We improved the tool-making process through experimentation and sharing knowledge. The Neanderthals did not. The Neanderthals used stone almost exclusively for tools. We used bone and ivory to make needles and other tools. We "tailored" our clothes and made ropes and nets. Our ability to obtain more food than we needed resulted in trading and the formation of far-ranging social networks. Status hierarchies, the accumulation of wealth, artistic efforts, laws, and story telling to preserve traditions followed, as more complex forms of cooperation were developed.

Whether we replaced or evolved from the Neanderthals, our ingenuity was especially evident in organizing cooperative efforts to increase our standard of living and the quality of our lives. Our success as a species is built on our ability to create and maintain high levels of positive interdependence.

❧[CONTROVERSY CONTRACT]❧

Major Learnings	Implementation Plans

Date _____   Date of Progress Report Meeting _____

Participant's Signature _____

Signatures of Other Group Members _____ _____

_____ _____ _____

EXERCISE MATERIALS

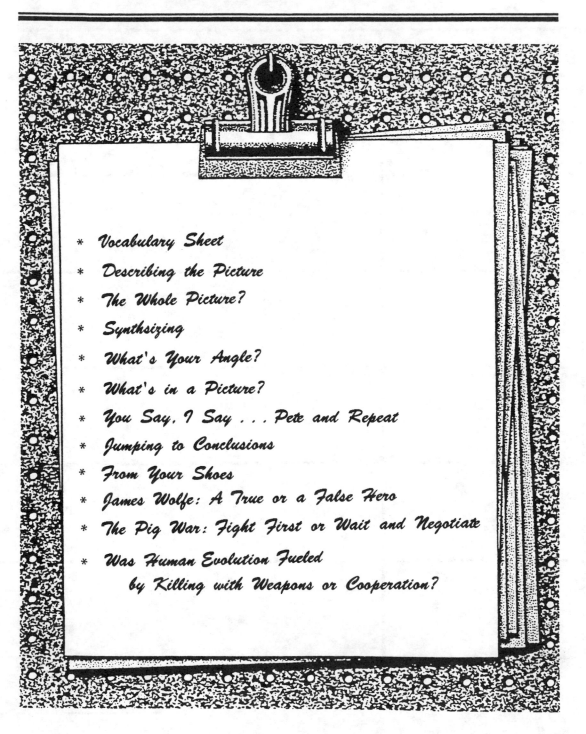

* *Vocabulary Sheet*
* *Describing the Picture*
* *The Whole Picture?*
* *Synthsizing*
* *What's Your Angle?*
* *What's in a Picture?*
* *You Say, I Say . . . Pete and Repeat*
* *Jumping to Conclusions*
* *From Your Shoes*
* *James Wolfe: A True or a False Hero*
* *The Pig War: Fight First or Wait and Negotiate*
* *Was Human Evolution Fueled*
   by Killing with Weapons or Cooperation?

VOCABULARY SHEET

Working with a partner, learn the definitions of the words below.

1. Define each word in two ways.

   First, write down what you think the word means.

   Second, look it up in the book and write down its definition.

   Note the page on which the definition appears.

   2. For each word write a sentence in which the word is used.

   3. Make up a story in which all of the words are used.

   4. Learn how to spell each word. They will be on your spelling test.

- **perspective**

- **perspective reversal**

- **egocentrism**

7:13

DESCRIBING THE PICTURE Exercise

1. Working cooperatively as a pair:

   a. **Write out a description of the person in the picture and plan how to teach the description to the other pair.** Each person needs an individual copy of the description. Include in your description the following:

1. Where is her nose?	4. Where is her ear?
2. Where is her eye?	5. What hair style is she wearing?
3. Where is her mouth?	6. What are her clothes like?

   b. **Plan how to advocate your description persuasively.** You may wish to make up a story about the person in the picture (who she is, what her personal history is like, and what she is doing).

2. **Present** your description to the other pair and listen carefully to their description.

3. **Advocate your perspective** and try to convince the other pair that they should adopt your perspective. Rebut their arguments against your perspective. Do not agree with the other pair until you are sure that your perspective has been given a fair and complete hearing.

4. **Reverse perspectives** by advocating accurately and fully the point of view of the other pair.

5. **Reach a decision** as to what the picture represents. Write out a full description of the picture that all members of the group can agree to.

6. Working **individualistically** write down (a) your strategies for advocating your position, (b) how you felt during the process, and (c) what you learned about how you manage conflict.

7. Repeat this lesson with other pictures that may be seen in two or more different ways.

DESCRIBING THE PICTURE (cont.)

7:15

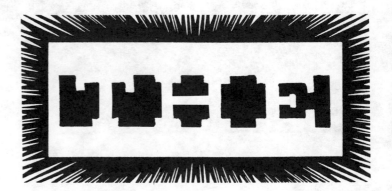

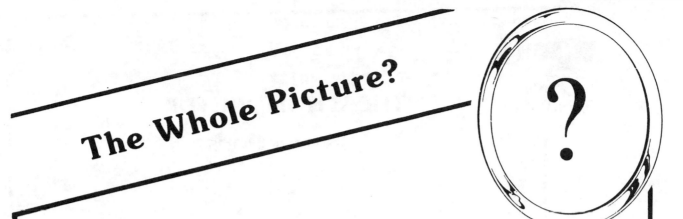

Task: You have been given a picture that is three-fourths covered by construction paper. Do not remove the cover and peak underneath it. Describe what you think the picture is about on the basis of the part you can see.

Cooperation: Agree on one description. Ensure that both of you are able to explain your description to members of other groups.

Procedure:

1. You and your partner have a copy of the picture covered except for one quadrant. Describe what they think the picture is about on the basis of what you can see. Each of you needs a copy of the picture and the description.

2. You have now been assigned to a group of four.

   a. Describe what you think the picture is about to the other group members. **You cannot show your picture to the other group members. Only verbal communication is allowed.** Give a complete and detailed description of your view.

   b. Listen carefully to the descriptions of the other group members.

   c. Challenge their view of the picture.

3. Uncover the whole picture and discuss:

   a. Where were descriptions accurate or inaccurate?

   b. Why is it important to get the whole picture of a conflict before you take action?

   c. What does the word **perspective** mean?

4. Practice saying:

   a. "I only know part of the picture."

   b. "I can't see the whole picture yet."

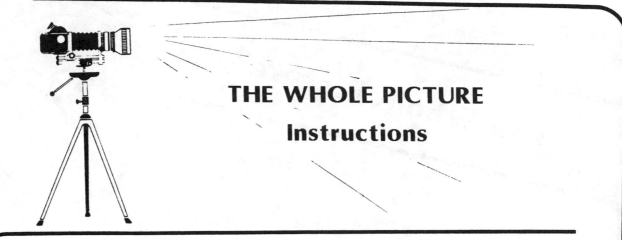

THE WHOLE PICTURE
Instructions

1. Take pieces of construction paper and cover all but one quadrant of the following picture. Attach the constructive paper with tape hinges so that the construction paper can be lifted. Cut a hole in the construction paper so that all of the picture is covered except for one-fourth.   One-fourth of your class should receive a copy of the picture with one quadrant exposed. In a class of 32 students, for example, 8 would receive a copy of the picture with the first quadrant exposed, 8 would receive a the picture with the second quadrant exposed, 8 would receive a the picture with the third quadrant exposed, and 8 would receive a the picture with the fourth quadrant exposed.

2. Divide the class into fourths. Within each fourth, give each student a copy of the picture with the same quadrant exposed. Organize each fourth into pairs. Give each pair a copy of previous page, **The Whole Picture**. Explain the task, the cooperation required, and the procedure. Then conduct the lesson.

3. Repeat this lesson by:

   a. Selecting a picture from a magazine or newspaper that would challenge your students.

   b. Having students bring in pictures that would fool the rest of the class.

7:19

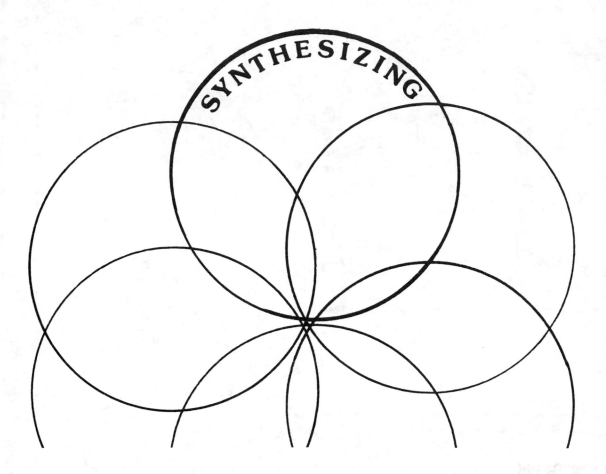

1. Teacher assigns students to pairs. Each pair is given a color wheel containing all the primary colors.

2. One student says, "I believe in yellow" and puts the yellow wheel forward. The other student says, "I believe in red" and puts the red wheel forward.

3. The two students then say, "Together we make green" and put their colors together.

4. The process is repeated several times. Students then discuss how to synthesize different ideas into a joint position that both can agree to.

WHAT'S YOUR ANGLE?

Task: The teacher has placed an object in the center of your group. Draw the object from your perspective. Then convince the other members of your group that your drawing is the correct way to see the object.

Cooperation: Agree on one description. Ensure that all of you are able to explain your description to members of other groups.

Procedure:

1. The teacher has placed an object in the center of your group. One of you is in front of the object, one of you is behind the object, and one of you is on each side of the object. Draw the object from your perspective.

2. Your group is supposed to agree on a description of how the object looks. Try to convince the other three members of your group that your drawing is the most correct way of seeing the object. Be persuasive and convincing.

3. Discuss:

   a. Why do objects look different from different angles?

   b. Why do different people see things differently?

   c. Why might you see things differently at two different times?

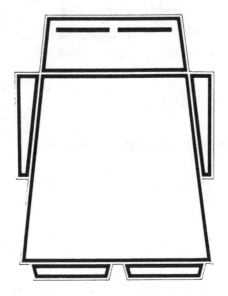

What's In a Picture?

1. The teacher cuts out a picture from a magazine or the newspaper for the lesson. The teacher then holds up the picture and shows it to the entire class.

2. Students, working individualistically:

   a. Write down three things that are important (or interesting) about the picture.

   b. Rank order the three things from most important (or interesting) to least important (or interesting).

3. Students are assigned to groups of three. Each student shares what he or she saw as important (or interesting) in the picture and her or his ranking. Students are reminded that there are no right or wrong answers.

4. Students discuss:

   a. Why do different people see different things in the picture?

   b. Why do different people rank the things they see in the picture differently?

   c. What influences decisions about importance?

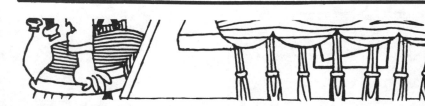

You Say, I Say . . . Pete and Repeat

1. Students sit in a circle of four.

2. One student begins by making a statement, such as "My favorite television show is _____."

3. The student on his or her right paraphrases by saying, "You say your favorite television show is _____. I say my favorite television show is _____."

4. The students continue around the circle, each student giving his or her opinion after paraphrasing the previous student's opinion.

5. Repeat the process several times until the students get quite fast in paraphrasing classmates.

6. The group of four is divided into two pairs. The teacher presents the class with a topic, such as "Who first discovered America?" The first person (**Pete**) talks for two or three minutes about the topic. The other person (**Repeat**) listens carefully. He or she can ask questions, but cannot criticize or disagree with what the person is saying.

7. Repeat paraphrases by saying, "You say _____ because _____. I say _____ discovered America because _____." This student now becomes Pete and talks for two or three minutes about the topic. The other student becomes Repeat and listens carefully, asking questions, but not criticizing or disagreeing.

8. Repeat the process several times, with one member of the pair giving his or her opinion after paraphrasing the other member's opinion. Students should practice until they get quite fast in paraphrasing classmates.

— JUMPING TO CONCLUSIONS —

1. Assign students to pairs. Ask them to define what **jumping to conclusions** means. Each pair shares its answer with the nearest pair, listens to the other pair's answer, and creates a new and better answer from the two definitions. The pairs then separate.

2. The teacher reads a description of an event, such as "Jeremy is laughing at Meg. Why?" "Betsy just hit Davy. Why?" "Jim refuses to talk to Chris. Why?"

3. Each student shares a possible conclusion with his or her partner. Before he or she can state a conclusion, however, he or she has to jump two or three feet forward. After both students have jumped to a conclusion, the teacher describes another event and the process is repeated.

4. For older students the Latin word, **Ergo** (which means **therefore**) may be used by students as they jump.

5. Students discuss:

   a. How does your perspective affect your conclusions?

   b. If you had a different perspective, would you make a different conclusion?

   c. How might jumping to conclusions cause problems with others?

   d. Has anyone ever jumped to conclusions about you?

∽ **From YOUR Shoes** ∾

1. Students are divided into pairs. Each pair needs two pairs of paper footprints. The footprints are attached to the floor so that they are facing each other. Each pair is also given two point-of-view cards defining positions in a controversy. Examples of point of view cards are:

    a. Students should be paid for every A they achieve; students should not be paid for achieving A's.

    b. Students should be assigned two hours of homework every night; students should not be assigned any homework.

    c. Students should be able to watch all the television they want; students should be limited to one-hour of television a night.

2. Students stand in their footprints:

    a. One student states the "pro" position on the issue giving several reasons to back up the position. The other student states the "con" position on the issue giving several reasons to back up the position.

    b. Students change places, standing in each other's footprints. They then paraphrase each other's position and reasons.

3. The procedure is repeated until students can change perspectives on the issue quickly and completely.

4. A variation is to take common fairy tales, such as **The Three Little Pigs** and have one student represent the pigs and the other student represent the wolf. Any story that has two or more positions may be used.

THE PIG WAR:

Fight First or Wait and Negotiate

In 1858, the gold of the Fraser River drew thousands of miners, mostly American, into Victoria from where they spilled out to the mainland in a pell-mell rush to find a rich deposit. Crime and chaos were common. Tensions rose between miners and Indians. James Douglas, as Lieutenant Governor in Victoria of the colony of Vancouver Island, had no authority over the mainland. However, since Douglas was also the Chief Factor of the Hudson's Bay Company in the area, he had some influence. So with a handful of soldiers and considerable bluster, Douglas started to enforce the rule of British law over the unruly newcomers.

In a time of slow communications, Douglas's urgent messages to London to send him some help took months. However, once they reached the colonial office, Her Majesty's Government quickly decreed the union of the mainland and Vancouver Island into a crown colony to be called British Columbia. They appointed Douglas as governor and sent him soldiers and ships in support.

The next year, 1859, brought a new problem for Douglas. It came from the ambiguity of the treaty to establish the boundary between the United States and British North America as the 49th parallel. From the middle of the Strait of Georgia, the treaty said, the boundary should follow south of the 49th parallel "the middle channel which separates the continent from Vancouver Island." However, there were three such channels as the map shows and both countries claimed the San Juan Islands in the Strait of Juan de Fuca. A joint British American commission failed to resolve the problem and in 1859 the islands were still in dispute.

Years earlier, in 1845, the Hudson's Bay Company (HBC) had claimed San Juan Island and in 1853 set up a sheep ranch. The US responded by appointing a customs officer in 1855 who seized 34 rams. However, this was not to be a ram war, but a pig war.

In 1859, a few Americans, disappointed with the Fraser goldfields, became squatters on the islands. One of them, Charles Lyman, started a small farm in the middle of the HBC ranch on San Juan. On June 15, Lyman became so angry with an HBC pig that had dug up his potatoes he shot the animal. A senior officer of the Hudson's Bay was visiting the island for a picnic and he supposedly ordered Lyman to pay $100 in compensation or be taken to Victoria for trial. Lyman refused.

THE PIG WAR (cont.)

At the end of July, a contingent of 60 soldiers from Fort Bellingham took possession of San Juan Island to "protect American settlers from Indians and the Hudson's Bay Company." The HBC manager ordered them off, but they ignored him.

Furious, Douglas sent the HMS **Tribune** with 31 guns and the Royal Marines to San Juan to get the American troops to evacuate and to prevent any further American landings. Although the **Tribune's** larger force and heavier guns would have easily destroyed the Americans, the captain hesitated. On August 1, the HMS **Satellite** joined the **Tribune**. However, the same day the Americans proceeded to unload another company of soldiers and a few howitzers.

Your task is to decide what Governor Douglas should do. At this moment, the Legislative Council is meeting and you are to take a seat as a member and join the debate. Should Douglas force the US troops off San Juan now before they can be reinforced or should he wait and seek a negotiated settlement first?

▬▬▬▬▬▬▬▬▬▬▬▬ **FIGHT FIRST**

Your position is that British Columbia needs to take strong measures now to keep the conflict to a minimum. The colony has the military might and the moral right to expel the American troops. The council should support Douglas's original decision to expel the Americans.

1. If British Columbia wishes the American troops gone with as little bloodshed as possible It must act swiftly. Douglas himself said, *It is better to have to cope with a small detachment than to wait until reinforcements from the Washington Territory make their dislodgement impractical with our present force.*

2. The British navy has the power to remove quickly the Americans or, better, to convince them to withdraw. The flagship, the HMS **Ganges** with its 84 guns, is the most powerful ship on the coast. If there was to be larger conflict, there are also the Royal Marines on the mainland. In addition, Douglas has said that in case of war, the Indian people, who still feel much hostility towards the Americans, would support Britain. He thinks 50,000 would join Britain's side.

3. During the Gold Rush, with only a handful of men, Douglas was able to bring into line a vastly greater number of Americans. He can do this again.

4. British Columbia has the moral right to expel the US soldiers. The American action is an illegal invasion of land that we claim to be our own.

5. If British Columbia does not stop the Americans at San Juan, they may be encouraged to advance on Victoria, New Westminster, and the whole of the colony. It was only a few years ago that American President Polk threatened to send an army to conquer the whole of the Pacific coast. The American miners on the Fraser River today in 1859 sing a song with this verse:

Soon our banners will be streaming
Soon the eagle will be streaming
And the lion - see it cower,
Hurrah, boys, the river's ours.

❧ Wait and Negotiate ❧

Your position is that British Columbia should first make every effort to resolve this dispute peacefully. Risking deaths over a small squabble is wrong. If given time, cooler heads should prevail and ownership of the islands will be settled fairly.

1. There is no point to risking lives if the conflict can be resolved by negotiation. The decision to occupy was made locally in the Washington Territory. Once the heads of government of the United States and Great Britain discuss the matter, it will be settled.

2. British Columbia is a British colony. Her Majesty's Government must be consulted before British Columbia risks a war with the United States.

3. Ownership of the islands is in dispute. Military action on San Juan Island would not be the same as defending British Columbia soil.

4. *It is silly to go to war over a pig* were the words of British Admiral Barnes once his ship, the Gange, reached the area. *The stakes here, whether a pig or an island, are not worth a war. The San Islands, though beautiful, are not valuable.*

5. If open hostilities start, the large number of United States citizens in the colony may cause trouble.

6. Even if Britain were to expel the Americans, eventually, the United States could send far more reinforcements than Britain would want to send to a place remote from London.

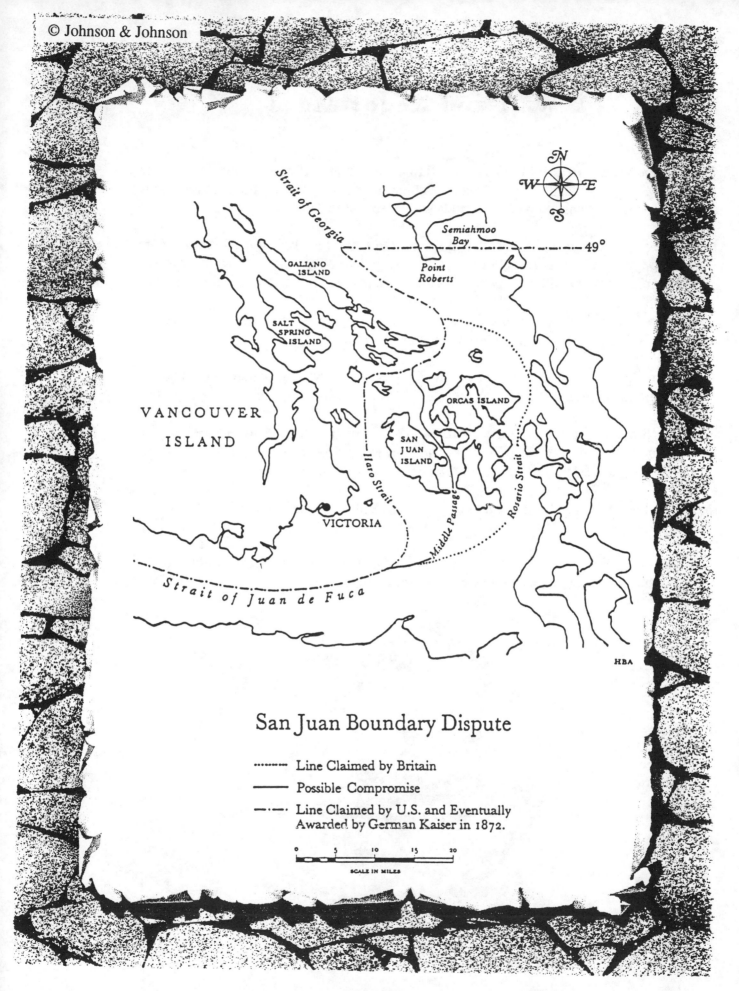

San Juan Boundary Dispute

.... Line Claimed by Britain

——— Possible Compromise

—·—· Line Claimed by U.S. and Eventually
Awarded by German Kaiser in 1872.

0   5   10   15   20
SCALE IN MILES

7 : 30

Chapter Eight: Using Controversy In Faculty Decision-Making Groups

Introduction

The best way ever devised for seeking the truth in any given situation is advocacy: presenting the pros and cons from different, informed points of view and digging down deep into the facts.

Harold S. Geneen, Former CEO, ITT

A large pharmaceutical company faced the decision of whether to buy or build a chemical plant (**Wall Street Journal**, October 22, 1975). To maximize the likelihood that the best decision was made, the president established two advocacy teams to ensure that both the "buy" and the "build" alternatives received a fair and complete hearing. An **advocacy team** is a subgroup that prepares and presents a particular policy alternative to the decision-making group. The "buy" team was instructed to prepare and present the best case for purchasing a chemical plant, and the "build" team was told to prepare and present the best case for constructing a new chemical plant near the company's national headquarters. The "buy" team identified over 100 existing plants that would meet the company's needs, narrowed the field down to twenty, further narrowed the field down to three, and then selected one plant as the ideal plant to buy. The "build" team contacted dozens of engineering firms and, after four months of consideration, selected a design for the ideal plant to build. Nine months after they were established, the two teams, armed with all the details about cost, (a) presented their best case and (b) challenged each other's information, reasoning, and conclusions. From the spirited discussion, it became apparent that the two options would cost about the same amount of money. The group, therefore, chose the "build" option because it allowed the plant to be located conveniently near company headquarters. This procedure represents the structured use of controversy to ensure high quality decision making.

In almost every meeting room within every organization, people are disagreeing with each other. Whether the organization is a business, an industry, a government agency, a hospital, a law firm, a family, or a school, disagreements occur as decisions are made and problems are solved. Involved participation in such situations means that different ideas, opinions, beliefs, and information will surface and clash (i.e., **controversy**). In the mining industry, for example, engineers are accustomed to address issues such as land use, air and water pollution, and health and safety. The complexity of the design of production processes, the balancing of environmental and manufacturing interests, and numerous other factors often create controversy. Most groups waste the benefits of such disputes, but every effective decision-making situation thrives on what controversy has to offer.

Figure 8.1 Decision Making In Schools

Step One: Establishing A Cooperative Context And Highlighting Interdependence

Step Two: Identifying And Defining The Problem Or Issue

Step Three: Gathering Information About The Problem

Step Four: Formulating And Considering Alternative Solutions

Step Five: Structuring Controversy Through Advocacy Subgroups

- Research And Prepare Position

- Present The Best Case Possible For Position

- Open Discussion To Refute Other Positions And REbut Attacks On Own Position

- Evaluating Strengths And Weaknesses Of Each Alternative

- Perspective Reversal

- Synthesis

Step Six: Implementing Decision And Evaluating Its Success

Overcoming Barriers To Effective Decision Making

Decision Making In Schools

It's a serious mistake for any leader to be surrounded by sycophants...The stronger and more self-assured a leader is the more likely he or she is to seek diversity of advice. If you are insecure or don't have confidence in yourself, then you're apt to listen to a narrow range of advice. I deliberately chose advisors with disparate points of view.

Jimmy Carter, Former President Of The United States

Faculty members, just like engineers, executives, politicians, and judges, have to make decisions to solve problems. Participating in controversies is just as powerful in schools as it is in business, industry, government, and other organizational settings. Whenever a problem occurs in a school or department, a decision has to be made as to which course of action the faculty will take to solve it. Decisions are by their very nature controversial, as alternative solutions are considered before agreement is reached. When a decision is made, the controversy ends and participants commit themselves to a common course of action.

The purpose of group decision making is to decide on well-considered, well-understood, realistic action toward goals every member wishes to achieve. A **decision** implies that some agreement prevails among group members as to which of several courses of action is most desirable for achieving the group's goals. **Decision making** is a process that results in a choice among alternative courses of action. There are five major characteristics of an effective decision (Johnson & F. Johnson, 1994):

1. The resources of group members are fully utilized.

2. Time is well used.

3. The decision is correct or of high quality. A **high quality decision** solves the problem, can be implemented in a way that the problem does not reoccur, and does **not** require more time, people, and material resources than the school can provide.

4. All the required faculty are fully committed to implementing the decision.

5. The problem-solving ability of the group is enhanced, or at least not lessened.

In a healthy faculty, spirited conflict among faculty members is inevitable whenever an important decision is made. Being able to initiate controversies and capitalize on their constructive outcomes are essential for faculty to (a) make high quality and effective decisions and (b) exchange expertise. To make high quality, creative decisions so that the school or department can achieve its goals or solve its problems, the expertise of different faculty members must be exchanged. Schools, like all other organizations, are filled with individuals who have expertise in their limited areas and must interact and make joint decisions with each other. Having the procedures and skills to exchange expertise and manage the resulting controversies are essential for reaching high quality decisions.

Problem Solving And Decision Making

In order to engage in a problem-solving procedure the cooperative nature of the school has to be reaffirmed. Faculty members must clearly perceive that they "sink or swim together." Competitors do not solve problems, they shift blame and point out each other's deficits. Within individualistic situations each person acts on his or her own without regard to or coordination with others. It is only within cooperative situations that joint effort can be taken to solve an organizational problem. Once a sense of cooperation is clearly highlighted, problem solving begins:

1. **Identify and define the problem.** Faculty members examine the discrepancy between what is actually taking place within the school and what they would like to take place within the school.

2. **Diagnose the existence, magnitude, and nature of the problem.** Valid information must be gathered about the existence of the problem. Then the information must be thoroughly discussed and analyzed to ensure that all faculty members understand it.

3. **Identify and analyze alternative courses of action to solve the problem.** Several alternative solutions must be identified and considered in order to find the one that will be maximally effective. A common error in decision-making situations is to prematurely decide on the first reasonable alternative that is suggested (this is called **satisficing**). What decision-making groups are supposed to do is choose the alternative course of action that maximizes their success (this is called **maximizing**). The faculty must ensure that each alternative gets full consideration and a fair and complete hearing. The only way to ensure that all alternatives are equally considered is to assign each to an advocacy subgroup whose responsibility is to present the best case possible for that alternative. The use of advocacy subgroups is described in the next section of this chapter.

4. **Make a decision about which course of action to take to solve the problem.** Such a decision may be made through consensus, two-thirds majority vote, a majority vote, or by an executive council can make the decision (see Johnson & F. Johnson, 1994).

5. **Implement the alternative chosen and evaluate its success in solving the problem**. If the problem is not solved, the procedure is repeated again.

To be effective, schoolwide problem solving requires:

1. Valid and complete information about the problem or issue.

2. Enough intellectual conflict and disagreement to ensure that all potential solutions get a fair hearing.

3. Free and informed choice.

4. Continuing motivation to solve the problem if the plan implemented does not work.

Establishing A Cooperative Context

It's easy to get the players. Getting them to play together, that's the hard part.

Casey Stengel

There are a number of classic errors made in solving problems within a school or department. The **first** and most severe is assuming that faculty will work cooperatively if they are placed in the same room. Faculty meetings may be characterized by competition and power conflicts among members or they may function more like "individualistic efforts with talking" than a cooperative effort. If you want faculty to work together productively, a clear cooperative structure must be established. The **second** fallacious assumption is that faculty have the leadership, decision-making, trust-building, communication, and conflict-management skills they need to work together effectively. Neither assumption is justified in most schools. Adults in our society typically do not have the small group and interpersonal skills to work cooperatively and even when they do they often do not use their skills because the situation is not clearly structured cooperatively.

What often happens in problem-solving situations is that faculty members stay psychologically uninvolved and uncommitted. They assume that the official chairperson will do all the work. Members can adopt a "leave it to George" attitude and expend decreasing amounts of effort and just go through the team-work motions. At the same time George may expend less effort in order to avoid the "sucker effect" of doing all the work. The responsibility to come up with innovative ideas can become so diffused that no one feels accountable. Conflicts among members may be managed destructively, causing members to become alienated from the task and each other. All such potential problems may be avoided by carefully and clearly structuring cooperation.

A school faculty is first and foremost a cooperative team. Like all cooperative teams, five basic elements need to be carefully structured (positive interdependence, individual accountability, face-to-face promotive interaction, social skills, and group processing). In order for effective controversy to occur among faculty members to ensure effective problem-solving and decision-making take place, the five basic elements have to be carefully and systematically structured.

Identifying And Defining The Problem Or Issue

The first step of the faculty is to identify and define the problem. A **problem** may be defined as a discrepancy or difference between an actual state of affairs and a desired state of affairs. Problem solving requires both an idea about where the school should be and valid information about where it is now. The more clear and accurate the definition of the problem, the easier it is to do the other steps in the problem-solving procedure. There are three steps in defining the problem:

1. Reaching agreement on what the desired state of affairs is.

2. Obtaining valid, reliable, directly verifiable, descriptive (not inferential or evaluative), and correct information about the existing state of affairs.

3. Discussing thoroughly the difference between the desired and actual state of affairs. Awareness of this discrepancy builds the commitment and motivation to solve the problem.

Because problem-solving groups often progress too quickly toward a solution to the problem without first getting a clear, consensual definition of the problem itself, faculty members should see to it that everyone understands what the problem is before trying to assess its magnitude.

Defining a workable problem is often the hardest stage of the problem-solving process. Suggestions for procedures are as follows:

1. List a series of statements about the problem. Describe it as concretely as possible by mentioning people, places, and resources. There should be as many different statements of the problem as the members are willing to give. Write them on a blackboard where everyone can see them. Avoid arguing about whether the problem is perfectly stated.

2. Restate each problem statement so that is includes a description of both the desired and actual state of affairs. Take out alternative definitions that are beyond the resources of the group to solve. Choose the definition that the group members agree is most correct. **The problem should be important, solvable, and urgent.**

3. Write out a detailed description of what school life will be like when the problem is solved. The more detailed and specific the scenario is, the better.

There are a number of potential barriers to identifying and defining problems. **The first is prematurely defining the problem**. The direction a group first takes in defining the problem may keep it from finding a successful solution (Maier, 1930); therefore, the group should be careful not to agree prematurely on the definition of its problem. **The**

second is a lack of clarity in stating the problem. Much of the initial effort of groups in solving a problem is directed toward orienting members to what the problem is. This phase is extremely important, and it deserves sufficient time and effort to identify the problem, to define it, and, through this process, to get the members involved in and committed to solving it. Often, groups are doomed to failure when they inadequately define the nature of their problem. **Third, a critical, evaluative, competitive climate** prevents creative and workable solutions from being discovered. A supportive, trusting, cooperative atmosphere is necessary for solving problems successfully. If group members are afraid that other members are evaluating their ideas, effective problem solving is destroyed. **Fourth, if group members have inadequate motivation to solve the problem a compelling solution will not be found.** Any problem-solving group must have the motivation to solve its problems. If the group members are not motivated, they must be persuaded to see the importance of the problem and the necessity for seeking a solution. Members who leave the work to others clearly lack motivation.

Gathering Information About The Problem

The second step in the problem-solving process is diagnosing the existence, magnitude, and nature of the problem. Valid information must be gathered. Then the information must be thoroughly discussed and analyzed to ensure that all faculty members understand it. Actual frequency of occurrence of the problem, the magnitude of the forces helping the school to move toward the desired state of affairs, and the forces hindering this movement need to be documented.

There are two major **barriers** to gathering valid information about the nature and magnitude of the problem. **The first is not getting the needed information.** When information is minimal, the definition of the problem will be inadequate, fewer alternative strategies for the solution will be generated, and potential consequences of those alternatives will not be properly explored. The result is relatively low-grade solutions. Great emphasis must be placed on fact finding in order to solve a problem effectively. **The second barrier is poor communication within the group.** Poor communication among group members has the same effect as the lack of information, with the added problem that it makes the implementation of any action that requires coordination among group members difficult. Effective communication among all group members is necessary for effective problem solving.

Without defining the problem correctly and specifically, it cannot be adequately understood. And without an accurate and precise understanding of the forces involved, the alternative strategies for the solution of the problem cannot be formulated.

Formulating And Considering Alternative Solutions

The overall purpose of faculty problem solving is to make a free and informed choice of a solution to the problem based on having and understanding the relevant information. To achieve that purpose, a cooperative structure must be established, the problem must be accurately identified and defined, and valid information about the existence, magnitude, and nature of the problem must be gathered and organized so it is easily understood. Once the nature and magnitude of the problem is accurately understood, alternative ways to solve it may be identified.

The **third step** in problem solving is identifying and analyzing alternative ways to solve the problem. Groups often make poor decisions because they (a) do not think of the proper alternative solutions and/or (b) do a poor job of evaluating and choosing among the alternatives considered. **Systematically evaluating each alternative and analyzing the advantages and disadvantages of each alternative before making a final decision are the most important factors in effective decision making.** The more explicit the systematic evaluation the less likely that an alternative will be overlooked or rationalized away. If decision makers do know what the alternatives are and have correctly diagnosed each alternative's inherent advantages and disadvantages, they will not choose a certain course of action unless its advantages are expected to exceed its disadvantages.

Identifying and analyzing alternative ways to solve the problem requires creative, divergent, and inventive reasoning. Such "higher-level" thinking and analysis comes primarily from intellectual disagreement and challenge, i.e., controversy. A major barrier to effective decision making and problem solving is **concurrence seeking**, which occurs when members inhibit discussion to avoid any disagreement and emphasize agreement. Controversy is structured within problem-solving groups through the use of advocacy subgroups.

Structuring Controversy Through Advocacy Subgroups

Controversy is structured within problem-solving groups through the use of advocacy subgroups. An **advocacy subgroup** consists of two (or three) members who (a) develop the assigned alternative in depth, (b) plan how to present the best case possible for the alternative to the rest of the faculty so that it receives a fair and complete hearing, and (c) advocate the alternative and attempt to convince the rest of the faculty to adopt the alternative. If each alternative is not presented sincerely and forcefully, it will not receive a fair hearing. In order to make an effective and high quality decision, the faculty assign members to advocacy groups and give each one alternative course of action to represent, the advocacy subgroups are given time to prepare their position and supporting rationale, each subgroup presents and elaborates its position and rationale, there is an open discussion in which subgroups argue their points-of-view and refute the other positions, members of each subgroup reverse perspectives and present another position as if it were their own, and the faculty synthesizes the best evidence and reasoning from all sides into a novel decision qualitatively better than any of the previous alternatives.

The purpose of controversy is **not** to choose the best of the alternatives. The purpose of controversy is to create a synthesis from the best evidence and reasoning from all the various alternatives. To do so, members have to keep conclusions tentative, accurately understand opposing perspectives, incorporate new information into their conceptual frameworks, and change their attitudes and position. This process is repeated until the differences in conclusions among group members have been resolved, a decision is reached, and the controversy has ended. The synthesis is created by the collision of adverse opinion.

Controversies tend to be constructive when the situational context is cooperative, there is some heterogeneity among group members, information and expertise is distributed within the group, members have the necessary social and cognitive skills, and the canons of rational argumentation are followed.

Forming Advocacy Subgroups

Once the alternative solutions to the problem have been identified, each is assigned to an advocacy subgroup of two members whose **tasks** are to (a) develop its alternative in depth and (b) plan how to present the best case possible for the alternative to the rest of the faculty. The goal is to make sure that the alternative receives a fair and complete hearing. The pair is to work **cooperatively**, preparing one presentation that both members will participate in equally.

1. Research And Prepare Position

The advocacy subgroup researches their position and get as much information to support it as possible. Members organize the available evidence to support their position based on their current information, experiences, and perspective. Preparing a position includes a thesis statement stating the alternative course of action, a rationale as to why the course of action is the one the faculty should adopt, and a conclusion that is the same as the thesis statement.

2. Present The Best Case Possible For Alternatives

Members of each advocacy subgroup present (and advocate) their position to the entire group with the intent of persuading the other group members of its validity. They are to be as sincere and thorough as they can in their presentation. They are to be as convincing as possible. In addition, they are to listen carefully to the presentation of the other advocacy subgroups. As they listen they are to take notes, clarify anything they do not understand, and write down the advantages of each alternative. They need to learn about the other alternative courses of action for at least two reasons:

1. To be able to challenge it and subject it to the fire of critical analysis. If they do not know the other positions, they cannot challenge them effectively.

2. To make a reasoned judgment about the advantages and disadvantages of each alternative proposed and hopefully to create a synthesis from the best information and reasoning from all positions.

3. Open Discussion

Faculty have an open discussion in which the advocacy subgroups argue their points-of-view and refute the other positions. **First**, members of each subgroup continue to advocate their position. They emphasize facts, evidence, and rationale. **Second**, all faculty members need to learn the advantages and disadvantages of each alternative course of action. The overall goal is to make a reasoned judgment about how to solve the problem. In order to do so, faculty members must carefully consider all the alternative courses of action and seek a synthesis that integrates the best reasoning from them all.

Third, each alternative course of action should be critically evaluated with doubts and objections freely expressed. In effect, each subgroup is a **devil's advocate** in criticizing the other positions. High quality decisions and conclusions are reached through a process of argument and counter-argument aimed at persuading others to adopt, modify, or drop positions. Members attempt to refute opposing positions while rebutting the attacks on their position.

When faced with (a) opposing positions with their rationales and (b) challenges to the validity of their own position and its rationale, faculty members experience uncertainty, conceptual conflict, and disequilibrium. This stimulates epistemic curiosity and divergent thinking and motivates an active search for more information, new experiences, and a more adequate cognitive perspective and reasoning in hopes of resolving the uncertainty. As a result faculty members reorganize and reconceptualize their conclusions, increasing the probability of creating a workable synthesis.

Evaluating Strengths And Weaknesses Of Each Alternative

In order to evaluate the strengths and weaknesses of each alternative being advocated, the factors typically considered are:

1. The advantages and disadvantages of each alternative course of action for the (a) faculty, (b) students, (c) parents and the community, and (d) any other relevant group. A balance sheet is completed for each course of action considered. A balance sheet

consists of listing the advantages (tangible gains) from adopting the alternative on one side and the disadvantages (tangible losses) on the other.

2. For each alternative course of action, the advantage and disadvantage should be rated on a ten-point scale from very high importance (10) to very little importance (1).

3. After a balance sheet is completed for each alternative course of action, the faculty as a whole:

   a. Compares the balance sheets and then ranks the alternative course of action from "most desirable" to "least desirable."

   b. Creates a synthesis based on the best evidence and reasoning from all the different alternatives.

4. Perspective Reversal

Members of each subgroup present the best case for one of the other alternative courses of action as if it were their own. All members must participate equally. They are to be forceful and persuasive, adding new arguments, facts, and rationale when it is possible. Other faculty members correct errors in their presentation and note omissions. The other faculty members will do the same. Faculty members strive to see the issue from all perspectives simultaneously. **Perspective reversal** is taking another frame of reference and sincerely and completely presenting their position as if it were one's own.

This perspective reversal ensures that each subgroup listens carefully to the other presentations and comprehends their rationales completely. Faculty members adapt their perspective and reasoning through understanding and accommodating the perspective and reasoning underlying the other alternatives. Being able to view the problem from a variety of perspectives simultaneously is emphasized.

5. Synthesis

Faculty members drop all advocacy, step back, strive for objectivity, and attempt to see the issue from a variety of perspectives. They look for new patterns within the body of evidence and generate a number of optional ways of integrating the evidence. The more alternatives suggested, the less group members will be "frozen" to their original positions. The faculty members summarize and synthesize the best evidence and reasoning from all sides of the issue into a joint position that all group members can agree to. Synthesizing involves at least three processes: (a) putting things together in fewer words, (b) creative insight, and (c) creating a new position that subsumes and unifies the previous ones. The previous positions are seen as parts to be combined into a whole.

Synthesis is a creative process that generally results in a group consensus as to what the decision should be. Perfect consensus means that everyone agrees what the decision should be. Unanimity, however, is often impossible to achieve. There are degrees of consensus. **Consensus** generally refers to unanimity in making a decision, but more precisely refers to unanimous commitment to implement the decision. Such commitment is based on group members believing they had a fair chance to influence what the decision is. When a decision is made by consensus, all members understand the decision and are prepared to support it. Members who continue to disagree or have doubts nevertheless say publicly that they are willing to give the decision a try for a period of time. Consensus is the best method for producing an innovative, creative, and high-quality decision that (a) all members will be committed to implementing, (b) uses the resources of all group members, and (c) increases the future decision-making effectiveness of the group. When consensus cannot be achieved, the faculty may wish to vote. A simple majority may rule, or the faculty may require a two-thirds majority. In either case, faculty members must believe that their views were given careful consideration and that the best case for what they believed was presented to the faculty as a whole.

Implementing Decision And Evaluating Its Success

Once a decision has been made, faculty meet again in their advocacy subgroups and note what each needs to do to implement the decision and evaluate its effectiveness. **Decision implementation** is a process of taking the necessary actions that result in the execution of the decision. This requires internal commitment to go out and do what the faculty have decided to do. As the decision is being implemented, the faculty (a) documents the extent to which implementation takes place (this is called **process evaluation**), (b) notes barriers to implementation, and (c) evaluates the success of the plan in solving the problem (this is known as **outcome evaluation**). If the faculty finds that its solution has been successfully implemented, but has failed to change substantially the current situation into the ideal state of affairs, a new solution must be chosen and implemented

until the group finds one that is effective. Evaluation often results in a new definition of a problem, a rediagnosis of the situation, and beginning of a new problem-solving sequence.

Finally, the faculty **process** how well they worked together and how they could be even more effective next time. The faculty then celebrate their success.

Barriers To Effective Decision Making

Pardon him, Theodotus: he is a barbarian, and thinks that the customs of his tribe and island are the laws of nature.

C. B. Shaw, **Caesar and Cleopatra**

Why do decisions often turn out to be wrong? Why is decision making in so many schools so hard? If, for example, the school budget has been cut and the school must dismiss half its teacher's aides, the faculty may have a difficult time making a decision as to how to redistribute the remaining aides throughout the building. Such decisions can create resentment and animosity among faculty members if they are not made effectively.

There are a number of barriers to making effective decisions. **The first is a failure to identify the proper alternative courses of action**. If a course of action is not identified, it cannot be considered and evaluated. **The second is premature elimination of courses of action without proper analysis and evaluation, or uninformed and premature choice.** For most people, ideas are fragile creations, easily blighted by a chill, or even indifferent, reception. As groups proceed in their problem-solving activities, they must avoid all tendencies to squelch each idea as it comes along; instead, they should create an atmosphere that supports the presentation and the pooling of a wide assortment of ideas. All alternative solutions should receive a fair hearing. Only then can the group avoid becoming fixated on the first reasonable solution suggested and critically evaluate the worth of all alternatives. Groups often make poor decisions because they (a) do not think of the proper alternative solutions and/or (b) do a poor job of evaluating and choosing among the alternatives considered. **Systematically evaluating each alternative and analyzing the advantages and disadvantages of each alternative before making a final decision are the most important factors in effective decision making.**

The third barrier is pressures for conformity. Pressures for conformity and compliance slow down the development of different and diverse ideas. Divergent thinking as well as convergent thinking are necessary for sound problem solving. **The fourth barrier is a lack of inquiry and problem-solving skills.** Some groups may need special training in how to use inquiry and problem-solving methods to advantage. Training may be accomplished through an expert member of the group, or the group may wish to call in an outside consultant. **The fifth barrier is a lack of procedures to aid analysis and synthesis.** The forces creating the problem must be understood and systematically analyzed in order for new alternatives to be created.

Perhaps the greatest barrier to effective decision making is the pressure toward concurrence within decision-making situations. **Concurrence seeking** occurs when group members inhibit discussion to avoid any disagreement or arguments and emphasize agreement. Most decision-making situations are dominated by concurrence-seeking (Walton, 1987). Within concurrence seeking there is a suppression of different conclusions, an emphasis on quick compromise, and a lack of disagreement. Group members become fixated on their own positions and little uncertainty arises as to the correctness of their conclusions. New information that may challenge their conclusions is avoided. Group members tend to restate the accepted conclusions without elaboration or exploration of the reasoning and rationale underlying the position. Opposing views are derogated and rejected. A failure to reconceptualize or understand different cognitive perspectives results. Concurrence seeking is close to the **groupthink** concept of Janis (1982) in which members of a decision-making group set aside their doubts and misgivings about whatever policy is favored by the emerging consensus so as to be able to concur with the other members. The underlying motivation of groupthink is the strong desire to preserve the harmonious atmosphere of the group on which each member has become dependent for coping with the stresses of external crises and for maintaining self-esteem.

Summary

Faculty (teachers, administrators, and support staff) are empowered to solve schoolwide problems when they are given the responsibility of deciding how the problem will be solved. A **decision** implies that some agreement prevails among group members as to which of several courses of action is most desirable for achieving the group's goals. Decision making by definition involves controversy, as different individuals prefer different courses of action to solve the problem and they must reach agreement as to what they will jointly do. Decision making is part of the larger problem-solving process. In order to solve a problem, a cooperative structure must be established. Faculty members identify and define a problem, collect valid and complete information about the problem's existence and magnitude, identify a number of alternative courses of action that may solve the problem, ensure that each alternative gets a fair and complete hearing, make a free and informed decision about which course of action to take to solve the problem in a way that creates continuing motivation to solve the problem if the plan does not work, and implement the chosen alternative and evaluate its success in solving the problem. To ensure that each alternative course of action gets a fair and complete hearing, the controversy procedure must be used. Each alternative is assigned to a pair of faculty members who are responsible for presenting the best case possible for that alternative. They research the issue and prepare their position. They present the best case for that position while listening carefully to the presentations of the other advocacy subgroups. An open discussion is then held in which faculty members challenge the evidence and reasoning of the other advocacy subgroups and defend their own position from attacks. Next, faculty members reverse perspectives and summarize the best case for the other alternatives. Finally, a decision is made based on a synthesis of the best evidence and reasoning from all the advocacy subgroups. Such a controversy process represents the best chance for an informed and reasoned decision to be made.

⟶⟨ CONTROVERSY CONTRACT ⟩⟵

Major Learnings	Implementation Plans

Date _____   Date of Progress Report Meeting   _____

Participant's Signature   _____

Signatures of Other Group Members   _____ _____

_____   _____   _____

VOCABULARY SHEET

Working with a partner, learn the definitions of the words below.

1. Define each word in two ways.

   First, write down what you think the word means.

   Second, look it up in the book and write down its definition.

   Note the page on which the definition appears.

2. For each word write a sentence in which the word is used.

3. Make up a story in which all of the words are used.

4. Learn how to spell each word. They will be on your spelling test.

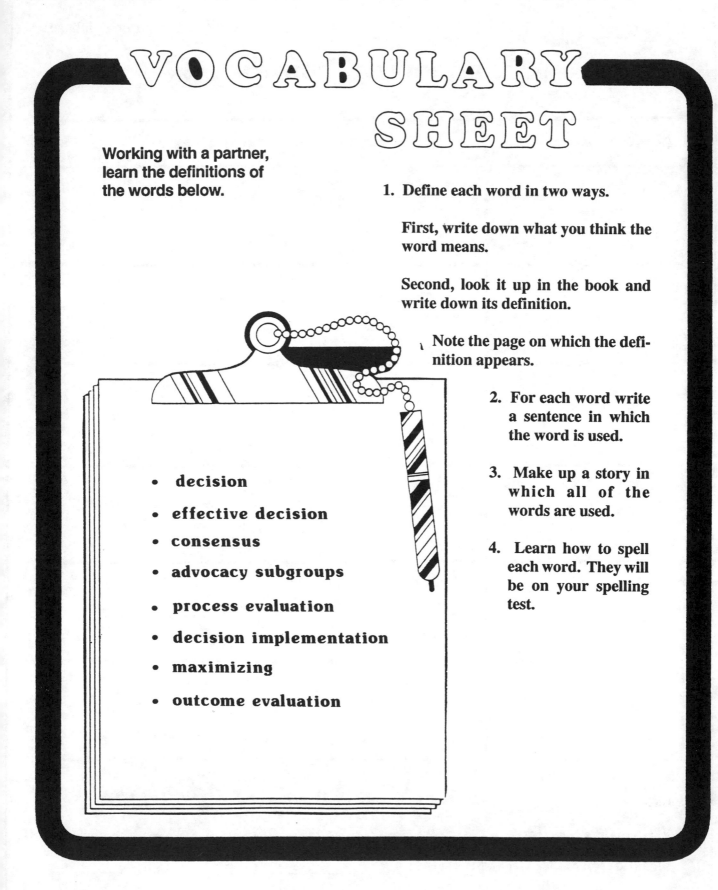

- decision
- effective decision
- consensus
- advocacy subgroups
- process evaluation
- decision implementation
- maximizing
- outcome evaluation

MAKING EFFECTIVE DECISIONS

1. What is the decision to be made?

2. What are the major alternative course of action?

   a.

   b.

   c.

3. My partner is:

   Our tasks are to research and prepare the best case possible for the assigned alternative and plan how best to convince the rest of the faculty of its soundness. This involves:

   a. Researching: Gather evidence to support the assigned position.

   b. Conceptualizing: Organize the evidence into a logical structure that provides a rationale for the position.

   c. Leaping To A Conclusion: Once the evidence is gathered and organized into a logical sequence, faculty must reach a tentative conclusion based on their current understanding of the issue.

   d. Presenting: Plan how to advocate for the alternative forcefully and persuasively.

   Cooperative: Work together to prepare one presentation that both of you agree with and are able to give. During the presentation and the rest of the controversy sequence both members should participate equally.

4. The best case for my alternative is:

   a. Thesis Statement:

   b. Rationale:

     1.

     2.

     3.

     4.

   c. Conclusion:

5. Presentation (everyone must participate, listen carefully, and write out the advantages for each alternative): For each course of action make and complete a table similar to the following.

Course Of Action

	Advantages	Rating	Disadvantages	Rating
Faculty				
Students				
Parents/Community				
Other				

6. Challenge and Refute:

   a. Everyone participates.

   b. Challenge and refute the evidence and reasoning supporting the other alternatives.

   c. Defend your alternative from the challenges of others.

Making Effective Decisions

    d. Write out disadvantages for each alternative.

    e. Add new advantages for each alternative.

    f. Begin rating the importance of each advantage and disadvantage.

7. Perspective-Reversal:

    a. Each person has to participate

    b. Present the best case for the other alternative as if it were your assigned position.

    c. Correct any misstatements of your position by the individuals who are presenting it.

    d. Try to hold all perspectives in mind simultaneously while you consider the problem to be solved.

8. Synthesize and Decide:

    a. Finish ratings.

    b. Take best evidence and reasoning from each alternative.

    c. Create syntheses.

9. The decision is:

10. My responsibilities in implementing the decision are:

    a.

    b.

    c.

11. How we will know if the problem is solved:

CLASSIC FALLACIES

Most fallacies in reasoning are apparent simply by knowing that they are common, not by applying the rules of deductive and inductive logic. We must constantly ask if people's words are meaning what they say and saying what the people mean. Then we must ask if they are inadvertently taking **some** for **all**, or taking an inductive leap too soon or in an errant direction. But logicians have identified six classic fallacies that often muddle discussions:

1. **Either-Or:** Assuming only two opposing positions such as, *Either you are a Republican or a Democrat.*

2. **Oversimplification:** Ignoring alternatives such as, *The best things in life are free.*

3. **Begging the Question:** Assuming as proven something that really needs proving such as, *This is another example of the boss getting all the credit.* This statement assumes that the boss never deserves the credit.

4. **Ignoring the Question:** Dealing with an issue different than the question being considered such as, *The price of living is going up, it's probably because of all the immigration.*

5. **Non Sequitur:** Making a conclusion that does not follow logically such as, *He's popular, he should be president.*

6. **Post Hoc, Ergo Propter Hoc:** Assuming that if an event occurred after another, that the first event caused the second, *Sunshine breeds black flies, because when the sun shines they come out.*

Working cooperatively with a partner, name and explain the fallacy in each of the following:

1. Either Ralph worked hard for his money, or else he was just lucky.

2. A student learns only what he or she wants to learn.

3. Free all political prisoners.

4. Ralph is rich. He must be dishonest.

5. He's sincere, he must be right.

6. He stayed up late and then won the race! Staying up late must make you run faster.

Chapter Nine: Summing Up

The Necessity For Controversy

When controversy is suppressed and concurrence seeking is emphasized, several defects in making decisions will appear. When NSAA, for example, decided to launch the space shuttle Challenger, engineers at the Morton Thiokol Company (which makes the shuttle's rocket boosters) and at Rockwell International (which manufactures the orbiter) had opposed the launch because of dangers posed by the subfreezing temperatures. The Thiokol engineers feared that the cold would make the rubber seals at the joints between the rocket's four main segments too brittle to contain the rocket's superhot gases. Several months before the doomed mission, the company's top expert had warned in a memo that it was a "*jump ball*" as to whether the seal would hold, and that if it failed "*the result would be a catastrophe of the highest order*" (Magnuson, 1986). In a group discussion the night before the launch, the engineers argued for a delay with their uncertain managers and the NASA officials who wanted to launch on schedule. Since the engineers could not **prove** there was danger, they were silenced (illusion of invulnerability). Conformity pressures were aimed at the engineers, such as when one of the NASA officials complained, "*My God, Thiokol, when do you want me to launch, next April?*" The NASA managers made a coalition with the Thiokol managers to shut the engineers out of the decision making (illusion of unanimity). Finally, to mindguard, the top NASA executive who made the final decision to launch was never told about the engineers' concerns, nor about the reservations of the Rockwell officials. Protected from the disagreeable information, he confidently gave the go-ahead to launch the Challenger on its tragic flight.

How could such faulty decision making take place. The answer is, because of the lack of controversy. NASA officials never gave the alternative of delaying the launch a fair and complete hearing. Disagreement was stifled rather than utilized. Often in group discussions if a margin of support for one alternative develops, then better ideas have little chance of being accepted. In mob lynching, for example, misgivings, if not immediately expressed, were drowned out. Drawing on biased information is evident in some group polarization experiments; often the arguments that surfaced in group discussion tended to be more one sided than those volunteered by individuals privately. Group discussions can exacerbate tendencies toward overconfidence, thereby heightening an illusion of judgmental accuracy (Dunning & Ross, 1988). Minority opinions can be suppressed. When initially only one member of a six-member group knew the correct answer, in almost 75 percent of the time the single member failed to convince the others because they were not given a fair and complete hearing (Laughlin, 1980; Laughlin & Adamopoulos, 1980). Group decision making often goes wrong because alternatives are not considered carefully, minority opinions are silenced, and disagreement among members' conclusions is suppressed.

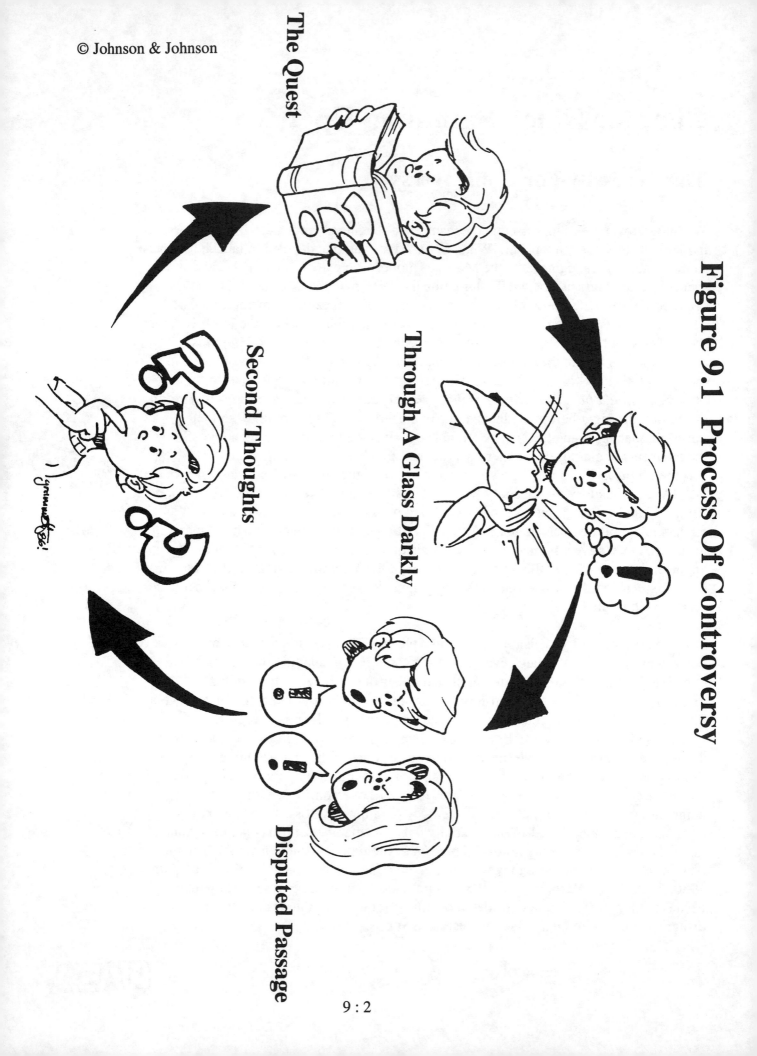

© Johnson & Johnson

The Quest

Second Thoughts

Through A Glass Darkly

Disputed Passage

Figure 9.1 Process Of Controversy

9 : 2

What is true in decision making situations is also true for learning situations. Stifling disagreement, seeking support for only one alternative view, drawing on biased information, suppressing information to make arguments one sided, creating an illusion of judgmental accuracy, becoming overconfidence, not considering alternative viewpoints, silencing minority opinions, and suppressing disagreement, all destroy the discovery of knowledge and "truth." Students have to learn how to be contributing members to a learning community in order to achieve the goals of the school and to prepare themselves for most careers where group decision making is an everyday occurrence. For classes and schools to be learning communities, four steps must be taken.

Step One: Create A Cooperative Context

The first factor in creating a learning community is creating positive interdependence among all members of the class or school. There are two possible contexts for conflict: cooperative and competitive (in individualistic situations individuals do not interact and, therefore, no conflict occurs). In a **competitive context** a valued commodity (such as grades) is scarce and individuals work against each other to win. Each person tries to defeat others. Within such a context individuals do not share information and are as likely to mislead as to clarify. Competitors are likely to misperceive the other's intentions and distort rival's actions. Competitors tend to be suspicious of and hostile toward each other. They tend to deny the legitimacy of the rival's goals and consider only their own interests. In a competitive context you go for the win and then walk away.

In a **cooperative context** individuals work together to achieve shared goals. The more honestly they communicate with each other, the more accurately they perceive each other's actions, the more they trust each other, and the more committed they are to each other's interests, the better able they are to achieve their mutual goals. In a cooperation context you solve the problem so that the joint effort to achieve mutual goals can continue.

The easiest way to create such a cooperative context and a learning community is to use cooperative learning procedures the majority of the day (Johnson, Johnson, & Holubec, 1993). Any lesson with any age student in any subject area may be taught cooperatively (Johnson, Johnson, & Holubec, 1993). In order to be cooperative, a lesson must include positive interdependence, face-to-face interaction among students, individual accountability, the use of collaborative skills, and the processing of how well the learning groups functioned. When done correctly, cooperative learning tends to promote higher achievement, greater motivation, more positive relationships among students, more positive attitudes toward the subject area and the teacher, greater self-esteem and psychological health, greater social skills, and many other important instructional outcomes. From making learning a cooperative effort, faculty may establish the mutual goal of searching for truth and knowledge and build commitment to achieving it. Increasing knowledge and understanding is achieved through cooperative interaction, not isolated thought. Truth and knowledge are consensual, based on intersubjectivity where different individuals reach the same conclusions and make the same inferences after considering theory and facts.

A detailed program on how to implement cooperative learning may be found in **Cooperation in the Classroom** (Johnson, Johnson, & Holubec, 1993) and **Advanced Cooperative Learning** (Johnson, Johnson, & Holubec, 1992).

Step Two: Create Intellectual Conflict

It's best that we should not all think alike. It's difference of opinion that makes horse races.

Mark Twain

The second step is to make intellectual conflict a way of life. Faculty need to engage students in intellectual conflicts within which they have to prepare intellectual positions, present them, advocate them, criticize opposing intellectual positions, view the issue from a variety of perspectives, and synthesize the various positions into one position.

The process through which intellectual conflict works is posited to be as follows (Johnson & Johnson, 1979, 1989). **First**, when students are presented with a issue or problem, they have an initial conclusion based on categorizing and organizing their current information and experiences and their specific perspective. **Second**, when asked to present their conclusion and its rationale to others, they engage in cognitive rehearsal, conceptually reorganize the rationale for their position as they present it, deepen their understanding of their position, and find themselves using higher-level reasoning strategies. **Third**, classmates present opposing positions (based on their information, experiences, and perspectives). This intellectual "disputed passage" causes students to become uncertain as to the correctness of their views. A state of conceptual conflict or disequilibrium is aroused. **Fourth**, the more uncertain students become, the more motivated they are to search actively for more information, new experiences, a more adequate perspective. Berlyne calls this active search epistemic curiosity. Like Macbeth (who said, "Stay, you imperfect speakers, tell me more."), students want more information. In their search, divergent attention and thought are stimulated and a higher-level reasoning process is sought in hopes of resolving their uncertainty. **Fifth**, students resolve their uncertainty by accommodating the perspective and reasoning of others and developing a new, reconceptualized, and reorganized conclusion. As Andre Gide said, "One completely overcomes only what one assimilates." Novel solutions and decisions are detected that are, on balance, qualitatively better. **Finally**, the process can then be repeated to promote even greater learning and understanding. There are hundreds of studies that valid this posited process (Johnson & Johnson, 1989).

Without intellectual conflict, a learning community in which faculty and students seek truth and knowledge cannot be achieved.

9 : 4

Step Three: Use Of Congruent Epistemology And Pedagogy

The third step is to make the epistemology and pedagogy used congruent with the need for joint action toward mutual goals and the continued presence of intellectual conflict. The epistemology resulting from (a) a competitive context in which students are ranked from highest to lowest performer and (b) making students passive recipients of lectures and reading mitigates against the formation of a learning community. Developing a learning community requires an epistemology based on the predominant use of cooperative learning and academic controversies. Since cooperative learning increases achievement, committed and caring relationships, increased social competencies, and a number of other important instructional outcomes (Johnson & Johnson, 1989), there will be little objection to making it the dominant mode of learning.

In addition to cooperative learning, faculty use academic controversies to create the intellectual conflict and internal disequilibrium needed to increase student critical thinking and use of higher-level reasoning strategies. **Controversy** exists when one student's ideas, information, conclusions, theories, and opinions are incompatible with those of another, and the two seek to reach an agreement. Within well structured controversies, students make an initial judgment, present their conclusions to other group members, are challenged with opposing views, become uncertain about the correctness of their views, actively search for new information and understanding, incorporate others' perspectives and reasoning into their thinking, and reach a new set of conclusions. The result is reasoned judgment.. Finding consenual truth requires mutual commitment to do so and intellectual disagreement and challenge. The combination of cooperative learning and academic controversies makes the epistemology and pedagogy congruent with faculty and students working together to accomplish mutual goals and engaging in continual intellectual conflict. These two instructional procedures thereby promote the creation of a true learning community.

Step Four: Establish A Peer Mediation Program

A soft answer turneth away wrath.

Bible

The fourth step is to establish a peer mediation program (see Johnson & Johnson, 1991). In a learning community, intellectual conflict is not the only type of conflict that arise. A **conflict of interests** exists when the actions of one person attempting to maximize his or her wants and benefits prevents, blocks, or interferes with another person maximizing his or her wants and benefits. When two students both want the same library book or want to use the computer at the same time, a conflict of interests exists. Conflicts among interests deal more with wants, needs, values, and goals than with differences in information and conclusions. Maintaining a learning community requires members to manage their conflicts of interests constructively. Doing so involves training students how to (a) negotiate constructive resolutions to their conflicts-of-interests (b) mediate the conflicts-of-interests occurring among fellow students. When conflicts among interests occur, settlements must be negotiated. Students, therefore, have to be taught the procedures and skills of negotiating. When students are unable to negotiate an acceptable agreement, they will turn to a mediator for help. **Mediation** exists when a neutral third person—a mediator—intervenes to help resolve a conflict between two or more people in a way that is acceptable to them. A mediator listens carefully to both sides and helps the disputants move effectively through each step of the negotiation sequence in order to reach an agreement that both believe is fair, just, and workable. Many schools have implemented peer mediation programs. The procedures for doing so are described in Johnson and Johnson (1991). Doing so provides the framework for ensuring that good relationships are maintained among community members.

Summary

Without these four factors (uniting goal to which faculty and students are committed, intellectual conflict as a way of life, an epistemology and pedagogy congruent with the first two, and a peer mediation program where all students are taught how to negotiate and mediate) schools and colleges cannot be learning communities. The key step, however, is teaching students how to engage in constructive intellectual conflicts by using academic controversies. In doing so, however, faculty need to understand:

1. The lure of suppressing intellectual conflict.

2. What is and is not an academic controversy.

3. How to respond when unanticipated controversies arise in the classroom.

4. The importance of academic controversy for teaching students how to be contributing citizens in a democracy.

The Lure Of Suppressing Intellectual Disagreement

Educators seem drawn to suppressing intellectual conflict within the classroom. Students are told not to talk to each other. All communication is to be directed at the teacher in response to direct questions. Students generally are expected not to intellectually challenge the teacher or each other. Much of the traditional teaching method of (a) lecture, (b) whole-class-discussion, and (c) individual worksheets eliminates most possibilities for intellectual disagreement and academic controversy. Teachers are generally anxious about the possibility of conflict being poorly managed within the classroom. Teachers generally have received no training in the procedures to use conflict for academic reasons. The diversity of students within most classrooms results in students have markedly different ideas about how intellectual conflicts should be managed. Teachers generally do not teach their students the procedure and skills students need to engage in constructive arguments. Conflicts, moreover, are often complex and take time to resolve. For these and many other reasons, academic conflicts are suppressed and avoided within most classrooms.

What Academic Controversy Is Not

There is often misunderstandings about conducting an academic controversy and dealing with controversial issues and controversial subject matter in the classroom. A **controversial issue** is an issue for which society has not found consensus, and is considered so significant that each proposed way of dealing with the issue has ardent supporters and adamant opponents. Controversial issues, by nature, arouse protest from some individual or group, since any position taken will be opposed by those who favor another position. The protest may result from a feeling that a cherished belief, an economic interest or a basic principle is threatened. Academic controversy is aimed at learning, not at resolving political issues within a community.

Second, in many places there are parents who are concerned about certain curriculum materials and topics for study. **Controversial subject matter** varies from school to school and community to community. Any issue or topic has the potential to become controversial at some time or place. Academic controversy is a procedure for learning, not specific subject matter, curriculum materials, or topics.

Academic controversies create interest in subject matter and motivate students to investigate issues and points-of-view they would not ordinarily be interested in. Controversial issues and subject matter are just the opposite. They involve issues that students may be so emotionally involved in and feel so strongly about that a rational discussion is difficult. When unplanned and/or highly emotionally charged issues arise in a class, however, faculty need a procedure and plan for dealing with them.

Unplanned Controversies

Unplanned controversies are often the result of information contributed in class that may not follow the content or direct line of learning prepared by the teacher. When unplanned controversies arise the teacher may wish to:

1. Give positive support to the student who raises the issue, unless it is distracting or irrelevant to the class.

2. The student should be given an opportunity to define his/her position and identify the source of his/her

information. All the rules of evidence and reasoned judgment apply.

3. If the topic clearly reflects a community sensitivity, teachers should contact their department head or appropriate administrator to explain in advance their plans to discuss it. The feelings and beliefs of the people in the community should be considered as the topic is discussed.

4. The librarian or media specialist should be told about the topic to be discussed so he/she can locate and make available useful references.

5. The academic controversy procedure should be used to structure and conduct the discussion.

6. The skills of focusing on the issue and not attacking or criticizing the person who raised the idea should be emphasized.

7. When the discussion is complete, the teacher should relate the importance of the topic and its discussion to the original purpose of the class so the students can see the significance of the topic to the course material.

Learning How To Be A Citizen In A Democracy

The word "democracy" comes from the Greek word **demokratia**, which is a combination of **demos** (the Greek word for people) and **kratos** (the Greek word for "rule"). One of the most impressive democracies the world has ever seen existed in the city of Athens in Ancient Greece. At its height in the 5th century B. C., Athens had an assembly of all citizens that met 10 times a year for an open exchange of ideas and opinions. Between such meetings, a council of 500 citizens elected annually did most of the important government work. The citizens of Athens believed that persuasion was preferable to warfare. At the beginning of Homer's **Iliad**, for example, Nestor stops a fight between Agamemnon and Achilleus and begins mediation by reminding them that **to be persuaded is better than fighting**.

One admirer of Athenian democracy was Thomas Jefferson. Jefferson believed that free and open discussion should serve as the basis of influence within society, not the social rank within which a person was born. Jefferson was fond of noting that *the first kings of Greece were elected by the free consent of the people*. Jefferson was also influenced by one of his professors at William and Mary School, Dr. William Small of Scotland. Small advocated a new method of learning in which students questioned and discussed, examining all sides of a topic, with scant regard for the pronouncements of established authorities. A few years before his death, Thomas Jefferson described his experiences as a student at the School of William and Mary in a letter to Dr. Thomas Cooper (1818): *I was bold in the pursuit of knowledge, never fearing to follow the truth and reason to whatever results they led, and bearding every authority which stood in the way.*

Based on the beliefs of Thomas Jefferson and his fellow revolutionaries, American democracy was founded on the premise that "truth" will result from free and open discussion in which opposing points of view are advocated and vigorously argued. In America we encourage rather than suppress the expression of opposing views because we have faith that truth will arise from the uninhibited clash of opposing views. Before a decision is made, every citizen is given the opportunity to advocate for his or her ideas. Once a decision is made, the minority is expected to go along willingly with the majority because they know they have been given a fair and complete hearing. To be a citizen in our democracy, individuals need to master the process of advocating one's views, challenging opposing positions, making a decision, and committing oneself to implement the decision made (regardless of whether one initially favored the alternative adopted or not).

Looking Forward

Thomas Jefferson based his faith in the future on the power of constructive conflict. There are numerous theorists who have advocated the use of intellectual conflict in instructional situations. There has been a reluctance to do so, perhaps due to a cultural fear of conflict, lack of procedures, and cultural and pedagogical norms discouraging the use of conflict. Academic controversy provides a clear procedure for faculty to use in promoting intellectual conflicts. There is strong research support indicating that academic controversy results in many positive benefits for students, including higher achievement, more positive relationships with classmates, and increased self-esteem. There is a clear theory as to the process by which controversy works that has been validated by numerous research studies. The teacher's role in conducting an academic controversy involves making a number of preinstructional decisions, explain the task and the controversy procedure, monitor the effectiveness of the controversy procedure, and evaluate students' achievement.

1. **Research And Prepare A Position:** Each pair takes their assigned position, gather evidence to support it, organize the evidence into a logical structure that provides a rationale for the position, plan how to advocate it forcefully and persuasively, and seek as complete an intellectual understanding of the issue as current knowledge allows. A persuasive argument consists of a thesis statement, a rationale, and a conclusion. The rationale consists of the evidence arranged in a sequence involving an outline, a hierarchy, a causal network, or a web network. Once the evidence is organized, both inductive and deductive logic is used to derive the conclusion.

2. **Present And Advocate Their Position:** Members of each pair make their presentation to members of the opposing pair. Students are to be as persuasive and convincing as possible. Members of the opposing pair are encouraged to take notes, listen carefully to learn the information being presented, and clarify anything they do not understand.

3. **Refute Opposing Position And Rebut Attacks On Their Own**: Students argue forcefully and persuasively for their position, presenting as many facts as they can to support their point of view. The group members analyze and critically evaluate the information and inductive and deductive reasoning of the opposing pair. They refute the arguments of the opposing pair and rebut attacks on their position. They discuss the issue following a set of rules to help them criticize ideas without criticizing people, differentiate the two positions, and assess the degree of evidence and logic supporting each position.

4. **Reverse Perspectives:** The pairs reverse perspectives and present each other's positions. In arguing for the opposing position, students are forceful and persuasive. They strive to see the issue from both perspectives simultaneously.

5. **Synthesize And Integrate The Best Evidence And Reasoning Into A Joint Position:** The four members of the group drop all advocacy and synthesize and integrate what they know into factual and judgmental conclusions that are summarized into a joint position to which all sides can agree. Synthesizing is a creative process that involves seeing new patterns in a body of evidence, viewing the issue from a variety of perspectives, and creating a new position that subsumes the previous ones.

Disagreeing with and criticizing another person's conclusions, however, will not always result in constructive controversy. It is only under certain conditions that intellectual attack results in a fun, spirited, and enlightening discussion. Through our research we have identified five of the conditions. Within a cooperative context controversy tends to promote open-minded listening to the opposing position, while within a competitive context controversy tends to promote a closed-minded orientation in which individuals are unwilling to make concessions to the opponent's viewpoint and refuse to incorporate any of the opponent's viewpoint into their own position. The more heterogeneous the students, the more frequently controversy occurs and the more informative it can be. Heterogeneity among individuals leads to potential controversy, and to more diverse interaction patterns and resources for achievement and problem-solving. The amount of relevant information distributed among students influences the constructiveness of the controversy. The more information individuals have about an issue, the more successful their problem solving. The more socially skilled students are, the better the controversy goes. Students especially need the ability to disagree with each other without creating defensiveness. Finally, the more students are able to engage in rational argument, the more constructive the controversy. Rational argumentation includes generating ideas, collecting and organizing relevant information, using inductive and deductive logic, and making tentative conclusions based on current understanding.

It is vital for citizens to seek reasoned judgment on the complex problems facing our society. Especially important is educating individuals to solve problems for which different points of view can plausibly be developed. To do so individuals must enter empathetically into the arguments of both sides of the issue and ensure that the strongest possible case is made for each side, and arrive at a synthesis based on rational thought. The skills required to implement the controversy procedure are intellectual skills that all school students are well advised to develop sooner or later. And engaging in a controversy can be fun, enjoyable, and exciting. Samuel Johnson once stated, *"I dogmatize and am contradicted, and in this conflict of opinions and sentiments I find delight."*

Now that you have reached the end of this book you are at a new beginning. Years of experience in using academic controversy are needed to gain real expertise in managing intellectual conflict constructively. The more students engage in the controversy process, the more they will learn, the more they will like each other, and the healthier they will be psychologically. It is through conflict that students grow, develop, learn, progress, and achieve. In the end you will find that academic controversies enrich rather than disrupt classroom life.

© Johnson & Johnson

⟆ CONTROVERSY CONTRACT ⟆

Major Learnings	Implementation Plans

Date _____ Date of Progress Report Meeting _____

Participant's Signature _____

Signatures of Other Group Members _____ _____

_____ _____ _____

The Timber Wolf

DAVID and ROGER JOHNSON

Minneapolis,
MN

Subject Area: Science, Social Studies

Grade Level: Intermediate, Secondary

Lesson Summary: Pairs of students prepare positions either for preserving the wolf as a protected species or for hunting and trapping wolves to keep their numbers limited. In groups of four the pairs prepare and present their positions, advocate their point of view while criticizing the opposing position, reverse perspectives, and then drop all advocacy to create a synthesis that all members agree to, and finally write a paper delineating and supporting their conclusion.

Instructional Objectives: Students will learn about the wolf, preservation of a species, the ecology of woodlands, and the relationships between predator and prey. In addition, they will learn the procedures involved in controversy and develop skills in organizing and conceptualizing evidence to support a position, thinking critically about other positions, seeing an issue from a variety of perspectives, and synthesizing diverse information and opinions.

Materials:

ITEM	NUMBER NEEDED
Situation Sheet	One per group
Procedure and Rules Sheets (See Penicillin Lesson)	One per group
Preserve the Wolf Briefing Sheet	One per group
Observation Sheet	One per group
Bibliography	One per group

Time Required: Three to five one-hour class periods

≈ Decisions ≈

Group Size: Four

Assignment to Groups: Maximize the heterogeneity within each group. Pair high and low readers together. If possible, pair males and females, minority and white, and handicapped and nonhandicapped students.

Roles: Assign the roles of:

- **Perspective Taker:** Restates the evidence and information supporting the opposing position.
- **Checker:** Ensures that both members of the pair can explain the assigned position and its supporting evidence and information.

≋ The Lesson ≋

Instructional Task:

This lesson presents the two major views about the timber wolf. Your task will be to gather as much information as possible about both sides of the issue, argue both points of view in order to examine them carefully, reach consensus as to whether the wolf should be preserved or managed, and present a reasoned, factual, and persuasive rationale as to why the decision is correct.

The procedure is as follows: You will be working in groups of four. During the first class period, your group of four will subdivide into pairs. One pair will be for preservation, the other for management of the wolf. You will be given readings and information to support your pair's position. You will have time to read and discuss your material with your partner and plan how best to advocate your assigned position so that (a) you learn the information and perspective within the articles and technical reports, (b) the opposing team is convinced of the soundness of your team's position, and (c) the members of the other pair learn the material contained within your readings.

During the second class period, both pairs will present their positions, and then engage in a general discussion in which they advocate their position, rebut the opposing position, and seek to persuade the opposing pair to adopt their position and reasoning. You will need to take notes and clarify anything you don't fully understand when the opposing team presents and advocates its position.

On the third day, the pairs will reverse positions and argue for the opposing side. Then you will drop your positions and, with the information and arguments you've accumulated, you will reach a consensus about the issue and prepare a group report detailing your group's decision and supporting it with information and rationale.

Positive Interdependence:

There are two group goals. First, the group is to produce a report detailing what should be done with the wolf. Second, all group members have to pass a test on the wolf. If all members get 80 percent correct on the test, each member will receive 10 bonus points.

Controversy Procedure:

See procedure sheet.

Individual Accountability:

Each group member will be given a test on the wolf to determine how much he or she learned. One student will be randomly selected from the group to present the final group report to the entire class.

Criteria for Success:

The group report will be evaluated on the basis of appropriate use of inductive and deductive reasoning to organize evidence into a coherent and reasoned conclusion that synthesizes the best from each perspective.

Expected Behaviors:

See rules sheet.

 Monitoring and Processing

Monitoring: While the students are working, watch to see how well they are doing the task. Energize any lagging pairs and help keep the class aware of the time limits. Use the observation sheet to observe formally the groups once each class period, so the groups will have it to use when they process the group interactions.

Intervening: If any student does not seem involved, ask him or her to tell you the position being advocated. If students are not following the rules, point this out and ask them to adhere to the rules. Praise good examples of criticizing ideas without criticizing the person and other controversy skills.

Processing: Either daily or at the end of the unit, give the groups the observation sheets you filled out on them and ask them to write down at least two comments about what went well in their group and one comment on what the group could do better next time. These are to be handed in with the report and kept on file. Then conduct a class discussion on what helped the groups fulfill their task effectively.

9:17

❧ The Wolf Situation ❧

Minnesota contains the last large stand of wolves in the continental United States. There are two major views toward the wolf. One is that wolves are a national treasure and should be a protected species and left to roam freely through Northern Minnesota. The other is that wolves are (a) a varmint that threatens domestic livestock and (b) a renewable resource to be managed for sport and revenue. Wolves should, therefore, be hunted and trapped to keep their numbers small and then confined to small areas that do not contain livestock and farms.

In 1973 the eastern timber wolf was classified as endangered in all of the lower 48 states, protecting it from all hunting and trapping. Minnesota boasts the only viable population of wolves at a stable 1,200 animals. Small populations also exist in Wisconsin (20 - 25) and on Isle Royal, Michigan (23). In 1978 ranchers and sportsmen were successful in persuading government officials to reclassify the wolf as "threatened" in Minnesota, which allowed government killing of wolves suspected of livestock predation. An effective predator control program in northern Minnesota has been in effect since that time.

You are a committee in the Minnesota Department of Natural Resources (DNR) who have been asked to make a recommendation as to the future classification of the gray wolf. The U.S. Fish and Wildlife Service (FWS) has been asked to approve a sport season for hunting wolves in Minnesota and to give the State of Minnesota full control over the wolf. In the past it has denied such requests on the basis that the wolf is protected under the Endangered Species Act. It has asked, however, for a full report and a recommendation from your committee. Two of you are from ecological groups that are deeply concerned with preserving the wolf and, therefore, wish the wolf to be reclassified as an "endangered species." Two of you are from farmer and rancher organizations who wish the control of the wolf to be given to the State of Minnesota so that wolves may be hunted and trapped. As a group you must make a plan for the future of the wolf that all four members can agree to. Share your position and its rationale with the group. Stick to your guns unless logically persuaded otherwise. At the same time, help your group achieve consensus on the issue.

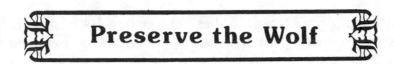

Preserve the Wolf

Your position is to preserve the wolf. You believe that it is time to dispel the myth of "the big bad wolf" and recognize that the wolf has a valuable role to play in the ecosystem and that we humans can adapt a little and compromise a little to share our space with this magnificent animal.

Whether or not you agree with this position, argue for it as strongly as you can. Take the preservation viewpoint honestly, using arguments that make sense and are rational. Be creative and invent new supporting arguments. Seek out information, ask members of other groups who may know. Remember to learn the rationale for both your position and the "manage" position. Challenge the "manage" position. Think of loopholes in the evidence and logic. Demand facts and information to back up their arguments.

You are members of a group at the University of Minnesota in Duluth. Your group works to promote preservation of the wolf by conducting awareness campaigns, lobbying at the state capitol, and by conducting expeditions into the wilderness to rack and observe wolves. You are adamantly opposed to the management efforts of the State Department of Natural Resources and fear the extinction of the wolf and its natural habitat.

1. The gray wolf represents a national treasure that is the last remnants of true wilderness left in the United States. Wolves have disappeared from 99 percent of their original range. Minnesota is one of the last states in America where wolves live. The wolf should be protected in this last 1 percent of their original habitat.

2. In the Endangered Species Act Congress mandated that the regulated killing of a member of a threatened species is prohibited except in the "extraordinary case where population pressures within a given ecosystem cannot otherwise be relieved." This is clearly not the case with Minnesota's wolf population which remains well within its biological carrying capacity.

3. Wolf depredation on Minnesota livestock is minor. Only 0.1 percent of livestock within wolf range and 0.3 percent of all Northern Minnesota farms have been affected. Wolves often eat some farm animals, but because farmers fail to remove the carcasses of dead animals. Farmers are only serving to entice the wolves.

4. According to government studies published in 1982, many cases of livestock depredation by wolves can be attributed to poor animal husbandry practices. Cattle are allowed to roam in forested areas or in remote open pastures where wolf encounters are more likely. Dead livestock are dumped in or near pastures, attracting wolves and giving them a taste for livestock. Proper disposal methods and better pasturing techniques would prevent many of the depredation problems.

5. Any farmer or rancher who suffers losses, verified as wolf kills, receives compensation through the Minnesota livestock compensation program. Domestic livestock does not need protection because owners will not lose financially from any killing of livestock by wolves.

6. A successful federal predator control program, under the direction of Dr. L. David Mech and Dr. Steven Fritts, has been operative since 1978. Under this program government trappers took 29 wolves in 1981 and 20 wolves in 1982. It is estimated that only 30 to 35 Minnesota wolves prey on livestock. The focus on the program has been to locate and trap only those wolves causing damage.

7. If control of the wolf is given over to the State of Minnesota, any and all wolves within a one-half mile radius of farms reported to have had depredation problems can be trapped. There will be no criteria for selecting trappers or for verifying wolf kills. No limit to the length of time trapping may be carried out will be given. The result will be indiscriminate killing of wolves.

8. Up to 400 wolves are killed illegally in Minnesota each year. A sport trapping season will officially sanction the public killing of wolves and an increase in illegal kills will occur.

9. Years of concerted effort on the part of environmental groups and millions of concerned citizens went into the creation of the Endangered Species Act. The classification needs to be changed back immediately or else all of this money and effort was wasted.

10. There has been a drop in the deer population in Minnesota due to having seven severe winters in a row.

11. There is a natural balance between the wolf and the deer. By killing the weak and sick deer, more food is left for the healthy deer. If humans kill wolves, they upset this natural balance.

 **Manage the Wolf**

Your position is that control over the gray wolf should be turned over to the State of Minnesota and a sport hunting and trapping season established. You believe that it is time to face the reality that wolves are dangerous animals running rampant in northern Minnesota and are threatening the economic survival of many farmers. Wolves must be trapped and shot to keep their population within reasonable limits.

Whether or not you agree with this position, argue for it as strongly as you can. Take the management viewpoint honestly, using arguments that make sense and are rational. Be creative and invent new supporting arguments. Seek out information, ask members of other groups who may know. Remember to learn the rationale for both your position and the "preserve" position. Challenge the "manage" position. Think of loopholes in the evidence and logic. Demand facts and information to back up their arguments.

You represent farmers and ranchers in northern Minnesota. They believe that to let the wolves roam free is nothing but a dream of some environmentalists who are not faced with the reality of the situation. To observe wolves is one thing, but to live with the threats they pose is quite another.

1. The gray wolf is a varmint that threatens domestic livestock and a renewable resource to be managed for sport and revenue.

2. A sport trapping season will reduce public antagonism toward wolves and, therefore, reduce the number of illegal kills.

3. The Minnesota Department of Natural Resources (DNR) has maintained for a long time that the Minnesota population of wolves is neither endangered nor threatened. Further, the DNR has maintained that the wolf must be actively managed to insure its survival.

4. The DNR has a history of fighting for the wolf. In 1965 the DNR attempted to have the Minnesota state legislature eliminate the antiquated bounty system on wolves. In the early 1970's, the DNR attempted to have the legislature elevate the timber wolf from an unprotected species to that of a game animal. Their recommendations, therefore, should be taken seriously.

5. Controlled hunting will protect the wolf and ensure its survival by lessening some of the rage against wolves by people who would exterminate this animal if given the opportunity. Unless a hunting season is established, illegal killing will grow.

6. A balance must be established between people and a great predator. Compromise and balance is the approach we should take. In some areas we can maintain a viable wolf population where wolves do not compete directly with humans. In other areas, the wolf must be managed and controlled if we are to avert wholesale destruction of the animal.

7. The **Federal Register** (vol. 48, no. 155, page 36256) of August 10, 1983, has this sentence included as a part of its statement relating to wolf predation on livestock--sheep, poultry, and cattle: "In areas where recurrent depredation appears, the Service is of the view that it would be consistent with sound conservation of the wolf to authorize a limited public trapping season for wolves, provided the wolf population density in the affected zones not fall below the level recommended by the Wolf Recovery Team."

8. The DNR plan providing a mechanism to control wolf encroachment into areas of human habitation is essential if illegal killing is to be eliminated. If the wolf is to remain a part of our priceless wildlife heritage we believe the DNR plan must be supported.

9. Farmers and ranchers believe that wolves are reproducing rapidly, the number of deer (their natural prey) is going down, and, therefore, wolves have taken to eating farm animals, including pet dogs. In 1965 we had 700,000 deer in Minnesota. Now we have only 200,000.

Wolf Hunter's Association

Preserve Our Deer . . . . Shoot a Wolf

I am a resident of northern Minnesota and, let me tell you, the wolf is not threatened or endangered in Minnesota. Wolves are reproducing rapidly, and they are a nuisance! The number of wolves has been increasing ever since the Federal Government started protecting them. And as the number of wolves goes up, the number of deer goes down. Deer have gotten so scarce that the wolves have taken to eating farm animals. Wolves eat the farmers' cows and sheep, and even eat their pet dogs! I should be allowed to hunt and trap these varmints.

I have no use for the wolf. Particularly now that it's illegal to kill them. I used to earn money collecting the bounty paid by the state for killing wolves. But the state's not paying bounties anymore, and I'm out of a job. Hopefully I can get work in the mines.

I heard they were planning to open a new mine near my home, but I'm afraid the Federal government will stop the mine from opening. Some people in the government think the wilderness needs to be preserved. They say it is an important habitat for the wolf. These people think that opening a mine will destroy the wilderness and the wolves along with it.

I don't think they need to worry about the wolves surviving. There hasn't been a decrease in the number of wolves since 1900. In fact, the number of wolves is increasing, and wolves have extended their range.

Wolves never were endangered. It was just luck that the wolf got on the list of endangered animals. It was part of a treaty between the U.S. and Pan America. No one in the government has done anything since then to determine on a factual basis whether there is any reason to have the wolf listed as endangered. They should have asked the people in northern Minnesota if there's a shortage of wolves!

The people up here, we know this country. We know the wolf. But nobody listens. Those slick timber wolves are wiping out our deer for sure! You figure it out for yourself. In 1965 we had 700,000 deer in Minnesota. Sure, there were some bad winters. But they took away the bounty on wolves and now we have only 200,000 deer.

9:23

I've heard people say that wolves only kill old or sick deer. That just isn't true. I've seen it with my own eyes. One winter the deer were weak because there wasn't enough food to feed them all. I saw herds of deer huddling on the edge of a lake that ran between the territories of two different wolf packs. Wolves don't usually leave their territory. But the wolves came, fast as lightening! The deer couldn't run fast enough in the deep snow to get away, and the wolf pack had a feast! Ate every deer in sight.

The wolf is a pest. They're not even content with taking the deer. Why, they've gone right into Babbitt to kill dogs. Right up to the back porch. I hear they chewed up one pup, doghouse and all!

And you should have been out at Julian B.'s farm. Some say there are over five wolf packs out there. The wolves are taking over his farm. They go right into the barn. Ate half his cattle. Ever since the Federal Government made Julian stop trapping and shooting wolves his cattle have become "easy pickings" for the wolves.

It's something all right. They had some people out there from the U.S. Fish and Wildlife Service (F.W.S.) for awhile. They sent out trappers and some wolfman with a PhD named Dr. Mech to help Julian. They weren't there long. Julian threw them off his property. He didn't think they were much help and decided he's take care of the wolves himself. I'd like to help Julian. Let me loose on the wolves. It wouldn't be long before they'd disappear from Julian's farm.

I wish the Federal government would mind their own business. They should let the state government decide what should be done about the wolves here in Minnesota. The people from the state know the wolf's a nuisance. They'd pay me to kill wolves that are eating farmer's livestock.

It's not enough to take the wolf off the list of endangered animals. They should add the wolf to the big game hunting list and allow people to hunt and trap wolves all year round. They certainly don't need to set aside any wilderness area for the wolves. Wolves can survive almost anywhere. The government doesn't have any business threatening people with a $20,000 fine for filling wolves. Wolves aren't endangered, we are! There is no balance of nature. Nature does not care about balance. The only balance there will ever be is if man helps nature achieve it. Both the deer and the people in Minnesota need me to kill wolves. Help me get the wolf off the list of endangered animals.

9:24

Dr. I Am Ecology

As a scientist I have been studying the wolf for many years so I can help the government make the best decision about what to do with the wolf. This is not an easy task. The issue is not one where there is one right answer or one wrong answer. I have to think a lot about all the people whose lives are touched by the wolf, and also what is the best decision for the wolf. The wolf is a beautiful animal and needs to be protected. But it simply isn't reasonable to say: Don't kill wolves.

A lot of people think wolves kill people, but any attacks by healthy wolves on human beings is extremely rare. When it comes to the farmer's livestock in northern Minnesota, however, wolf attacks do happen. For the wolf, all livestock are easy to catch and this hurts the farmer. The farmers can't make money when the wolves eat their animals and that's why wolves can't be allowed to live in farming areas.

When humans and wolf were far apart, they did not get in each other's way. But now that people are taking more and more land, they are living closer to where the wolf lives. And the forests up north are getting too old to provide good food for the deer, so the deer are moving south where farmers live where there are good forests with the needed food. The wolves follow the deer, and that's where a lot of the problems begin. The wolf is a meat eater, and when the wolf is near where people farm, the wolf will eat the farmer's animals. Wolves and humans can't co-exist. But there's no reason why wolves can't be allowed to remain in the wilderness.

In the wilderness areas, wolves live mostly on deer. Deer have great speed and are very alert which means the wolves don't have a lot of success in catching deer. The wolf pack usually ends up with unfit deer: the young, old, crippled, sick, or otherwise inferior deer. By killing inferior deer, the wolf makes sure only the healthiest, strongest deer survive. Those deer that do survive have more food. These deer live longer, grow healthier, and produce a greater number of healthy babies.

Hunters think the wolves take too many deer. They are afraid that there won't be any deer left for them to hunt. Wolves are partly responsible for the decrease in deer, but there are other reasons that are more important. Winters are hard on deer in Minnesota, and we had seven severe winters in a row. Deer can stand cold weather but when you combine several hard winters with deep snow and malnutrition from lack of food, you have an animal who is very weak. In this condition, the deer can't protect themselves from the wolves.

9:25

Wolves have the advantage in deep, heavy snow. Also, when the snow is deep, deer frequently gather on the ice of lakes. Wolves can run faster than deer on ice. At times like this, the wolves not only eat healthy deer, but they eat more than they need to survive. But, I know of no scientist in the state that has evidence that wolves are really hurting deer hunting. Of greatest importance is the habitat problem. Without considerably more logging or fires to improve the food situation for the deer in northern Minnesota, the future of the deer is dim. Any continued decrease in the number of deer will result in fewer wolves. It is important to take care of the land for both the deer and the wolves.

I think there are a number of things that can be done. The best thing to do with the wolf is to make some areas just for the wolf and some areas where the trappers can trap the wolf. Where the wolf is taking the livestock the wolf should either be killed or moved to an area far from the farmer. We tried to do that on Julian B.'s farm where the wolf was bothering his animals, but he wouldn't let us help much, and threw us off his farm. We need the cooperation of the farmer if this plan is to be successful.

People need to realize that for the wolf's own good the wolf must be kept in the wilderness. So I think that in the wilderness areas like the B.W.C.A., the wolf should be considered endangered and fully protected. In this area no one could hunt or trap the wolf, and the wolf could live in its packs freely roaming the land.

There should be another area where the wolf is listed as threatened, which would allow the wolf to be hunted and trapped. This should help in those areas where wolf and man do not get along. There should be a hunting season in this area which would mean that the wolf isn't hunted all year long. If the wolf were hunted all year long it would decrease the possibility of them having enough babies to keep the pack healthy.

Some plan needs to be taken soon, and I think my plan of having different areas for the wolf would make sure that the wolf lives on, and also help in the areas where humans and wolf come into conflict. Then as scientists like myself keep studying more about the wolf and humans and the deer, we can change the plan to meet the needs of all animals and people involved. I hope our work will provide a better understanding of the wolf, and will help the government take actions that will protect the wolf in the last small area where wolves continue to live. It seems to me that this is the least we can do.

9:26

Julian B. Farmer

I am a dairy farmer in northern Minnesota, and I think something needs to be done to control the wolves. I know there must be a place for the wolf to live, but there must also be a place for our cattle. My family has farmed on this land successfully for years. But recently I almost went out of business because wolves were eating my cattle. My grandfather had trouble with wolves. But in his day you just shot a few wolves and the others learned not to come around. But now it is against the law to kill a wolf, and the wolves have learned they can eat my cattle without being harmed. They come right into the barn and eat our animals.

So far I've lost 28 cattle. I'm worried because soon the cows will be going out into the summer pasture alone. The new calves will be born at this time and they are easy pickings for the wolves.

The United States Fish and Wildlife Service (F.W.S.) knows there are five or more wolf packs in the area around my farm. They sent trappers and a scientist named Dr. Mech to help me. The trappers caught 61 wolves on my farm. These wolves were taken to Superior National Forest, but this is only 30 miles from my farm, and the wolves keep returning to eat my cattle.

It really upsets me to watch my livestock disappear. And the state trappers aren't very helpful. It's not their fault. By law they aren't allowed to catch a wolf unless I can prove the wolf ate one of my animals. I know the wolves did away with my cattle, but it isn't easy to prove. All I know is that the cows are gone and they sure didn't drown in Lake Superior!

I saw two wolves on the road yesterday. The logging around here has attracted the deer. The fresh cedar browse is ideal deer food. But while we are feeding the deer, we also are attracting the wolves. The wolves have broke me completely. I go down to the bank and ask for another loan, and they look at me and say: Well, now, Julian. How's the wolf situation out your way? You ever heard of a banker who wants to go on lending money to feed wolves?

I've lost about $10,000 worth of cattle in the last three years. I can't wait any longer for federal action. I've got a family to feed and I'm going to get rid of some wolves, one way or another. It's gotten so bad my children are afraid to go into the barn. One night we heard the dogs barking and went out to the barn. A wolf had eaten most of a full-grown cow. We were afraid that the wolf was still in the barn. I don't care what anyone says, I don't think it is safe for the children.

I just wish they'd allow me to shoot wolves that come onto my farm. I wouldn't have to kill many. As soon as the wolves catch on that they are being shot at they'll leave and stay away from my farm.

I think the best thing to do is allow the state to make the laws about what should be done with the wolf. The state wants to take the wolf off the list of endangered animals. They would have an annual hunting and trapping season when hunters could kill wolves for sport. And they would let me shoot wolves anytime they come onto my farm.

We farmers don't mind if wolves live in the wilderness, but the wolves are still considered an endangered animal when they get outside of the wilderness so we can't shoot them. And we farmers are not in the business of raising livestock to feed wolves. I don't want to see all of the wolves killed. I think we should help the wolf to survive in the wilderness. I just want to farm and raise cattle where I was born, and where my father farmed before that, and keep my animals safe from the wolves.

9:28

Ms. Sierra

As an active member of H.O.W.L. (Help Our Wolves Live) I am trying to make sure that the wolf is totally protected. Wolves need this protection because some people think wolves are a nuisance and kill them. Trappers also want to kill wolves so they can earn money selling their pelts to fur companies. It is important that the Federal government protect the wolf by listing wolves as an endangered animal. This will help save the wolf because the government forbids the filling of endangered animals.

I disagree with hunters who say that wolves are eating all the deer. I know there aren't as many deer now as there used to be, but it sure isn't because of the wolf. I read a study by the wolf scientist, Dr. Mech. He found out that the reason why there are fewer deer is because we had seven severe winters in a row. There wasn't enough food for the deer so they starved to death.

Dr. Mech said that the growth of the trees made it difficult for the deer to survive. Deer eat plants and low limbs of trees. The trees where the deer live have grown so big that the deer can't reach the limbs and get the food they need to eat. Many deer have died because of lack of food.

Wolves certainly aren't responsible for the decreasing number of deer. The truth is that the wolves help the deer be healthier. Wolves help the deer by killing old and sick deer that would die anyway. When the wolves take the sick and old deer, more food is left for the healthy deer. If the wolves didn't eat some of the deer, all of the deer would be weak from hunger. These weakened deer would die in a severe winter.

The wolf has a useful role in the balance of nature. Only a certain number of animals can survive on a given piece of land. If more animals are living in an area than the land can provide for, the number of natural enemies increase to kill off some of the animals. If natural enemies, like the wolf, are not around the area becomes overpopulated, and adult deer die from starvation. Nature provides a proper balance of wolves and deer. Humans upset this balance by killing wolves.

Wolves also need to be protected from the farmers. Farmers blame the wolf for killing their livestock, but more farm animals are killed in accidents than are eaten by wolves. Sure, some wolves have eaten a few of the farmer's animals, but wolves mostly live on deer and moose, not cattle.

Even when wolves attack farm animals there is no need for the farmers to kill the wolves. The Federal government is aware that farmers survive on the money they earn from their cattle. And they have agreed to pay farmers for each animal that is killed by a wolf. They've even hired trappers to catch wolves that come onto their farms. They take the wolves they catch up to the Superior National Forest and release them. There sure aren't any farm animals up in the forest that the wolves could harm!

And that farmer, Julian B., who is worried about the safety of his children because of all those wolves living near his farm; he really has nothing to be afraid of. Wolves don't hurt human beings. Even when you walk into their den, wolves are as gentle as my pet dog, Rover. No one in the United States has ever been harmed by a wolf, unless the wolf was sick with rabies.

The Federal government needs to protect the wolf. But the Department of Natural Resources (D.N.R.) wants the Federal government to allow the State to make the laws about the wolf and how it should be protected in Minnesota. I think giving control to the state would be a disaster! The State has never done anything to help the wolves. They used to have a bounty on the wolf and paid trappers $50 for each wolf they killed. Fortunately, the Federal government made them stop this when they changed the law. But the D.N.R. wants people to be allowed to hunt and trap wolves again. I think the D.N.R. is more concerned about making the hunters happy than in saving the wolf.

The wolf needs help. Wolves have disappeared from 99% of the original range, and Minnesota is one of the last states in America that has any. I'm proud that Minnesota has a wilderness area in which the wolves can survive. But some of the people in northern Minnesota want to develop this land. They want to be allowed to mine peat and copper in this area, destroying one of the last places where wolves can live. We need to preserve our wilderness because it is an important habitat for the wolf. Something needs to be done soon to make sure that the wolf stays on the endangered list, and to preserve our wilderness, or we may never see of hear a wolf again. H.O.W.L.

# THE WOLF SPEAKS

We are the wolf. We have many qualities that make us a superior animal. We keep the deer strong. Our body is finely tuned to meet our needs in the setting in which we live. The build of our body, our sharp sense of smell and hearing, our intelligence, the place we occupy within the social structure of our pack, and even the ways we communicate with each other, all help us survive.

We are hunters. We chase, attack, and kill deer and moose and any other animal that we need to eat to live. Our large chest and strong legs make it easy for us to run in deep snow. We can walk easily on logs, rocks, and other hard and uneven surfaces because our paws have a large, hard pad. We can run for 9 hours a day at 5 miles per hour and if we need to we can run up to speeds of 25 miles per hour while chasing the deer and moose.

To catch and eat our prey we have 42 teeth. Some of our teeth help us hold onto our prey while other teeth do the cutting and chewing. When we catch an animal, we eat all of it and leave nothing to waste. Each of us eats up to 20 pounds of meat in one sitting because we often have to go for two weeks at a time without eating. It is not easy to find and catch the food we need to live.

We have a very sharp sense of smell that is one hundred times more sensitive than that of humans. We can smell any animal within 300 yards of us and then, if we want to, we can try to catch it. We also have keen hearing. We can hear other wolves howling up to four miles away. This helps us reunite with each other after a long chase and keeps the pack together. We need the pack in order to live.

We hunt and live as part of a pack. Since the animals we chase and sometimes catch are much bigger than we, we have to have the help of the pack to catch and kill my food. We are a very structured team in which every member has his or her position or rank. Each wolf knows his or her place in the pack, and therefore knows how it should behave and act with others. The leader of the pack is called the alpha (al-fuh) wolf. He dominates all other members of the pack. He leads in the hunt, and controls and guides the activities of the members of the pack. There is never any question as to who should act first and who should follow. Some of us are called dominant because we are the first to act in most situations. Others of us are called subordinate, because we wait for others to lead or act. The clear ranking of all members of the pack helps us survive by keeping us highly organized and efficient. This is important because we need each other to live. We couldn't catch enough food to live if we did not hunt and work together.

Our success in working together comes from our ability to communicate with each other and our intelligence. We have many ways of communicating with each other and showing each other how we feel. We use our faces and our tails to show we are happy or angry. We communicate with each other by howling, barking, whimpering and growling. All of these different ways of communicating help us keep order in the pack. Keeping order helps us survive.

Can you see how interesting and valuable we are? We may not always catch our prey, like the moose or the deer, but with our excellent body construction, keen senses, high level of social organization and communication, and intelligence, we know we deserve to live and survive.

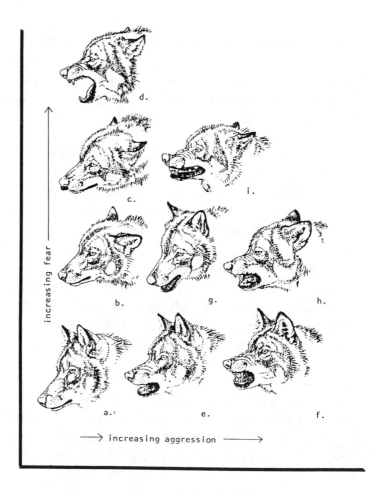

9:32

The Deer Speaks

We are the deer. We have many qualities that make us a superior animal. Our body is finely tuned to meet our needs in the setting in which we live. The build and coloring of our body, our sharp senses of smell, eyesight, and hearing, and our ability to communicate that danger approaches to other deer in the herd, help us survive by escaping our predators.

Our first defense is camouflage. When we are born we are spotted for the first four days of their lives. Since we do not move we blend in with the ground they are laying on. Because of this coloring, we are hidden from the wolf and other predators.

Our second defense is speed. We have long legs that help us run quickly and escape from predators who want to eat us. We can run for short periods of time at speeds up to 35 miles per hour. We can leap over objects as high as 8 feet off the ground while my predators have to run around the same object. Our hoofs give us a good grip on hard ground so we can run faster through the thick forests.

Our third defense is attack. Our strong hoofs and legs help us protect ourselves. We can bash in the skull of an animal with our hoofs when we are cornered. If we have a choice, however, we prefer to run.

Our best defense is sensing predators when they are far away and we can run away with little danger. Our sense of smell is highly developed to alert us to danger so we can escape in time. We can smell odors up to one third of a mile away. At night we go to the lower land areas because warm air sinks and we can smell the scents of danger. During the day we go up on hills and ridges because the warm air carries the scent of danger up to us so we can run away in time.

Our eyesight is amazing. We see the slightest movement immediately. Our eyes can focus on the object or animal that has moved. We instantly freeze and study whatever has attracted our attention. The freezing helps camouflage us so that the predator cannot tell that we are around. We will run for safety at moment so slight as even the blinking of a human eyelid.

Our ears are large and are as sensitive as a radar antenna. We constantly turn and twist our ears to scan and screen the air for any possible sound of danger. No sound is too slight to escape our attention. We also listen for the warning calls of the other animals in the forest for their warning calls and follow their advice.

9:33

We believe that there is safety in numbers. What one of us does not see or hear, another will. We have many ways to communicate danger to each other. Sometimes we snort. The snort sounds like a big sneeze. It clears our noses so we can smell the air better to pick up the scent of danger. It also warns the other deer that something strange is happening. Sometimes our snort startles our enemies into making a move so we can use our excellent eyesight to see where they are.

We have other ways of communicating to each other than danger may be near. We stamp our feet. The hairs on our backs rise just enough to catch the eyesight of the other deer. This tells them there is danger. Then when we bound away, the white hair on our tails stands up and our tails wag back and forth so our fawns can easily follow us through the dark forest.

We need only an area of about one square mile to live in. We get to know our land very well. We know where to hide from our predators.

Can you see how interesting and valuable we are? We camouflage ourselves, we run fast and jump high, we smell, hear, and see danger, we stay in herds because doing so provides more eyes, ears, and noses to sense danger, we tell each other when to run and hide, and we know where to hide because we live all our lives in a small area. We are beautiful animals that give many people pleasure just to see us running through the woods. Many people love to take our picture, paint us, and write stories about us. We are gentle and beautiful creatures who harm no one. We know we deserve to live and survive.

9:34

Wolf Bibliography

Primary Sources

American Zoologist. (1967). Ecology and behavior of the wolf. **7(2).**

Allen, D. L. (1979). **Wolves of Minong: Their vital role in a wild community.** Boston: Houghton Mifflin Co.

Hall, R. L., & Sharp, H. S. (1979). **Wolf and man: Evolution in parallel.** New York: Academic Press.

Harrington, F. H., & Mech, L. D. (1978). Howling at two Minnesota wolf pack summer homesites. **Canadian Journal of Zoology, 56,** 2024-2028.

Harrington, F. H., & Mech, L. D. (1979). Wolf howling and its role in territory maintenance. **Behavior, LXVII.**

Harrington, F. H., & Mech, L. D. (1982). An analysis of howling response parameters useful for wolf pack censusing. **Journal of Wildlife Management, 46(3).**

Harrington, F. H., & Paquet, P. C. (Eds.)(1982). **Wolves of the world: Perspectives of behavior, ecology and conservation.** New Jersey: Noyes Publications.

Lopez, B. H. (1978). **Of wolves and men.** New York: Charles Scribner's Sons.

Mech, L. D. (1970). **The wolf.** Garden City, NY: American Museum of Natural History, Natural History Press.

Peterson, R. O. (1978). **Wolf ecology and prey relationships on Isle Royale.** Washington, DC: U.S. Government Printing Office, National Park Service Scientific Monograph Series (No. 11).

Theberge, J. B. (April, 1971). Wolf music. **Natural History,** 37-42.

Young, S., & Goldman, E. A. (1964). **The wolves of North America, Vols. I and II.** New York: Dover Publishing Co.

Zimen, E. (1981). **The wolf: A species in danger.** New York: Delacorte Press.

Secondary Sources and Additional Readings on Wolves

Clarkson, E. (1975). **Wolf country: A wilderness pilgrimage.** New York: E.P. Dutton Co.

Crisler, L. (1958). **Arctic wild.** New York: Harper and Brothers Publishing.

Crisler, L. (1968). **Captive wild.** New York: Harper and Brothers Publishing.

Department of Lands and Forests. **Wolves and coyotes in Ontario.** Toronto, Ontario, Canada.

Fiennes, R. (1976). **The order of wolves.** Indianapolis: Bobbs Merrill.

Fox, M. (1980). **The soul of the wolf.** Boston: Little Brown and Co.

Mech, L. D. (October, 1977). Where can the wolf survive? **National Geographic Magazine, 152(4),** 518-537.

Murie, A. (1944). **The wolves of Mount McKinley.** Washington, DC: Fauna of National Parks, U.S. Series No. 5.

Pimlott, D. H., & Kolenosky, G. B. (1969). **The ecology of the timber wolf in Algonquin Provincial Park.** Toronto, Ontario, Canada: Department of Lands and Forest.

Rutter, R. J., & Pimlott, D. (1968). **The world of the wolf.** Philadelphia: Lippincott.

Theberge, J. B. **Wolves and wilderness.** Toronto, Ontario, Canada: Dent.

Canids

Bekoff, M. (Ed.) (1978). **Coyotes: Biology, behavior and management.** New York: Academic Press.

Ewer, R. (1973). **The carnivores.** Ithaca, New York: Cornell University Press.

Fox, M. W. (1970). The central nervous system. In A. C. Anderson (Ed.), **The beagle as an experimental dog.** Iowa State University Press.

Fox, M. W. (1971). **Behavior of wolves, dogs, and related canids.** New York: Harper and Row.

Fox, M. W. (1975). **The wild canids.** New York: Van Nostrand Reinhold Co.

Lorenz, K. (1953). **Man meets dog.** Baltimore: Penguin Book.

McLoughlin, J. C. (1983). **The canine clan.** New York: Viking Press.

Mery, F. (1968). **The life history and magic of the dog.** New York: Grosset and Dunlap.

Official American Kennel Club (1961). **The complete dog book.** Garden City, New York: Garden City Books.

Field Guides

Burt, W. H., & Grossenheider, R. (1964). **A field guide to mammals.** Boston: Houghton Mifflin Co.

Fritts, S. H., & Weaver, J. L. (1979). Comparison of coyote and wolf scat diameters. **Journal of Wildlife Management, 43(3).**

Hamilton, W. J., & Whitaker, J. O. (1979). **Mammals of Eastern United States.** Ithaca, NY: Comstock Publishing.

Harris, R. B., & Ream, R. **A comparative study of wolf (Canis Lupus) and dog (canis familiaris) tracks.** School of Forestry, University of Montana.

Murie, O. (1954). **A field guide to animal tracks.** Boston: Houghton Mifflin Co.

Ream, R., & Mattson, U. (June, 1979). **Wolf identification: Fieldguide.** Missoula, Montana: Montana Forest Conservation Experiment Station, University of Montana.

Rue, L. L. (1981). **Furbearing animals of North America.** New York: Crown Publishers.

Seton, E. T. (1921). **The book of woodcraft.** New York: Garden City Publishers.

Specific Science/Biology/Zoology Topics

Adorjan, A. S., & Kolenosky, G. B. (1969). **A manual for the identification of hairs of selected Ontario mammals.** Toronto, Ontario, Canada: Research Sec. Report No. 90, Ministry of Natural Resources.

Buffum, H. E. (Ed.)(1924). **The household physician.** New York: Brown-Flynn Publishing Company.

DeBlase, A. F., & Martin, R. E. (1974). **A manual of mammalogy.** Dubuque, Iowa: W. C. Brown.

Getty, R. (Ed.) (1975). **Sisson and Grossman's anatomy of domestic animals.** Philadelphia: W. B. Saunders Company.

Henshaw, R., et al. (March 3, 1972). Peripheral thermoregulation: Foot temperature in two Arctic canines. **Science, 175,** 988-990.

Johnson, W. H., et al. (1962). **General biology.** New York: Holt, Rinehart and Winston.

Rand McNally Atlas of the Body and Mind.(1976). New York: Rand McNally Company.

Rothman, R., & Mech, L. D. (1979). Scent marking in lone wolves and newly formed pairs. **Animal Behavior, 27,** 750-760.

Schwarze, D. M. (Ed.) (1976). **Chemical signals in vertebrates.** New York: Plenum Press.

Whittaker, J. O. (1970). **Introduction to psychology.** Philadelphia: Saunders.

Wilson, E. O. (1975). **Sociobiology: The new synthesis.** Cambridge, MA: Harvard Press.

History and Legend

Caras, R. (1966). **The Custer wolf.** Boston: Little Brown and Company.

Lopez, B. H. (1977). **Giving birth to Thunder Sleeping with His Daughter Coyote Builds North America.** Kansas: Sheed Andrews and McMeel Inc.

White, T. H. (1960). **The bestiary: A book of beasts.** New York: G. P. Putnam's Sons.

Young, S. (1970). **The last of the loners.** London: Macmillan Company.

Other Wolf Stories

Hellmuth, J. (1964). **A wolf in the family.** New York: New American Library.

Lawrence, R. D. (1980). **Secret go the wolves.** New York: Holt, Rinehart and Winston.

Leslie, R. F. (1974). **In the shadow of a rainbow.** New York: New American Library--Signet.

Maclean, C. (1977). **The wolf children.** New York: Hill and Wang, Farrar, Straus Giroux.

Mowat, F. (1963). **Never cry wolf.** New York: Dell Laurel Edition.

Stone, G. (1975). **A legend of wolf song.** New York: Dell Book.

Children's Books

Craighead-George, J. (1972). **Julie of the wolves.** New York: A Harper Trophy Book, Harper and Row.

DeJonge, J. E. (1979). **Anaku--the true story of a wolf.** Grand Rapids, Michigan: Baker Book House.

Fox, M. E. (1973). **The wolf.** New York: Coward, McCann and Geoghegan.

Hansen, R. (1981). **Wolves and coyotes.** New York: Platt and Munk Publishers.

Harris, J., & Pahl, A. (1976). **Endangered predators.** New York: Doubleday.

Hogan, P. Z. (1979). **The life cycle of the wolf.** Milwaukee: Raintree Children's Books.

Monjo, F. N. (1971). **The Jezebel wolf.** New York: Simon and Schuster.

Reigot, B. P. (1980). **Wolves.** New York: Scholastic Book Services.

Seton, E. T. (1951). **Wild animals I have known.** Racine, WI: Whitman Publishing Company.

Education Using Wolves

Steps to Our Social World, Social Studies Department, Toronto Board of Education, Toronto, Ontario, Canada.

GLOSSARY

Advocacy: Presenting a position and providing reasons why others should adopt it.

Advocacy subgroup: Two (or three) members of a decision-making group who (a) develop an alternative in depth, (b) plan how to present the best case possible for the alternative to the rest of the faculty so that it receives a fair and complete hearing, and (c) advocate the alternative and attempt to convince the rest of the faculty to adopt the alternative.

Aggression: Attempt to hurt someone or destroy somthing.

Ambiguous Claim: A claim that can be interpreted in two or more very different ways.

Anger: A defensive emotional reaction that occurs when we are frustrated, thwarted, or attacked. Anger is a righteous but defensive reaction to frustration and aggression based on a unidimensional perceptual focus, a physical demand to take action, and a belief that we must get our way.

Arbitration: The submission of a dispute to a disinterested third party who makes a final and binding judgment as to how the conflict will be resolved.

Argumentum Ad Hominem: Directing arguments at the opponent rather than at his or her ideas. Examples are the **genetic fallacy** (an attempt to discredit an argument by questioning the motives of the arguer), **argumentum ad personam** (an appeal to personal interest—he wants x because it will benefit him), and **accusing the opponent of inconsistency**.

Arguing from Analogy: When the outcome of a proposed course of action is predicted by citing the outcome of some previous similar course of action.

Asserting the Consequence: The following fallacy of deductive logic. All A are B. C is B. Therefore, C is A. An example is: All wars are preceded by arms buildups. We have had an arms buildup. Therefore, we will have a war.

Arbitration: The submission of a dispute to a disinterested third party who makes a final and binding judgment as to how the conflict will be resolved.

Belief: Something thought to be true but yet beyond the reach of verification through our senses (it cannot be measured, weighted, or counted).

Causal Network: Information organized into a sequence so that one or more events are shown to have caused another.

Cognitive Perspective: The cognitive organization being used to give meaning to a person's knowledge. Also, the structure of a person's reasoning.

Common fate: When you cannot succeed unless the other person succeeds and the other person cannot succeed unless you succeed. You sink or swim together.

Competitive Learning: Students working against each other to achieve a goal that only one or a few can attain. You can attain your goal if and only if the other students involved cannot attain their goals.

Concept: A name of a person, place, thing, or event that has certain characteristics.

Conceptual Conflict: Conflict that exists when incompatible ideas exist simultaneously in a person's mind or when information being received does not seem to fit with what one already knows.

Conceptualize Organizing evidence into a logical structure that provides a rationale for a position.

Conflict: The occurrence of incompatible activities. An activity that is incompatible with another activity is one that prevents, blocks, or interferes with the occurrence or effectiveness of the second activity. Incompatible activities may originate in one person, between two or more people, or between two or more groups.

Conflict of interests: When the actions of one person attempting to reach his or her goals prevent, block, or interfere with the actions of another person attempting to reach his or her goals.

Concurrence seeking: When group members inhibit discussion to avoid any disagreement or arguments and emphasize agreement.

Consensus: Unanimity in making a decision or at least unanimous commitment to implement the decision (based on group members believing they had a fair chance to influence what the decision is).

Controversy: Conflict that exists when one person's ideas, information, conclusions, theories, and opinions are incompatible with those of another and the two seek to reach an agreement.

Cooperative Base Groups: Cooperative learning groups used to provide long-term support and assistance for academic progress.

Cooperative Learning: Students work together to accomplish shared goals. Students seek outcomes that are beneficial to everyone involved.

Co-Orientation: Operating under the same norms and adhering to the same procedures.

Debate: Two or more individuals argue positions that are incompatible with one another and a judge declares a winner on the basis of who presented their position the best.

Decision: Agreement among group members as to which of several courses of action is most desirable for achieving the group's goals.

Decision making is a process that results in a choice among alternative courses of action.

Decision implementation is a process of taking the necessary actions that result in the execution of the decision.

Deductive Reasoning: Applying a generalization to specific instances through syllogisms made up of a major premise, minor premise, and conclusion.

Denying the Antecedent: The following fallacy in deductive logic. All A are B. C is not A. Therefore, C is not B. An example is: All cowboys ride horses. Pecos Bill is not riding a horse. Therefore, Pecos Bill is not a cowboy.

Developmental Conflict: A recurrent conflict that cycles in and out of peak intensity as the person develops socially. When recurrent incompatible activities between adult and child based on the opposing forces of stability and change within the child cycles in and out of peak intensity as the child develops cognitively, socially, and physically.

Differentiation: Seeking out and clarifying differences among members' ideas, information, conclusions, theories, and opinions.

Divergent Thinking: Generating a variety of ideas (fluency) and more classes of ideas (flexibility) about how to solve a problem.

Dualistic Thinking: Seeing the world in terms of two categories, right or wrong, and accepting the opinion of authority without question.

Effective Decision: A decision made so that the resources of group members were fully utilized, time was well used, the decision was correct or of high quality, all group members are fully committed to implementing the decision, and the problem-solving ability of the group is enhanced, or at least not lessened.

Egocentrism: The embeddedness in one's own viewpoint to the extent that one is unaware of other points of view and of the limitation of one's perspective.

Ego-Oriented Efforts: Efforts focusing on proving one is "right" and "better" than the other people involved.

Epistemic Curiosity: Active search for more information in hopes of resolving uncertainty, disequilibrium, or conceptual conflict.

Errors of Judgment: Flaws in reasoning that occur in the process of sorting out and assessing evidence.

Errors of Perception: Faulty ways of seeing reality preventing persons from being open-minded even before they begin to think.

Errors of Reaction: Defensive ways to preserve a self-image.

Euphemism: Substitution of a mild expression for a blunt one. Euphemisms are expressions that are intended to soften the meaning of certain information but employ vague words that are unsupportable as claims.

Fact: A thing, state, or event that is verifiable by (a) the senses (measuring, weighing, and counting) or (b) making an inference from physical data so strong as to allow no other explanation.

Fallacy of Many Questions: Asking a series of questions all at once rather than asking only one question at a time.

Fallacy of a Question with a Presupposition: A question that cannot be given any answer without the answerer conceding a point that is in dispute ("Do you still beat your wife?" or "How do you explain the deterioration of the economy?").

Fermenting Skills: The social and cognitive skills involved in challenging groupmates' conclusions and evidence and defending one's own position from attack.

Fixation: A mind set fixed on one thing so that the person is unable to think of or see alternatives.

Formal Cooperative Learning Groups: Cooperative learning groups used to teach specific academic content.

Formulating Skills: Social and cognitive skills that provide the mental processes needed to build deeper level understanding of the material being studied, to stimulate the use of higher quality reasoning strategies, and to maximize mastery and retention of the material supporting both the student's assigned position and the opposing position.

Fundamental Attribution Error: Belief that other people's behavior is caused by their personalities and nature while one's own behavior is caused by circumstances and situational factors.

Goal: An ideal and desired state of affairs that people value and are working to achieve.

Goal structure: The type of social interdependence specified among individuals as they strive to achieve their goals.

Group Processing: Discussion of how well group members are achieving their goals and maintaining effective working relationships among members.

Groupthink: Members of a decision-making group setting aside their doubts and misgivings about whatever policy is favored by the emerging consensus so as to be able to concur with the other members.

Hasty Conclusion: A conclusion drawn without enough evidence for choosing it over others.

Ignoratio Elenchi: Missing the point. It is an attempt to discredit the opponent's position by disproving an assertion that the opponent has not actually made.

Individual Accountability: When the performance of each individual student is assessed and the results given back to the group and the individual.

Individualistic Learning: Students working by themselves to accomplish learning goals unrelated to those of their classmates.

Inductive Reasoning: Taking known facts, information, experiences, and evidence and making a "likely" conclusion.

Informal Cooperative Learning Groups: Cooperative learning groups used to ensure active cognitive processing of information during a lecture or direct teaching.

Integration: Combining the information, reasoning, theories, and conclusions of the group members into a single position that satisfies them all.

Maximizing: Choosing the alternative course of action that maximizes group success in a decision-making situation.

Mediation: When a neutral and impartial third party actively assists two or more people (called disputants) to negotiate a constructive resolution to their conflict. The Latin root "mediare" means "to divide in the middle."

Meaningless Claim: A claim that includes contrived terms intended to promote a false impression.

Mind Map: An expanded web network that has four major features: (a) key idea, (b) sub-ideas, (c) supporting ideas, and (d) connectors that show relationships.

Mutual causation exists when whether you succeed or fail depends both on your own efforts and the efforts of the other person. You must depend on the other person to help you succeed and he or she must depend on you to help him or her succeed.

Negotiation is a process by which persons who have shared and opposed interests and want to come to an agreement try to work out a settlement.

Norms: Shared expectations about the behavior that is appropriate within the situation.

Opinion: An unproven belief or judgment.

Oppositional Interaction: Students discouraging and obstructing each other's efforts to achieve. Students focus both on increasing their own achievement **and** on preventing any classmate from achieving higher than they do.

Outcome Evaluation: The evaluation of the success of the plan in solving the problem.

Outline: Evidence arranged into a sequence of major ideas each followed by supportin ideas.

Overgeneralization: A generalization that far exceeds the facts that accompany it.

Oversimplification: Conclusion that omits essential information or ignores the complexity of a causal relationship and thereby distorting reality.

Paraphrasing: Restating, in your own words, what the person says, feels, and means.

Perspective: A person's way of viewing the world and his or her relation to it.

Perspective Reversal: Taking the frame of reference and position of another person and sincerely and completely presenting them as if they were one's own.

Perspective Taking: The ability to understand how a situation appears to another person and how that person is reacting cognitively and emotionally to the situation.

Persuasive Argument: A thesis statement or claim followed by a rationale that leads the audience to a clearly defined conclusion that is the same as the thesis statement.

Plausible Claims: Claims that are self-evident on the basis of common knowledge.

Positive Interdependence: Students perceive that they are linked with others in a way that one cannot succeed unless the other members of the group succeed (and vice versa) and/or that they must coordinate their efforts with the efforts of their groupmates to complete a task. They perceive that they "sink or swim together."

Probabilistic Thinking: Knowledge is available only in degrees of certainty between zero (no chance of being valid) and one-hundred percent (absolutely certain).

Problem: A discrepancy or difference between an actual state of affairs and a desired state of affairs.

Problem Solving: Adopting a course of action that eliminates the discrepancy or difference between an actual and a desired state of affairs.

Process Evaluation: The documentation of the extent to which implementation takes place.

Promotive Interaction: Students helping, assisting, encouraging, facilitating, and supporting each other's efforts to learn, achieve, complete tasks, and produce in order to reach the group's goals.

Qualifier: Words such as "probably," "sometimes," "never," and "always" that communicate how confident the speaker is in his or her claim.

Rationale: Arranging evidence in a logical order that leads to the conclusion that the claim is "true."

Reasonable Claim: A claim that is supportable for the context in which it is stated.

Rebuttal: Rebuilding one's case after it has been attacked by the opponent.

Refutation: Attacking another person's position in an attempt to cast significant doubt on and/or show the inadequacies of the evidence and reasoning so that the other person (or interested other people) will be willing to change his or her mind.

Relativistic Thinking: Right or wrong depends on your perspective and, therefore, anyone's view of right or wrong is as valid as anyone's else's on most questions. Authorities and experts are seen as only sometimes being right.

Rhetorical Question: A statement (usually a broad or exaggerated one) expressed as a question to which there can be only one answer, in the hope that the listener will draw the desired conclusion on his or her own. "Do you want a President who cares nothing about the poor in our society?" is an example.

Reduction Ad Absurdum: Directly challenging the assumptions on which the other's arguments are based by suggesting that if the assumptions were uniformly applied they would lead to absurd conclusions.

Reservation: Words such as "unless" and "until" that communicate the circumstances under which the speaker would decide not to defend a claim.

Role Reversal: Having two participants in a conflict reverse roles and play each other during a role play.

Satisficing: Prematurely choosing on the first reasonable alternative that is suggested in a decision-making situation.

Shifting the Burden of Proof: Demanding that the challenger disprove the assertion rather than the person making the assertion.

Social Perspective Taking: The ability to understand how a situation appears to another person and how that person is reacting cognitively and emotionally to the situation.

Stereotype: Judgment that prevents people from seeing important differences among individual people, places, and things.

Supportable Claim: A claim that can be supported by evidence in the form it is stated.

Syllogism: A three part chain of deductive reasoning in which two statements (a generalization known as a major premise and a specific factual statement known as a minor premise) are brought together to arrive at a conclusion (a new assertion).

Synthesis: Integrating a number of different ideas and facts into a single position. Combining two positions into a new one that subsumes the other two.

Task Involvement: The quality and quantity of the physical and psychological energy that individuals invest in their efforts to achieve.

Task-Oriented Efforts: Efforts focusing on contributing to a process of making the best decision possible or achieving the goal.

Thesis Statement or Claim: An assertion that the presenter wants accepted as "true." Sometimes known as a claim.

Unwarranted Assumptions: When people take too many underlying premises for granted and, therefore, do not ask useful questions and explore possibilities.

Vague Claim: A claim that is impossible to support because there is no distinct meaning conveyed by the claim.

Venn Diagram: Two or more overlapping circles within which a person lists what is similar and what is different about two (or more) concepts.

Web Network: A wheel in which a main idea, important fact, or conclusion is in the center, with supporting ideas and information radiating from it.

 © Johnson & Johnson

REFERENCES

Allen, V. (1965). Situational factors in conformity. In L. Berkowitz (Ed.), **Advances in experimental social psychology**, Vol. 2 (pp. 133-175). New York: Academic Press.

Allen, V. (1976). **Children as teachers: Theory and research on tutoring**. New York: Academic Press.

Allport, G., & Postman, L. (1945). The basic psychology of rumor. **Translations of New York Academy of Sciences, Series II, 8,** 61-81.

Ames, G., & Murray, F. (1982). When two wrongs make a right: Promoting cognitive change by social conflict. **Developmental Psychology, 18,** 892-895.

Anderson, N., & Graesser, C. (1976). An information integration analysis of attitude change in group discussion. **Journal of Personality and Social Psychology, 34,** 210-222.

Annis, L. (1983). The processes and effects of peer tutoring. **Human Learning, 2,** 39-47.

Argyris, C. (1964). **Integrating the Individual and the Organization.** New York: John Wiley.

Asch, S. (1952). **Social psychology.** Englewood Cliffs, NJ: Prentice-Hall.

Asch, S. (1956). Studies of independence and conformity: A minority of one against a unanimous majority. **Psychological Monographs, 70,** 416.

Bach, G., & Wyden, P. (1969). **The Intimate Enemy.** New York: William Morrow.

Bahn, C. (1964). **The interaction of creativity and social facilitation in creative problem solving.** Doctoral dissertation, Columbia University. Ann Arbor, MI: University Microfilms, 65-7499.

Bargh, J., & Schul, Y. (1980). On the cognitive benefits of teaching. **Journal of Education Psychology, 72,** 593- 604.

Bartlett, F. (1932). **Remembering**. Cambridge, England: Cambridge University Press.

Beach, L. (1974). Self-directed student group and college learning. **Higher Education**, 3, 187-200.

Beilin, H. (1977). Inducing conservation through training. In G. Steiner (Ed.), **Psychology of the 20th century, Piaget and beyond** (Vol. 7). Zurich: Kindler.

Benware, C. (1975). **Quantitative and qualitative learning differences as a function of learning in order to teach another**. Unpublished manuscript, University of Rochester. (As cited in E. L. Deci, **Intrinsic motivation.** New York: Plenum Press).

Berlyne, D. (1957). Uncertainty and conflict: A point of contact between information theory and behavior theory concepts. **Psychological Review**, **64**, 329-339.

Berlyne, D. (1960). **Conflict, arousal, and curiosity**. New York: McGraw-Hill.

Berlyne, D. (1963). Exploratory and epistemic behavior. In S. Koch (Ed.), **Psychology: A study of science**, Vol. 5. New York: McGraw-Hill.

Berlyne, D. (1965). Curiosity and education. In J. Krumboltz (Ed.), **Learning and the educational process.** Chicago: Rand-McNally.

Berlyne, D. (1966). Notes on intrinsic motivation and intrinsic reward in relation to instruction. In J. Bruner (Ed.), **Learning about learning** (Cooperative Research Monograph No. 15). Washington, D. C.: U. S. Department of Health, Education, and Welfare, Office of Education.

Berlyne, D. (1971). **Aesthetics and psychobiology**. New York: Appleton-Century-Crofts.

Bigelow, R. (1972). The evolution of cooperation, aggression, and self- control. In J. K. Cole and D. D. Jensen (Eds.), **Nebraska Symposium of Motivation** (pp. 1-58). Lincoln: University of Nebraska Press.

Blake, R., & Mouton, J. (1969). **Building a dynamic corporation through grid organization and development.** Reading, MA: Addison-Wesley.

Blatt, M. (1969). **The effects of classroom discussion upon children's level of moral judgment**. Unpublished doctoral dissertation, University of Chicago.

Blatt, M., & Kohlberg, L. (1973). The effects of classroom moral discussion upon children's level of moral judgment. In L. Kohlberg (Ed.), **Collected papers on moral development and moral education.** Harvard University: Moral Education and Research Foundation.

Bolen, L., & Torrance, E. (1976). **An experimental study of the influence of locus of control, dyadic interaction, and sex on creative thinking**. Paper presented at the American Educational Research Association, San Francisco, April.

Borys, S., & Spitz, H. (1979). Effect of peer interaction on the problem-solving behavior of mentally retarded youths. **American Journal of Mental Deficiency**, **84**, 273-279.

Botvin, G., & Murray, F. (1975). The efficacy of peer modeling and social conflict in the acquisition of conversation. **Child Development**, **45**, 796-799.

Boulding, E. (1964). Further reflections on conflict management. In R. Kahn and E. Boulding (Eds.), **Power and conflict in organizations**. New York: Basic Books, 146-150.

Bruner, J. (1961). **The process of education**. Cambridge, MA: Harvard University Press.

Bruner, J., & Minturn, A. (1955). Perceptual identification and perceptual organization. **Journal of Genetic Psychology, 53,** 21-28.

Burdick, H., & Burnes, A. (1958). A test of "strain toward symmetry" theories. **Journal of Abnormal and Social Psychology, 57,** 367-369.

Cook, H., & Murray, F. (1973, March). **Acquisition of conservation through the observation of conserving models.** Paper presented at the meetings of the American Educational Research Association, New Orleans.

Coser, L. (1956). **The function of social conflict.** Glencoe, IL: Free Press.

Crockenberg, S., & Nicolayev, J. (1977). **Stage transition in moral reasoning as related to conflict experienced in naturalistic settings.** Paper presented at the Society for Research in Child Development, New Orleans, March.

Davison, M. (1987). Personal communication.

Dearborn, C., & Simon, H. (1958). Selective perception: A note on the departmental identification of executives. **Sociometry, 23,** 667-673.

Deutsch, M. (1962). Cooperation and trust: Some theoretical notes. In M. Jones (Ed.), **Nebraska symposium on motivation.** Lincoln: University of Nebraska Press, 275-319.

Deutsch, M. (1969). Conflicts: Productive and destructive. **Journal of Social Issues, 25,** 7-43.

Deutsch, M. (1973). **The resolution of conflict.** New Haven, CT: Yale University Press.

Deutsch, M., & Gerard, H. (1955). A study of normative and informational social influences upon individual judgment. **Journal of Abnormal and Social Psychology, 51,** 629-636.

DeVries, D., and Edwards, K. (1973). Learning Games and Student Teams: Their Effects on Classroom Process. **American Educational Research Journal, 10,** 307-318.

Doise, W., & Mugny, G. (1979). Individual and collective conflicts of centrations in cognitive development. **European Journal of Social Psychology, 9,** 105-108.

Doise, W., Mugny, G., & Perret-Clermont, A. (1976). Social interaction and cognitive development: Further evidence. **European Journal of Social Psychology, 6,** 245-247.

Dunnette, M., Campbell, J., & Jaastad, K. (1963). The effect of group participation on brainstorming effectiveness of two industrial samples. **Journal of Applied Psychology, 47,** 30-37.

Dunning, D., & Ross, L. (1988). **Overconfidence in individual and group prediction: Is the collective any wiser?** Unpublished manuscript, Cornell University.

Falk, D., & Johnson, D. W. (1977). The effects of perspective-taking and ego-centrism on problem solving in heterogeneous and homogeneous groups. **Journal of Social Psychology, 102**, 63-72.

Feffer, M., & Suchotliff, L. (1966). Decentering implications of social interaction. **Journal of Personality and Social Psychology, 4**, 415-422.

Festinger, L., & Maccoby, N. (1964). On resistance to persuasive communications. **Journal of Abnormal and Social Psychology, 68**, 359- 366.

Fiedler, F., Meuwese, W., & Oonk, S. (1961). An exploratory study of group creativity in laboratory tasks. **Acta Psychology, 18**, 100-119.

Fisher, R. (1969). An each one teach one approach to music notation. **Grade Teacher, 86**, 120.

Flavell, J. (1963). **The developmental psychology of Jean Piaget**. Princeton, NJ: Van Nostrand.

Flavell, J. (1968). **The development of role-taking and communication skills in children**. New York: Wiley.

Foley, J., & MacMillan, F. (1943). Mediated generalization and the interpretation of verbal behavior: V. Free association as related to differences in professional training. **Journal of Experimental Psychology, 33,** 299-310.

Follet, M. (1940). Constructive conflict. In H. Metcalf & L. Urwick (Eds.), **Dynamic administration: The collected papers of Mary Parker Follet** (pp. 30-49). New York: Harper.

Freud, S. (1930). **Civilization and its Discontents.** London: Horgarth.

Frick, F. (1973). **Study of peer training with the Lincoln Training System** (AFATC Report KE 73-116). Harrison, MS: Keesler Air Force Base.

Gartner, A., Kohler, M., & Reissman, F. (1971). **Children teach children: Learning by teaching.** New York: Harper & Row.

Gelman, R. (1978). Cognition development. **Annual Review of Psychology, 29**, 297-332.

Gerard, H., & Greenbaum, C. (1962). Attitudes toward and agent of uncertainty reduction. **Journal of Personality, 30**, 485-495.

Glidewell, J. (1953). **Group emotionality and production.** Unpublished doctoral dissertation, University of Chicago.

Goldman, M. (1965). A comparison of individual and group performance for varying combinations of initial ability. **Journal of Personality and Social Psychology, 1,** 210-216.

Greenwald, A., & Albert, R. (1968). Acceptance and recall of improvised arguments. **Journal of Personality and Social Psychology, 8**, 31-35.

Guilford, J. (1956). The structure of intellect. **Psychological Bulletin, 33**, 267-293.

Gunderson, B., & Johnson, D. W. (1980). Building positive attitudes by using cooperative learning groups. **Foreign Language Annals, 13**, 39-46.

Hall, J., & Williams, M. (1966). A comparison of decision-making performance in established ad hoc groups. **Journal of Personality and Social Psychology, 3**, 214-222.

Hall, J., & Williams, M. (1970). Group dynamics training and improved decision making. **Journal of Applied Behavioral Science, 6**, 39-68.

Hammond, K. (1965). New directions in research on conflict resolution. **Journal of Social Issues, 11**, 44-66.

Hammond, K., & Boyle, P. (1971). Quasi-rationality, quarrels, and new conceptions of feedback. **Bulletin of the British Psychological Society, 24**, 103-113.

Hoffman, L., Harburg, E., & Maier, N. (1962). Differences in disagreements as factors in creative problem solving. **Journal of Abnormal and Social Psychology, 64**, 206-214.

Hoffman, L., & Maier, N. (1961). Sex differences, sex composition, and group problem solving. **Journal of Abnormal and Social Psychology, 63**, 453-456.

Hogan, R., & Henley, N. (1970). **A test of the empathy-effective communication hypothesis.** Report No. 84, Center for Social Organization of Schools. Baltimore: Johns Hopkins University.

Hovey, D., Gruber, H., & Terrell, G. (1963). Effects of self-directed study on course achievement, retention, and curiosity. **The Journal of Educational Research, 56**(7), 346- 351.

Hunt, J. (1964). Introduction: Revisiting Montessori. In M. Montessori (Ed.), **The Montessori method.** New York: Shocken Books.

Inagaki, K. (1981). Facilitation of knowledge integration through classroom discussion. **Quarterly Newsletter of the Laboratory of Comparative Human Cognition, 3**, 26-28.

Inagaki, K., & Hatano, G. (1968). Motivational influences on epistemic observation. **Japanese Journal of Educational Psychology, 16**, 221-228.

Inagaki, K., & Hatano, G. (1977) Application of cognitive motivation and its effect on epistemic observation. **American Educational Research Journal, 14**, 485-491.

Inhelder, B., & Sinclair, H. (1969). Learning cognitive structures. In P. H. Mussen, J. Langer, & M. Covington, (Eds.), **Trends and issues on developmental psychology,** 2-21. New York: Holt, Rinehart & Winston.

Iverson, M., & Schwab, H. (1967). Ethnocentric dogmatism and binocular fusion of sexually and racially discrepant stimuli. **Journal of Personality and Social Psychology, 7,** 73-81.

Inhelder, B., & Sinclair, H. (1969). Learning cognitive structures. In P. Mussen, J. Langer, & M. Covington (Eds.), **Trends and issues in developmental psychology** (pp. 2-21). New York: Holt, Rinehart & Winston.

Janis, I. (1982). **Groupthink: Psychological studies of policy decisions and fiascoes.** Boston, MA: Houghton-Mifflin.

Johnson, D. W. (1970). **Social psychology of education.** New York: Holt.

Johnson, D. W. (1971). Role-reversal: A summary and review of the research. **International Journal of Group Tensions, 1,** 318-334.

Johnson, D. W. (1971). Students against the school establishment: Crisis intervention in school conflicts and organization change. **Journal of School Psychology, 9,** 84-92.

Johnson, D. W. (1973). **Contemporary social psychology.** Philadelphia: Lippincott.

Johnson, D. W. (1974a). Communication and the inducement of cooperative behavior in conflicts: A critical review. **Speech Monographs, 41,** 64-78.

Johnson, D. W. (1975a). Cooperativeness and social perspective taking. **Journal of Personality and Social Psychology, 31,** 241- 244.

Johnson, D. W. (1975b). Affective perspective-taking and cooperative predisposition. **Developmental Psychology, 11,** 869-870.

Johnson, D. W. (1977). Distribution and exchange of information in problem-solving dyads. **Communication Research, 4,** 283-298.

Johnson, D. W. (1978). Conflict management in the school and classroom. In D. Bar-Tal & L. Saxe (Eds.), **Social psychology of education: Theory and research,** pp. 199-326. New York: Hemisphere.

Johnson, D. W. (1979). **Educational psychology.** Englewood Cliffs, NJ: Prentice-Hall.

Johnson, D. W. (1980). Group processes: Influences of student-student interaction on school outcomes. In J. McMillam (Ed.), **The social psychology of school learning.** New York: Academic Press.

Johnson, D. W. (1991). **Human relations and your career** (3rd ed.). Englewood Cliffs, NJ: Prentice-Hall.

Johnson, D. W. (1993). **Reaching out: Interpersonal effectiveness and self- actualization**. (5th ed.) Englewood Cliffs, NJ: Prentice-Hall.

Johnson, D. W., & Johnson, F. (1994). **Joining together: Group theory and group skills**. (4th ed.) Englewood Cliffs, NJ: Prentice-Hall.

Johnson, D. W., Johnson, F.,& Johnson, R. (1976). Promoting constructive conflict in the classroom. **Notre Dame Journal of Education**, **7**, 163-168.

Johnson, D. W., & Johnson, R. (1974). Instructional goal structure: Cooperative, competitive, or individualistic. **Review of Educational Research**, **44**, 213-240.

Johnson, D. W., & Johnson, R. (1979). Conflict in the classroom: Controversy and learning. **Review of Educational Research**, **49**, 51-61.

Johnson, D. W., & Johnson, R. (1983). The socialization and achievement crises: Are cooperative learning experiences the solution? In L. Bickman (Ed.), **Applied Social Psychology Annual 4**. Beverly Hills, CA: Sage Publications.

Johnson, D. W., & Johnson, R. (1984). Building acceptance of differences between handicapped and nonhandicapped students: The effects of cooperative and individualistic problems. **Journal of Social Psychology**, **122**, 257-267.

Johnson, D. W., & Johnson, R. (1985). Classroom conflict: Controversy versus debate in learning groups. **American Educational Research Journal**, **22**, 237-256.

Johnson, D. W., & Johnson, R. (1988). Critical thinking through structured controversy. **Educational Leadership**, **45**(8), 58-64.

Johnson, D. W., & Johnson, R. (1988). **Teaching students to manage conflict constructively by involving them in academic controversies**. Paper given at the annual meetings of American Association for the Advancement of Science, February.

Johnson, D. W., & Johnson, R. (1989). **Cooperation and competition: Theory and research**. Edina, MN: Interaction Book Company.

Johnson, D. W., & Johnson, R. (1992). Encouraging thinking through constructive controversy. In Davidson, N., & Worsham, T. (Eds.), **Enhancing Thinking Through Cooperative Learning**. New York: Teachers College Press.

Johnson, D. W., & Johnson, R. (1992). Pro-con: Structuring academic controversy. In Stahl, R. (Ed.), **Cooperative learning: Making it work in social studies**. Boston, MN: Addison-Wesley.

Johnson, D. W., & Johnson, R. (1992). Structuring academic controversy. **Cooperative Learning, 12**(2), 8-11.

Johnson, D. W., & Johnson, R. (1993). Creative and critical thinking through academic controversy. **American Behavioral Scientist, 37**, 40-53.

Johnson, D. W., & Johnson, R. (1994). **Learning together and alone: Cooperative, competitive, and individualistic learning** (4th ed.). Englewood Cliffs, NJ: Prentice-Hall (first edition, 1975).

Johnson, D. W., & Johnson, R. (1994). **Leading the cooperative school** (2nd Edition). Edina, MN: Interaction Book Company.

Johnson, D. W., & Johnson, R. (1994). Structuring academic controversy. In S. Sharan (Ed.), **Handbook of cooperative learning methods**, pp. 66-81. Westport, CN: Greenwood Press.

Johnson, D. W., & Johnson, R. (1995). **Teaching students to be peacemakers** (3rd Edition). Edina, MN: Interaction Book Company.

Johnson, D. W., Johnson, R., & Holubec, E. (1993). **Circles of learning: Cooperation in the classroom** (4th ed.). Edina, MN: Interaction Book Company.

Johnson, D. W., Johnson, R., & Holubec, E. (1993). **Cooperation in the classroom** (5th ed.). Edina, MN: Interaction Book Company.

Johnson, D. W., Johnson, R., & Maruyama, G. (1983). Interdependence and interpersonal attraction among heterogeneous and homogeneous individuals: A theoretical formulation and a meta-analysis of the research. **Review of Educational Research, 53,** 5-54.

Johnson, D. W., & Johnson, R., Pierson, W., & Lyons, V. (1985). Controversy versus concurrence seeking in multi-grade and single-grade learning groups. **Journal of Research in Science Teaching, 22**(9), 835-848.

Johnson, D. W., Johnson, R., & Smith, K. (1986). Academic conflict among students: Controversy and Learning. In R. Feldman, (Ed.). **Social psychological applications to education**. Cambridge University Press.

Johnson, D. W., Johnson, R., & Smith, K. (1989). Controversy within decision-making situations. In M. Rahim (ed.), **Managing conflict: An interdisciplinary approach** (pp. 251-264). New York: Praeger.

Johnson, D. W., Johnson, R., Smith, K., & Tjosvold, D. (1990). Pro, con, and synthesis: Training managers to engage in constructive controversy. In Sheppard, B., Bazerman, M., & Lewicki, R. (eds.), **Research on negotiation in organizations**, Volume 2 (pp. 135-170). Greenwich, CT: JAI Press, 1990.

Johnson, D. W., Johnson, R., & Scott, L. (1978). The effects of cooperative and individualized instruction on student attitudes and achievement. **Journal of Social Psychology, 104**, 207-216.

Johnson, D. W., Johnson, R., & Smith, K. (1991). **Active learning: cooperation in the college classroom.** Edina, MN: Interaction Book Company.

Johnson, D. W., Johnson, R., & Smith, K. (1993). Structured controversy / constructive controversy. **Cooperative Learning and College Teaching, 3**(3), 14-15.

Johnson, D. W., Johnson, R., & Tiffany, M. (1984). Structuring academic conflicts between majority and minority students: Hindrance or help to integration. **Contemporary Educational Psychology, 9**, 61-73.

Johnson, D. W., Maruyama, G., Johnson, R., Nelson, D., & Skon, L. (1981). Effects of cooperative, competitive, and individualistic goal structures on achievement: A meta-analysis. **Psychological Bulletin, 89,** 47-62.

Johnson, R., Brooker, C., Stutzman, J., Hultman, D., & Johnson, D. W. (1985). The effects of controversy, concurrence seeking, and individualistic learning on achievement and attitude change. **Journal of Research in Science Teaching, 22**, 197-205.

Jones, E., & Aneshansel, J. (1956). The learning and utilization of contravaluant material. **Journal of Abnormal and Social Psychology, 53**, 27-33.

Judd, C. (1978). Cognitive effects of attitude conflict resolution. **Journal of Conflict Resolution, 22**, 483-498.

Kalven, H., & Zeisel, H. (1966). **The American jury.** Boston: Little & Brown.

Kaplan, M. (1977). Discussion polarization effects in a modern jury decision paradigm: Informational influences. **Sociometry, 40**, 262-271.

Kaplan, M., & Miller, C. (1977). Judgments and group discussion: Effect of presentation and memory factors on polarization. **Sociometry, 40**, 337-343.

Keasey, C. (1973). Experimentally induced changes in moral opinions and reasoning. **Journal of Personality and Social Psychology, 226**, 30-38.

Kleinhesselink, R., & Edwards, R. (1975). Seeking and avoiding belief-discrepant information as a function of its perceived refutability. **Journal of Personality and Social Psychology, 31**, 787-790.

Knechel, S., Maruyama, G., & Petersen, R. (1990). The impact of strategies to enhance minority influence on decision making in educational groups. In H. Woxman & C. Ellet (Eds.), **The study of learning environments**: Vol. 4 (pp. 68-79). Houston, TX: College of Education, University of Houston.

Knight-Arest, I., & Reid, D. (1978). **Peer interaction as a catalyst for conservation acquisition in normal and learning-disabled children**. Paper presented at the Eighth Annual Symposium of the Jean Piaget Society, Philadelphia, May.

Kohlberg, L. (1969). Stage and sequence: The cognitive-developmental approach to socialization. In D. Goslin (Ed.), **Handbook of socialization theory and research** (pp. 347- 480). Chicago: Rand McNally.

Kouzes, J., & Posner, B. (1987). **The leadership challenge**. San Francisco: Jossey-Bass.

Kuhn, D., Langer, J., Kohlberg, L., & Haan, N. (1977). The development of formal operations in logical and moral judgment. **Genetic Psychological Monographs, 55**, 97-188.

Langer, E., Blank, A., & Chanowitz, B. (1978). The mindlessness of ostensibly thoughtful action: The role of "placebic" information in interpersonal interaction. **Journal of Personality & Social Psychology, 36**, 635-642.

Laughlin, P. (1980). Social combination processes of cooperative problem-solving groups on verbal intellective tasks. In M. Fishbein (Ed.), **Progress in social psychology** (Vol. 1). Hillsdale, NJ: Lawrence Erlbaum.

Laughlin, P., & Adamopoulos, J. (1980). Social combination processes and individual learning for six-person cooperative groups on an intellective task. **Journal of Personality and Social Psychology, 38**, 941-947.

Laughlin, P., Branch, L., & Johnson, H. (1969). Individual versus triadic performance on a unidimensional complementary task as a function of initial ability level. **Journal of Personality and Social Psychology, 12**, 144-150.

LeCount, J., Evens, J., & Maruyama, G. (1992, April). **It's a tough world out there...for men: Students' attitudes toward gender socialization pressures following a constructive controversy**. Paper presented at annual meeting of the American Educational Research Association, San Francisco.

LeCount, J., Maruyama, G., Petersen, R., & Basset, F. (1991, April). **Minority empowerment strategies and group decision making processes**. Paper presented at the annual meeting of the American Educational Research Association, Chicago.

LeFurgy, W., & Woloshin, G. (1969). Immediate and long-term effects of experimentally induced social influence in the modification of adolescents' moral judgments. **Journal of Personality and Social Psychology, 12**, 104-110.

Levine, J., & Murphy, G. (1943). The learning and forgetting of controversial material. **Journal of Abnormal and Social Psychology, 38**, 507-517.

Levine, R., Chein, I., & Murphy, G. (1942). The relation of the intensity of a need to the amount of perceptual distortion: A preliminary report. **Journal of Psychology, 13**, 283-293.

Lord, C., Ross, L., & Lepper, M. (1979). Biased assimilation and attitude polarization: The effects of prior theories on subsequently considered evidence. **Journal of Personality and Social Psychology, 37,** 2098-2109.

Lowin, A. (1969). Further evidence for an approach- avoidance interpretation of selective exposure. **Journal of Experimental Social Psychology, 5,** 265-271.

Lowry, N, & Johnson, D. W. (1981). Effects of controversy on epistemic curiosity, achievement, and attitudes. **Journal of Social Psychology, 115,** 31-43.

Luchins, A. (1942). Mechanization in problem solving: The effect of Einstellung. **Psychological Monographs, 54**(6, Whole No. 248).

Lund, S. (1980). **Group decision-making: The effects of controversy and systematic evaluation on vigilant information processing.** Unpublished doctoral dissertation, University of Minnesota, Minneapolis.

Maass, A., & Clark, R. (1984). Hidden impact of minorities: Fifteen years of minority influence research. **Psychological Bulletin, 95,** 428-450.

Magnuson, E. (1986, March 10). A serious deficiency: The Rogers Commission faults NASA's flawed decision-making process. **Time,** pp. 40-42, international edition.

Maier, N. (1930). Reasoning in humans. **Journal of Comparative Psychology, 10,** 115-143.

Maier, N. (1970). **Problem-solving and creativity in individuals and group.** Belmont, CA: Brooks/Cole.

Maier, N., & Hoffman, L. (1964). Financial incentives and group decision in motivating change. **Journal of Social Psychology, 64,** 369-378.

Maier, N., & Solem, A. (1952). The contributions of a discussion leader to the quality of group thinking: The effective use of minority opinions. **Human Relations, 5,** 277-288.

Maitland, D., & Goldman, J. (1974). Moral judgment as a function of peer group interaction. **Journal of Personality and Social Psychology, 30,** 699-704.

McClelland, D., & Atkinson, J. (1948). The projective expression of needs: I. The effect of different intensities of the hunger drive on perception. **Journal of Psychology, 25,** 205- 222.

McKeachie, W. (1986). **Teaching tips—a guidebook for the beginning college instructor** (3rd. Edition). Lexington, MA: D. C. Health.

Miller, S., & Brownell, C. (1975). Peers, persuasion, and Piaget: Dyadic interaction between conservers and nonconservers. **Child Development, 46,** 992-997.

Moscovici, S., & Faucheaux, C. (1972). Social influence, conformity bias, and the study of active minorities. In L. Berkowitz (Ed.), **Advances in Experimental Social Psychology** (Vol. 6, pp. 149-202). New York: Academic Press.

Moscovici, S., & Lage, E. (1976). Studies in social influence III: Majority versus minority influence in a group. **European Journal of Social Psychology, 6**, 149-174.

Moscovici, S., Lage, E., & Naffrechoux, M. (1969). Influence of a consistent minority on the responses of a majority in a color perception task. **Sociometry 32**, 365-380.

Moscovici, S., & Nemeth, C. (1974). Social influence II: Minority influence. In C. Nemeth (Ed.), **Social psychology: Classic and contemporary integrations** (pp. 217-249). Chicago: Rand-McNally.

Mugny, G. (1980). **The power of minorities**. London: Academic Press.

Mugny, G., & Doise, W. (1978). Socio-cognitive conflict and structure of individual and collective performers. **European Journal of Social Psychology, 8**, 181-192.

Murray, F. (1972). Acquisition of conservation through social interaction. **Development of Psychology, 6**, 1-6.

Murray, F. (1978). Development of intellect and reading. In F. Murray, & J. Pikulski (Eds.), **The acquisition of reading** (pp. 55-60). Baltimore: University Park Press.

Murray, F. (1981). The conservation paradigm: Conservation of conservation research. In D. Brodzinsky, I. Sigel, & R. Golink off (Eds.), **New directions in Piagetian theory and research** (pp. 143-175). Hillsdale, NJ: Lawrence Erlbaum Associates.

Murray, F. (1982). Teaching through social conflict. **Contemporary Educational Psychology, 7**, 257-271.

Murray, F. (1983). **Cognitive benefits of teaching on the teacher**. Paper presented at American Educational Research Association Annual Meeting, Montreal, Quebec.

Murray, F., Ames, G., & Botvin, G. (1977). Acquisition of conservation through cognitive dissonance. **Journal of Educational Psychology, 69**, 519-527.

Murray, J. (1974). Social learning and cognitive development: Modeling effects on children's understanding of conservation. **British Journal of Psychology, 65**, 151-160.

Neisser, U. (1954). On experimental distinction between perceptual process and verbal response. Journal of Experimental Psychology, 47, 399-402.

Nel, G., Helmreich, R., & Aronson, E. (1969). Opinion change in the advocate as a function of the persuasibility of his audience: A clarification of the meaning of dissonance. **Journal of Personality and Social Psychology, 12,** 117-124.

Nemeth, C. (1976). **A comparison between conformity and minority influence.** Paper presented at the International Congress of Psychology, Paris.

Nemeth, C. (1986). Differential contributions of majority and minority influence. **Psychological Review, 93**(1), 23- 32.

Nemeth, C., & Kwan, J. (1985a). Originality of word associations as a function of majority vs. minority influence. **Social Psychology Quarterly, 48,** 277-282.

Nemeth, C., & Kwan, J. (1987). Minority influence, divergent thinking, and detection of correct solutions. **Journal of Applied Social Psychology, 17,** 788-799.

Nemeth, C., Mayseless, O., Sherman, J., & Brown, Y. (1990). Exposure to dissent and recall of information. **Journal of Personality and Social Psychology, 58,** 429-437.

Nemeth, C., Swedlund, M., & Kanki, B. (1974). Patterning of the minorities' responses and their influence on the majority. **European Journal of Social Psychology, 4**(1), 53- 64.

Nemeth, C., & Wachtler, J. (1974). Creating the perceptions of consistency and confidence: A necessary condition for minority influence. **Sociometry, 37,** 529-540.

Nemeth, C., & Wachter, J. (1983). Creative problem solving as a result of majority vs. minority influence. **European Journal of Social Psychology, 13**(1), 45-55.

Nicholls, J. (1983). Conceptions of ability and achievement motivation: A theory and its implications for education. In S. Paris, G. Olson, & H. Stevenson (Eds.), **Learning and motivation in the classroom,** pp. 211-237. Hillsdale, NJ: Erlbaum.

Nijhof, W., & Kommers, P. (1982). **Analysis of cooperation in relation to cognitive controversy.** Second International Conference on Cooperation in Education, Provo, Utah, July.

Nisbett, R., & Ross, L. (1980). **Human inference: Strategies and shortcomings of social judgment.** Englewood Cliffs, NJ: Prentice-Hall.

Noonan-Wagner, M. (1975). **Intimacy of self-disclosure and response processes as factors affecting the development of interpersonal relationships.** Unpublished doctoral dissertation, University of Minnesota.

Palmer, P. (1990). Good teaching. **Change,** (January/February), 11-16.

Palmer, P. (19). Community, conflict, and ways of knowing. **Change,** (September/October), 20-25.

Palmer, P. (1991). The courage to teach. **National Teaching and Learning Forum, 1**(2), 1-3.

Palmer, P. (1992). Divided no more. **Change,** (Mach/April), 11-17.

Pellegrini, A. (1984). Identifying causal elements in the thematic-fantasy play paradigm. **American Education Research Journal, 21**, 691-701.

Pepitone, A. (1950). Motivational effects in social perception. **Human Relations, 3**, 57-76.

Perret-Clermont, A. (1980). **Social interaction and cognitive development in children.** London: Academic Press.

Peters, R., & Torrance, E. (1972). Dyadic interaction of preschool children and performance on a construction task. **Psychological Reports, 30**, 747-750.

Piaget, J. (1948). **The moral judgment of the child** (2nd ed.). Glencoe, IL: The Free Press.

Piaget, J. (1950). **the psychology of intelligence.** New York: Harcourt.

Postman, L., & Brown, D. (1952). The perceptual consequences of success and failure. **Journal of Abnormal and Social Psychology, 47**, 213-221.

Putnam, L., & Geist, P. (1985). Argument in bargaining: An analysis of the reasoning process. **Southern Speech Communication Journal, 50**, 225-245.

Rensberger, B. (1984, April). What made humans human? **New York Times Magazine**, pp. 80-81, 89-95.

Rest, J., Turiel, E., & Kohlberg, L. (1969). Relations between level of moral judgment and preference and comprehension of the moral judgment of others. **Journal of Personality, 37**, 225-252.

Rogers, C, (1970). Towards a theory of creativity. In P. Vernon (Ed.), **Readings in creativity.** London: Penguin.

Rosenshine, B, & Stevens, R. (1986). Teaching Functions. In M. Wittrock (Ed.), **Handbook of research on teaching** (3rd Ed., pp. 376-391). New York: Macmillan.

Sarbin, T. (1976). Cross-age tutoring and social identity. In V. Allen (Ed.), **Children as teachers: Theory and research on tutoring.** New York: Academic Press.

Sigel, I., & Hooper, F. (Ed.) (1968). **Logical thinking in children: Research based on Piaget's theory.** New York: Holt, Rinehart & Winston.

Silverman, I., & Geiringer, E. (1973). Dyadic interaction and conservation induction: A test of Piaget's equilibration model. **Child Development, 44**, 815-820.

Silverman, I., & Stone, J. (1972). Modifying cognitive functioning through participation in a problem-solving group. **Journal of Educational Psychology**, 63, 603-608.

Simmel, G. (1955). **Conflict**. New York: Free Press.

Simon, H. (1976). **Administrative behavior: A study of decision-making processes in administrative organization** (3rd ed.). New York: Free Press.

Sinclair, H. (1969). Developmental Psycho- linguistics. In D. Elkind and J. Flavell (Eds.), **Studies in cognitive development: Essays in honor of Jean Piaget** (pp. 315- 336). New York: Oxford University Press.

Smedslund, J. (1961a). The acquisition of conservation of substance and weight in children: II. External reinforcement of conservation and weight and of the operations of addition and subtraction. **Scandinavian Journal of Psychology**, 2, 71-84.

Smedslund, J. (1961b). The acquisition of conservation of substance and weight in children: III. Extinction of conservation of weight acquired `normally' and by means of empirical controls on balance. **Scandinavian Journal of Psychology**, 2, 85-87.

Smith, K. (1980). **Using controversy to increase students' achievement, epistemic curiosity and positive attitudes toward learning.** Unpublished Doctoral Dissertation, University of Minnesota.

Smith, K., Johnson, D. W., & Johnson, R. (1981). Can conflict be constructive? Controversy versus concurrence seeking in learning groups. **Journal of Educational Psychology**, 73, 651- 663.

Smith, K., Johnson, D. W., & Johnson, R. (1982). Effects of cooperative and individualistic instruction on the achievement of handicapped, regular, and gifted students. **Journal of Social Psychology**, 116, 277-283.

Smith, K., Johnson, D. W., & Johnson, R. (1984). Effects of controversy on learning in cooperative groups. **Journal of Social Psychology**, 122, 199-209.

Snyder, M., & Cantor, N. (1979). Testing theories about other people: The use of historical knowledge. **Journal of Experimental Social Psychology**, 15, 330-342.

Swann, W., & Reid, S. (1981). Acquiring self- knowledge: The search for feedback that fits. **Journal of Personality and Social Psychology**, 41, 1119-1128.

Tanford, S., & Penrod, S. (1984). Social influence model: A formal integration of research on majority and minority influence processes. **Psychological Bulletin**, 95, 189-225.

Taylor, D., Altman, I., & Sorrentino, R. (1969). Interpersonal exchange as a function of rewards and costs and situational factors: Expectancy confirmation-disconfirmation. **Journal of Experimental Social Psychology**, 5, 324-339.

Tjosvold, D. (1974). Threat as a low-person's strategy for bargaining: Social farce and tangible outcomes. **International Journal of Group Tensions, 4**, 494-510.

Tjosvold, D. (1982). Effects of approach to controversy on superiors' incorporation of subordinates' information in decision-making. **Journal of Applied Psychology, 67**, 189-193.

Tjosvold, D. (1990). Flight crew collaboration to manage safety risks. **Group and Organizational Studies, 15**, 177-191.

Tjosvold, D., & Deemer, D. (1980). Effects of controversy within a cooperative or competitive context on organizational decision-making. **Journal of Applied Psychology, 65**, 590-595.

Tjosvold, D., & Johnson, D. W. (1977). The effects of controversy on cognitive perspective-taking. **Journal of Educational Psychology, 69**, 679-685.

Tjosvold, D., & Johnson, D. W. (1978). Controversy within a cooperative or competitive context and cognitive perspective-taking. **Contemporary Educational Psychology, 3**, 376- 386.

Tjosvold, D., & Johnson, D. W. (Eds.). (1983). **Productive Conflict Management: Perspectives for Organizations.** New York: Irvington.

Tjosvold, D., Johnson, D. W., & Fabrey, L. (1980). The effects of controversy and defensiveness on cognitive perspective-taking. **Psychological Reports, 47**, 1043-1053.

Tjosvold, D., Johnson, D. W., & Lerner, J. (1981). Effects of affirmation of one's competence, personal acceptance, and disconfirmation of one's competence on incorporation of opposing information on problem-solving situations. **Journal of Social Psychology, 114**, 103-110.

Torrance, E. (1961). Can group control social stress in creative activity? **Elementary School Journal, 62**, 139-394.

Torrance, E. (1970). Influence of dyadic interaction on creative functioning. **Psychological Reports, 26**, 391-394.

Torrance, E. (1971). Stimulation, enjoyment, and originality in dyadic creativity. **Journal of Educational Psychology, 62**, 45-48.

Torrance, E. (1973). **Dyadic interaction in creative thinking and problem solving.** Paper read at American Educational Research Association, New Orleans, February.

Triandis, H., Bass, A., Ewen, R., & Midesele, E. (1963). Teaching creativity as a function of the creativity of the members. **Journal of Applied Psychology, 47**, 104-110.

Turiel, E. (1966). An experimental test of the sequentiality of developmental stages in the child's moral judgment. **Journal of Personality and Social Psychology, 3**, 611- 618.

Turiel, E. (1973). Stage transition in moral development. In R. Travers (Ed.), **Second handbook of research on teaching** (pp. 732-758). Chicago: Rand McNally.

Tversky, A., & Kahneman, D. (1981). The framing of decisions and the psychology of choice. **Science, 211**, 453-458.

Van Blerkom, M., & Tjosvold, D. (1981). The effects of social context on engaging in controversy. **Journal of Psychology, 107**, 141-145.

Vinokur, A., & Burnstein, E. (1974). Effects of partially shared persuasive arguments on group-induced shifts. **Journal of Personality and Social Psychology, 29**, 305-315.

Wallach, L., & Sprott, R. (1964). Inducing number conservation in children. **Child Development, 35**, 1057-1071.

Wallach, L., Wall, A., & Anderson, L. (1967). Number conservation: The roles of reversibility, addition-subtraction, and misleading perceptual cues. **Child Development, 38**, 425-442.

Walton, R. (1987). **Interpersonal peacemaking.** Reading, MA: Addison-Wesley.

Watson, G., & Johnson, D. W. (1972). **Social psychology: issues and insights.** Philadelphia: Lippincott.

Webb, N. (1977). **Learning in individual and small group settings**. (Technical Report #7). Stanford, CA: Aptitude Research Project, School of Education, Stanford University.

Wilson, R. (1987). Toward Excellence in Teaching. In L. Aleamoni (Ed.), **Techniques for evaluating and improving instruction** (pp. 9-24). San Francisco: Jossey-Bass.

Woholwill, J., & Lowe, R. (1962). Experimental analysis of the development of the conservation of number. **Child Development, 33**, 153-167.

Worchel, P., & McCormick, B. (1963). Self-concept and dissonance reduction. **Journal of Personality, 31**, 589-599.

Zajonc, R. (1965). Social facilitation. **Science, 149**, 269-272.

Zimbardo, P. (1965). The effect of effort and improvisation on self-persuasion produced by role playing. **Journal of Experimental Social Psychology, 1**, 103-120.